# PICKING THE BONES

For Sheila Tate and John Lewis

# PICKING THE BONES

Reclaiming the Past from the Politicians

## GEOFFREY REGAN

Cartoons by
Matt Buck

MAINSTREAM
PUBLISHING
EDINBURGH AND LONDON

First published in Great Britain in 2004 by
MAINSTREAM PUBLISHING COMPANY (EDINBURGH) LTD
7 Albany Street
Edinburgh EH1 3UG

ISBN 1 84018 830 8

A catalogue record for this book is available from the British Library

Typeset in Times and Univers BQ

Printed in Great Britain by
Mackays of Chatham plc

# *Contents*

# *Introduction*

Thought for the Day by Abraham Lincoln
'Do I not destroy my enemies when I make them my friends?'

In his novel *Nineteen Eighty-Four*, George Orwell observed, 'Who controls the past controls the future, who controls the present controls the past.' It is the use of the past to control the future that is the theme of this book.

Politicians have always sought the authority of history to validate their agendas and, in doing so, have been prepared to distort and misrepresent past events to win contemporary support. It should not be assumed that democratic states are immune to the sort of tactics employed in the totalitarian state envisaged by Orwell. Far from it. Democracies have witnessed some of the most sophisticated methods of political control that have ever been attempted, notably during the anti-Soviet campaigns of the Cold War and in the recent Global War on Terror, or GWOT. What is particularly worrying is the way in which politicians have been prepared to preside over an erosion of civil liberties in both Britain and the United States. They have invoked crude patriotism and a process that newspaperman and political commentator H.L. Mencken described in *In Defence of Women* as: 'The whole aim of practical politics is to keep the populace alarmed by menacing it with an endless series of hobgoblins, all of them imaginary.'

We were told that Britain and the United States carried out a pre-emptive attack on Iraq on 19 March 2003 because intelligence sources were certain that Saddam Hussein posed a real and impending threat to British and American targets. According to international law, the only scenario which ever justifies such pre-emptive action is when the threat posed is imminent and real. In a dossier produced by the British Government in September 2002, it was asserted that recent intelligence from an Iraqi source reported Saddam Hussein could launch weapons of mass destruction (WMD) within 45 minutes against British and American targets. This information was then taken up by the British press and formed the basis for a wave of sensational stories which portrayed Iraqi capabilities as a looming and increasing threat to the world.

This was an insult to common sense.

In fact, after a decade of UN sanctions, Iraq was a mere shadow of the military power she had been in 1991 during the first Gulf War. Saddam Hussein's regime in Iraq constituted no realistic threat to her neighbours, least of all to America's ally Israel, a regional superpower with huge stocks of weapons of mass destruction.

The British Government's September dossier made an unconvincing case for pre-emptive war. What made matters worse was the shabby nature of the dossier, part of which, far from reflecting recent intelligence, had been copied from a 12-year-old Ph.D. thesis prepared by a Californian student, Dr Ibrahim al-Marashi. Such a careless approach to an issue of war and peace, which had serious implications for British citizens as well as Iraqis, reflected badly on Tony Blair's Government.

I did not believe what was in the dossier for the following reasons:

- It is military common sense to deduce that the weapons of mass destruction that could be employed within 45 minutes were battlefield munitions, not long-range missile-borne weapons, and therefore posed no threat at all to targets beyond the battle zone. Yet the distinction was not made by those preparing the dossier.

- The intelligence information on Iraq's weapons of mass destruction was out of date and Saddam Hussein had no delivery systems for long- or medium-range weapons. This information must have been known to US intelligence with its satellite intelligence capabilities.

- In the period since the first Gulf War in 1991, Saddam Hussein had made no overt threats against any of his neighbours and certainly none against Britain or the United States.

What was apparent to me, I reasoned, must be even more obvious to military intelligence personnel. They, as well as the political establishment in both Britain and the United States, knew that Saddam had been thoroughly cowed by UN sanctions and by Anglo-American military deterrence, and had made no threats against any of his neighbours. Many people around the world, including Hans Blix and his team of UN inspectors, and a substantial number of experts in both Britain and the United States, doubted the evidence on weapons of mass destruction presented by Britain and the US immediately prior to the war, notably the evidence offered by Colin Powell before the Security Council in February 2003.

And yet Britain and the United States claimed the right to launch a pre-emptive attack on Iraq, basing their case on the imminent threat of attack by Saddam Hussein on his neighbours or on British and American targets. When the British press seized upon this and began to print their lurid headlines, Tony Blair and his supporters, knowing what the truth was – at least as far as the available intelligence could inform them – chose not to correct the misinterpretation and allowed the British people to be misled into believing that Saddam Hussein could really carry out strikes against British targets within 45 minutes with chemical, biological or even, possibly, nuclear munitions.

While the Hutton Report into the death of David Kelly may have been right to reject Andrew Gilligan's assertion that the 45-minute claim was used deliberately to exaggerate the threat from Iraq – which was tantamount to accusing Tony Blair of lying to Parliament and the British people – the claim was clearly based on faulty intelligence.

The question that Hutton, to the bewilderment of the British people, did not address was why the 45-minute claim was allowed to develop into a 'scare story' which Tony Blair chose not to refute. His intelligence advisers knew that there was no threat to Britain from any Iraqi strategic weapons, so one is entitled to ask why these people did not inform the Prime Minister that a misleading impression was being created in the country, which, though helpful to those pressing for an immediate strike against Saddam Hussein, could not be used without allegations of impropriety? Neither Tony Blair nor his advisers chose to intervene at this point, and so at a time when the public deserved the best and most accurate information on a subject of great national importance, they were subjected to inaccurate information resulting from faulty intelligence and a misleading interpretation of it.

At this point I decided to commit some of my thoughts to print and the idea of this book was born.

## PICKING THE BONES

While Tony Blair, after the publication of the Hutton Report, insisted on receiving an apology from the BBC, Andrew Gilligan and the leader of the Conservative Party, Michael Howard, he can surely see that he must apologise for the actions he took as a result of faulty intelligence information.

- He must apologise first and foremost to the Iraqi people for invading their country, killing their people, wrecking their cities, seizing their oilfields and overthrowing their leader.
- He must apologise to the friends and families of British military personnel killed or injured during a war which he cannot now justify on the original grounds.
- He must apologise to the British taxpayer for the money he used to fund an unnecessary and illegal war.
- He must apologise to the United Nations for ignoring the Security Council and pursuing a war of aggression against Iraq.
- He must apologise to Britain's allies, notably France and Germany, for the absurd campaign used against them to justify the war.
- He must apologise to the British people for a) trying to change the *casus belli* after the war was over and no WMD had been found, and b) sullying Britain's reputation through joining an aggressive and illegal war against a Third World nation.

David Kay, head of the Iraq Survey Group, admitted early in 2004 that Iraq probably never had any weapons of mass destruction at all – something Hans Blix had already concluded months before. Furthermore, US Secretary of State Colin Powell has said it is an open question whether Iraqi WMD will ever be found. When these conclusions are set alongside George W. Bush's redefinition of WMD in January 2004 as 'weapons of mass destruction-related programme activity', it is easy to see how Tony Blair must be feeling very lonely while proclaiming his continuing belief that the WMD will eventually be found. Human beings are never more frightening than when they are convinced beyond reason that they are right. There is a fanaticism about Tony Blair that seems unsuited to a British democrat and is closer to the mythocrats in the United States. Honest men acknowledge their errors and apologise to those they have harmed.

# INTRODUCTION

I have no reason to think that men like Dick Cheney or Donald Rumsfeld are uncomfortable over their failure to find weapons of mass destruction. They had business to conclude with Saddam Hussein. Now that they have both him and his country, they have all the justification they need. Others are joining their ranks. I fear that Tony Blair, as a man of principle, has succumbed to the fundamentalism and the unprincipled opportunism of the Bush administration. Ironically, this makes his pursuit of self-justification more of a problem than the shoulder shrugging of the Americans. Blair's adoption of an 'end justified the means' approach is highly questionable. Aldous Huxley spoke of this when he said, 'The end cannot justify the means, for the simple and obvious reason that the means employed determine the nature of the end produced.'

This book was born out of the anger I felt when Tony Blair showed himself willing to use the techniques of American politicians to win an argument the British people had rejected. He began by advocating actions through the United Nations Security Council but ended colluding with American attempts to bully the members of the council into supporting pre-emptive action against Iraq. Many people – myself included – hoped that Blair had cast himself in the role of brakeman to the runaway American train. However, when the time came to dig in his heels and slow the juggernaut, he simply climbed aboard and waved farewell to international law and multilateralism.

If the *casus belli* for war against Iraq was invalid because Saddam Hussein had no stockpiles of chemical, biological and possibly even nuclear weapons, which could be used at short notice against British and American targets, then the subsequent war was a war of aggression. Parliament and the British people never agreed to any war for regime change, and collateral advantages accruing from overthrowing a vile dictator cannot be used retrospectively to justify the war. Nor, to my mind, can weapons, found nine months or more after the war ended, be used to justify the war itself when their existence and location could not be proved at the beginning of the conflict. In my view, this war was an illegal one, the casualties on the Iraqi side were unlawfully inflicted and the Coalition governments are consequently guilty of a serious war crime.

Sometimes the road to hell is paved with good intentions. And, whatever democratic future Tony Blair might think he is offering the Iraqi people, he cannot overlook the fact that through his decision to invade their country in March 2003, he and George W. Bush have put them through hell. As Gandhi once observed, 'What difference does it make to the dead, the orphans and the homeless, whether the mad destruction is wrought under the name of totalitarianism or the holy name of liberty or democracy?'

If the callous and boastful American proclamation that they would 'Shock and Awe' the people of Baghdad reflected anything more than the shallow mentalities of the Bush administration, it certainly did not reveal any sincere feelings for an oppressed people who were being freed from a vile tyranny. Paraphrasing war veteran Daniel Berrigan on Vietnam, the war in Iraq in 2003 was run to show the world, and particularly the Third World, where exactly it stands in relation to American technology. For me, it brought to mind an anecdote from the intense Normandy fighting in 1944. Emerging from the shattered city of St-Lô, one American soldier said to another, 'We sure liberated the hell out of this place.'

A thought from the eminent British sociologist and historian Christopher Dawson seems particularly appropriate at this point in time. In *The Judgement of Nations* he stated, 'As soon as men decide that all means are permitted to fight an evil, then their good becomes indistinguishable from the evil that they set out to destroy.' We overlook this at our peril. The greatest acts of state terrorism have been perpetrated by two democratic states, Britain and the USA, operating from the moral high ground. Civilian casualties in central Europe from the hunger blockade of the First World War or the strategic bombing of the Second World War far exceed those resulting from terrorist activity by any group – national or otherwise – in the twentieth century. Even the casualties of the terrible events of 9/11 are minuscule when viewed alongside those inflicted on enemy civilians on a nightly basis in Germany or Japan between 1942 and 1945.

It is double-talk to suggest that a noble cause can ever justify the slaughter that will be inflicted during warfare on innocent civilians in the name of democracy, freedom, peace or whatever. A democracy, in theory at least, does not initiate wars except in the name of its people. Thus it is sometimes necessary for politicians to create a 'myth of war', of the kind favoured by Winston Churchill, to assure the people that their cause is just. This 'myth' then becomes a weapon of the media, which convinces the reading and listening public that they have justice on their side. Just as individual enemies like Saddam Hussein are demonised to make it easier for people to treat them harshly, so some nations are stigmatised in order to justify the most violent military action against them. It becomes easier to justify doing terrible things if you can portray the enemy as deserving it.

Peter Ustinov's comment in the script of *Romanoff and Juliet* that, 'At the age of four with paper hats and wooden swords we're all generals. Only some of us never grow out of it' could apply to Winston Churchill, who loved to play with toy soldiers as a little boy and never let go of the habit. While Churchill has been much admired for 'mobilising the English language and sending it into battle', he mobilised a lot of people as well, encouraging them to give their all for fancy phrases that could have been found inside Christmas crackers from Fortnum & Mason. In America it is noticeable that the most warlike politicians are often the ones who skipped military service. Nevertheless, the rhetoric of war serves one important purpose: it kills the stench of the real thing.

The United States no longer has a history as such, only a mythology, and modern Americans are slaves to those who control these myths. Heroification of the American past has created a 'selective, collective memory', which is set in stone for most Americans on Mount Rushmore. A critical approach to history flourishes in the universities but never raises its liberal head in America's schools or homes. It is unwelcome for anyone, even an apprentice stonemason, to try to apply a Cromwellian wart to the chin of one of America's 'great stone faces'.

Heroes from America's past may have got drunk, kicked the dog, cheated on their wives and shot a few more Native Americans than was absolutely necessary, but Americans do not need to know about it. For Americans, history, like modern warfare, has been sanitised. The tricky bits – like racism and slavery – have been erased or excised. All Americans learn as children the 'foundation myth': that America was created on the 'good idea' of Freedom. Nobody dares to mention the thought that tormented one of the greatest of the Founding Fathers, Thomas Jefferson. The Declaration of Independence expressed the fundamental truth that 'All Men are Created Equal' – yet the man who wrote it was a slaveholder, the country based upon it maintained a system of slavery and Jefferson himself had at least one child by a slave woman and kept the child as a slave for himself. With that skeleton inside the cupboard, the door must have taken some shutting!

Jefferson's ally in making the world safe for hypocrisy was Woodrow Wilson, the father of US idealism. Unfortunately, the man behind the myth was the most racist president in American history, a man who suspended civil liberties in wartime and whose principle of self-determination at Versailles in 1919 condemned Europe to a re-run of the world war in 1939.

The political use of stereotyping opponents on racial lines is thoroughly disreputable, however it has become common since 1945. The diplomacy in the Security Council prior to the recent war in Iraq disintegrated into a virtual playground scuffle when the Americans began insulting their French opponents. Stereotyping by American politicians was used to muddy the waters of the debate. The accusation that the French were 'cheese-eating surrender monkeys' appealed to the lowest common denominator in the American and British media and ensured that sensible debate would be lost in a welter of prejudice and racism.

Hard upon the heels of the failed WMD argument came Bush and Blair demanding regime change on the grounds that Saddam Hussein was a war criminal. This accusation was irrefutable. On the other hand, war crimes and human-rights abuses have been widespread in the twentieth century. Interestingly enough, the United States has itself been responsible for some of the worst war crimes, like those perpetrated by American troops in the Philippines, Vietnam or Latin America, and these should be made known as an antidote to American triumphalism.

America's belief in her own exceptionalism has won her few friends since 1945. Her claims to be the world's great liberator had given hope to a world emerging from the horrors of the worst war in history. However, more recent claims by the religious right that America is the land of God's 'chosen people' are so unilateral, divisive and self-righteous that they would be laughable were they not backed up by such a formidable military arsenal. They are a product of religious brainwashing. With history revealing nothing but America's blessed mission, critical thinking has almost completely ceased in the United States.

Americans must begin to face up to the truth of their own violent history or else they will never master terrorism by understanding its roots. While Americans treat their militarism as almost a weekend pastime, one is forced to reflect on the words of British writer John Rae in his book *The Custard Boys*:

> War is, after all, the universal perversion. We are all tainted: if we cannot experience our perversion at first hand we spend our time reading war stories, the pornography of war; or seeing war

films, the blue films of war; or titillating our senses with the imagination of great deeds, the masturbation of war.

America surely does not want to be seen by the rest of the world as embodying George Orwell's symbol of the future from *Nineteen Eighty-Four*, a boot stamping on a face forever: the boot US army issue; the face, that of a Third World child. It is doubtful if America will ever be completely free from terror because it comes from within, not from outside. It came to America with the first settlers who crossed the Atlantic and US presidents have been using it ever since to maintain their hold on a democratic people. This is the future for those who abandon their history and fail to remember who they are by forgetting who they were.

# CHAPTER 1

## *Shock and Awe*

In the infamous British dossier of September 2002, Tony Blair used the phrase that has echoed heartlessly down the years since 1914, 'We have no quarrel with the Iraqi people.' Those who are about to die are saluted. The millions of civilians who have perished at the hands of democratic forces in the past 100 years have succumbed with these reassuring words ringing in their ears. Nobody meant them any harm but they were the price that had to be paid for their unpopular leadership.

Britain, as a signatory of the Geneva and Hague conventions of 1899 and 1907 which forbade the specific targeting of civilians in warfare, chose to do exactly that in both world wars. America's decision to drop the atomic bomb on Hiroshima and Nagasaki specifically targeted civilians. Since 1945 the United States has targeted civilians by its use of air power in numerous conflicts.

Only the enemy uses WMD, so that Iraq's mustard gas weapons are always classified as WMD, but America's far more destructive Tomahawk missiles are scalpels in a sanitised war, disinfected before they are fired and wrapped in a condom for 'Safe War'. That might be seen as a case of double standards. On the other hand, the 'God of Battles' has always ridden with the winners and the 'Legions of the Damned' with the losers.

In 1946, George Orwell observed, 'In our time, political speech and writing are largely the defence of the indefensible.'[1] Just a year after the bombing of Hiroshima, Nagasaki and Dresden, and while the Morgenthau Plan was still playing a part in the American treatment of

17

defeated Germany, these terrible actions, which rival the Holocaust in their sheer horror, were being justified by men like Winston Churchill, Franklin D. Roosevelt and Harry S Truman on the grounds that they saved lives, ensured peace and liberated the oppressed.

In fact, some of the greatest examples of state terrorism have been committed in the name of democracy. Orwell refers to this political rhetoric as 'newspeak', which is the use of language for the specific political purpose of mind control rather than communication.

In the immediate aftermath of the 2003 Iraq War, George W. Bush showed that he had learned at least one lesson from his predecessors in the White House. After visiting soldiers wounded in the fighting in Iraq, Bush said, 'I reminded them and their families that the war in Iraq is really about peace.'[2]

Ouch! That hurt.

In the months preceding the 2003 war in Iraq, the United States and, to a lesser extent, the United Kingdom, witnessed an unprecedented campaign of Orwellian 'newspeak', including two examples of which 'Big Brother' himself would have been proud. Both the terms 'Axis of Evil' and 'Shock and Awe' prove that whoever controls the thesaurus of the past will surely have a free hand with the dictionary of the future.

In the field of psychobabble, nothing quite matches the phrase 'Shock and Awe', first used in 1996 by the military strategist Harlan K. Ullman. His theory was that America's technological superiority should enable her to pursue a strategy that would aim to 'deter and overpower an adversary through the adversary's perception and fear of his vulnerability and our own invincibility'.[3] This vision of a high-tech, low-casualty war became the basis for the attack on Iraq in March 2003, in which Baghdad would be hit by up to eight hundred cruise missiles in the first two days of the war. The missiles would destroy everything that made life in Baghdad liveable. 'We want them to quit. We want them not to fight,' Ullman told CBS reporter David Martin, 'so you take the city down. You get rid of their power, water. In two, three, four, five days they are physically, emotionally and psychologically exhausted.'[4]

This is Orwellian double-talk for state terrorism. The psychological torment of the Iraqi civilian population uncovers the lie in the claim that the Americans came as liberators and that their argument was with Saddam Hussein and his minions, not the Iraqi people. Moreover, to 'Shock and Awe' a civilian population in this way is clearly at odds with the idea that the war was part of the Global War on Terror. Terrorists would not be affected in the slightest way by the sight of Iraqi women and children suffering at the hands of American bullies, who, by every hostile step they took, confirmed why the terrorists felt justified in resisting them. Every missile that crashed into downtown Baghdad created new recruits for terrorist organisations, as had happened many times the world over from Belfast to Beirut, from the West Bank to Panama.

Ironically, one is left wondering who read Ullman's book more closely – the Pentagon or al-Qaeda? Surely the most remarkable example of 'Shock and Awe' since the atomic bombs were dropped on Japan in 1945 was the destruction of the Twin Towers of the World Trade Center in New York on 11 September. The sheer terror and panic generated in the minds of the American people on that day may never be equalled. The knee-jerk reaction of the American government showed how much al-Qaeda had gained in 'showing' the Americans how vulnerable they were. The result was that Bush blundered in choosing Iraq as an opponent in the war against terror. President Bush's advisers, as Robin Cook has demonstrated, chose to make Saddam Hussein an example to the Third World. Those who opposed America's world hegemony could expect a similar fate. As Cook wrote, 'The truth is that the US chose to attack Iraq not because it posed a threat but because the US knew Iraq was weak and expected its military to collapse.'[5] Now that is double-think: to make a pre-emptive attack on an enemy state on the grounds that it is an imminent threat, in the full knowledge that the state is militarily incapable of presenting any such threat and will collapse easily. In the world of advertising, the Trade Descriptions Act would be invoked. In politics, however, there is no political regulator to save the general public from such outrageous misrepresentation.

## But Who was Shocked and Who was Awed by the War in Iraq?

Terrorism expert Jessica Stern wrote that President Bush had 'taken a country that was not a terrorist threat and turned it into one'.[6] Ironically, in her opinion, the war had created 'precisely the situation the administration has described as a breeding ground for terrorists: a state unable to control its borders or provide for its citizens' rudimentary needs'. Vincent Cannistraro, former CIA director of counter-terrorism, further observed, 'There was no substantive intelligence information linking Saddam to international terrorism before the war. Now we've created the conditions that have made Iraq the place to come and attack Americans.'[7] Professor of Human Rights Practice Michael Ignatieff concluded:

The foreign fighters who have crossed into Iraq from Syria, Iran and Palestine to join Hussein loyalists in attacks on American soldiers know how much is at stake. Bloodying American troops, forcing a precipitate withdrawal, destroying the chances for a democratic Iraq would inflict the biggest defeat on America since Vietnam and send a message to every Islamic extremist in the region: Goliath is vulnerable.[8]

## Weapons of Mass Destruction

Am I the only person in the world who does not know what a 'weapon of mass destruction' is?

For example, is a 'weapon of mass destruction' a four-engined Lancaster bomber flying over Bremen in 1944 carrying a full load of high explosive bombs? Or is a 'weapon of mass destruction' a four-engined Lancaster bomber flying over Bremen in 1944 after it has been specially prepared to carry anthrax or poison gas?

No? Well, I am confused.

What about an American plane spraying Agent Orange in Vietnam in 1968?

No? Am I missing something?

What about American armoured earthmovers burying Iraqi troops alive in their trenches in 1991?

No? I think I'm beginning to see.

These are not 'weapons of mass destruction' because *we* used them and we were the winners, and the winners not only get to write the history but to make the definitions. But what exactly is a 'weapon of mass destruction'? After all, someone ought to know.

'Weapons of mass destruction are a threat to all who love freedom, liberty and democracy – that means you, voter!'

In Britain, Tony Blair ordered political debate to cease as soon as British soldiers went into action. So I still do not have an answer to my question, but I persevere. Is a 'weapon of mass destruction' a battlefield munition of more than usual effectiveness or is it a device designed for use against civilians, as by a terrorist group or rogue nation?

The distinction seems important to me. It suggests that the intentional use of a weapon must be a defining factor, otherwise collateral damage caused by any battlefield munition – as when a missile misses its legitimate target and hits, say, the Chinese Embassy in Belgrade, or a baby food factory in Baghdad, or a mental asylum in Grenada – would see the missile condemned as a 'weapon of mass destruction', which would have to be stored in a bunker deep under the Arizona desert so that UN inspectors could never find it.

Clearly, in 2003, Iraq possessed battlefield munitions, artillery shells for example, which could be used to fire chemical or biological weapons against enemy troops. The armies of all modern states have this capability. Moreover, many more states – at short notice – could produce the illegal substances to fill them. The technology is not advanced. Would the use of such illegal munitions in a battlefield situation be effective against troops equipped with protective suits and antidotes? It is very doubtful that such munitions would be as effective in modern warfare as conventional munitions. The value of such illegal weapons is more psychological. These are 'terror' weapons only because politicians convince their populations that being gassed is somehow worse than being blown into small pieces by high explosives.

The Americans recently admitted that they were developing battlefield tactical nuclear weapons, probably designed to destroy deep defences or missile silos. Again, the psychological effect of the word 'nuclear' would be out of all proportion to the threat posed to men on or under the ground. However, it triggers images of mushroom clouds and the total destruction of Hiroshima and Nagasaki.

What would alter the capability of these weapons and turn them into potential WMD would be a delivery system designed to make them a threat to targets many hundreds of miles, possibly even thousands of miles, from the battlefield. One of the defining points, therefore, in the definition of 'weapons of mass destruction' must be the range over which they could be employed, not merely their localised effect on the battlefield. The mere capacity to create toxins or gases is secondary to the capacity to deliver them.

While the term 'weapon of mass destruction' may have won itself a future in dictionaries of political quotations, it has been so loosely used that it no longer has language's usual function of communicating meaning and aiding understanding. Instead, its function is to convey a whole hamper of subconscious messages. It is itself a 'weapon of mass destruction': it destroys the very language from which it is formed. It has not been defined because its meaning is not fixed but constantly shifting as the politics which created it adjust to the changing world.

**The Rhetoric of War**

In 1914, as a naval rather than a military power, Britain thought in terms of economic victory over the Central Powers rather than the sort of battlefield victory that the French or Germans might have wished – a kind of Austerlitz or a Königgrätz which 'tied up the loose ends' all in one go. The British way was slower and more insidious, psychological as much as physical. It aimed to destroy a soldier's morale, so that in his mind or when he went home on leave he saw his stick-legged, Lowry-esque children starving in the streets. How must it have felt to the German soldiers in 1918, reduced to a virtual starvation diet of black bread and turnips, to know that in the trenches opposite the British and American soldiers ate chocolate and smoked Virginia tobacco?

In 1914, First Lord of the Admiralty Winston Churchill had already found the Achilles heel of the Central Powers. As a student of British military history he knew that the British way had always been to take part in as little of any war as could conceivably bring about a political victory. This was generally achieved by allying with a land power – in this case France – whose army could tire the enemy in static land engagements in which their casualties would be heavy, while British naval power would blockade the enemy coastline and slowly starve her to death. It was not pretty, but it worked.

Churchill's name has always been associated with the Dardanelles campaign against Turkey in 1915. His predilection for alternative strategies envisaged the city of Constantinople, the first Christian city and the capital of the eastern Roman Empire for 1,000 years, under the guns of British battleships. In the hope of driving the Muslim population out of the city, overthrowing their government and pulling Turkey out of the war, the First Lord of the Admiralty envisaged that the new super-dreadnought, *Queen Elizabeth*, on loan from the Grand Fleet at Scapa Flow, would terrify the population with its 15-inch guns, each armour-piercing shell of which was as tall as a man. At point-blank range of just a few miles, the *Queen Elizabeth* and as many as a dozen other British battleships would have been able to destroy Constantinople and inflict on the civilian population carnage never seen until the slaughter of Dresden, Hiroshima and Nagasaki in 1945. But, alas, exponents of the 'What if?' school of counterfactuals never saw the merits of Churchill's plan and so the original aim of the Dardanelles operation was written out and replaced by the unimaginative and truly incompetent Gallipoli campaign, where the 'mass destruction' was equally shared by the soldiers of the British Empire and Turkey.

Intermission. Dim lights.


**Victory at Sea 1916 (Please put on your rose-tinted glasses)**
In 1916, in smoky halls up and down the length of wartime Britain, flickering images on newsreels conveyed a kind of truth to patriotic Britons. It was communicated via a special kind of 'Britspeak' or 'Britview', a language exploited by British politicians to convince everyone they were fighting not just for the Britain of the present day but also for parallel universes in which the Britain of Nelson, Marlborough, Prince Rupert and Drake coexisted. Here, other nations like Germany or Napoleonic France, or the Spain of Philip II might threaten to invade England but against their apparently overwhelming military strength Britain possessed 'might'. The courage of the foreign invaders quailed before British 'pluck', 'valour' and 'gallantry'. Their soldiers, content to face danger against the enemy, were written out of history and fell back in humiliation at the 'peril' of facing an English 'foe'. Britain's 'weapons of mass destruction' were hidden beneath a whole body of literature. The English had learned to write the enemy off the battlefield.

Viewing the Battle of Jutland on the flickering screens hastily erected in village halls, squire's son and blacksmith's boy rubbed shoulders in the wonderful equality of a propagandist's war. Audiences viewed the misty seas between Britain and Denmark with a sense of nostalgia for a golden past. With a seemingly limitless vista of mighty leviathans covering the seas like creatures from Arthurian legend, the Battle of Jutland was like the medieval affrays at Agincourt or Crécy. At Jutland, however, it was a cleaner war, between men in armoured ships, with the unpleasant realities flushed away to the bottom of the North Sea for some future marine archaeologist to discover.

Belching smoke, the silent dreadnoughts of the Royal Navy sailed out of Scapa Flow with the battle-cruisers *Lion* and *Tiger*, *Princess Royal* and *Queen Mary*, sleek and beautiful, combining feline speed with the efficient killing capacity of a predator. Commanding the 'Splendid Cats' was the handsome and debonair Sir David Beatty, whose name seemed to have been especially chosen from a list of heroic surnames supplied by English Heritage: Drake and Frobisher, Collingwood and Nelson, Benbow and Hood. Names like these have resonated throughout British history and their like spirit runs through the veins of every true Briton.

Behind the sleek shapes of Beatty's 'Cats' came the armoured might of dreadnought battleships, successors to the knights who rode with the Black Prince and Hotspur through the pages of Unstead's medieval histories. In his flagship, the appropriately named *Iron Duke*, was Sir John Jellicoe, whose name was carved at Buckler's Hard on the Solent from the New Forest oak where King William Rufus fell. A thousand years of naval mastery rode with the names of *Invincible*, *Indomitable*, *Indefatigable*; names a delight to the Scrabble-playing clerks of the Admiralty but unpronounceable to the Jack tars of the lower decks, though still etched into their very souls like seaside rock. In the serried ranks of the battle squadrons pouring out from the wild and lonely waters of Scapa Flow – *Hercules*, *Ajax*, *Agamemnon*, *Bellerophon*, *Neptune* – they were all there, bearing witness to the public-school obsession with classics. *Thunderer*, *Conqueror* and *Superb* reverberated in the mind of First Lord of the Admiralty Winston Churchill. He had once suggested naming a new battleship 'Oliver Cromwell' but had had his knuckles rapped by King George V . . .

Meanwhile, off the coast of Suffolk at Harwich, the destroyer HMS *Cheerful* was conducting its own personal war against Frau Hilda Holzenbeim of Nussbaumstrasse 34, Wiesbaden. Belying its name, the destroyer, deadliest of Britain's 'weapons of mass destruction', intercepted a Dutch freighter out of Rotterdam heading for Hamburg with a cargo of grain and root vegetables. The *Cheerful* escorted the neutral vessel into a British port where the cargo was impounded. It was just an everyday event for the destroyer, a victory with no casualties in the deadliest, if probably the least known, of all campaigns in the First World War. Yet . . .

Stop the film!

. . . One of the greatest state atrocities of the twentieth century was taking place and nobody seemed to notice. Was it merely that nobody knew? Or did nobody care? The Royal Navy does not include it in its battle honours. Winston Churchill never referred to HMS *Cheerful*'s 'finest hour' yet Britain was fighting 'in the food queues, in the doctors' surgeries and in the children's shoe shops'.

Britain's deliberate and calculated 'starvation policy' during the First World War was directed against the civilians of the Central Powers. Between 1914 and 1919 the naval blockade was the chosen strategy of the Royal Navy. Unlike the saturated aerial bombing of Germany during the Second World War, which grew out of the RAF's inability to accurately bomb military targets, the blockade was naval policy from the start of the war. First Lord of the Admiralty Winston Churchill freely admitted that Britain's navy aimed 'to starve the whole German population – men, women and children, old and young, wounded and sound – into submission'.[9]

The naval blockade was a war crime that violated the Hague Convention of 1907, which only listed food as 'contraband' when it was intended for enemy military personnel, not civilians. Yet, H.G. Wells felt the policy was entirely justified, claiming, 'Every sword that is drawn against Germany is a sword drawn for peace.'[10] Double-talk had begun, soon to be followed by phrases such as 'the war to end all wars' and others.

When Germany retaliated with her U-boat campaign against the British navy, she explained to prominent neutrals, notably the US, that the Royal Navy was slowly strangling her civilian population. However, Germany's complaints were brushed aside by Colonel House, adviser to President Woodrow Wilson, with the curious reasoning, 'England is not exercising her power in an objectionable way, for it is controlled by a democracy.'[11]

By 1917, the war on the domestic fronts was engendering the racial hatred absent from the common soldiers who went to war in 1914. States, rather than armies or even individuals, were fighting to the death and national policies were revealing a darker purpose, redolent of eugenics and Social Darwinism. In C. Paul Vincent's book *The Politics of Hunger*, the author refers to a 'zoological warfare', a war of extermination apparent in the views of men like Lord Baden-Powell, who chillingly expressed satisfaction that the German race was being ruined through starvation. A British journalist picked up the prevalent mood when he wrote of 'tens of thousands of Germans now in the wombs of famished mothers' who were 'destined for a life of physical inferiority'. Even more terrible, the same writer projected a grim future for the Germans 'not yet conceived'.[12] This was the politics of racial hatred with a capital 'H'. In France, Prime Minister Clemenceau expressed his satisfaction at the development of the starvation policy on the grounds that 'there are 20 million Germans too many'.[13]

By the time Jutland was fought off the coast of Denmark, Frau Holzenbeim and her family were surviving on a meagre diet of black bread, slices of sausage without fat and a ration of 3 lb of potatoes a week. For those at the Admiralty who had named Jellicoe's battleships *Superb*, *Conqueror* and *Valiant*, the titles 'Emaciated', 'Starved' and 'Gaunt' had no place in the official records.

In Germany and Austria-Hungary, the potato crop failed and terrible starvation struck in the winter of 1916–17, known as the 'Turnip Winter', during which turnips became the only food widely available for the poor. Malnutrition was widespread throughout the civilian population, with an average diet reduced from 3,400 calories in 1914 to just 1,000 in 1916.

Food rationing was an attempt to equalise the suffering of the people but not everybody was prepared to suffer equally. One grand lady was seen on a German station platform struggling with an enormously heavy case. Seeing her obvious distress several gentlemen hurried to help her but as they lifted her luggage it fell open to reveal half a pig inside. Her explanation is, unfortunately, not in the records but would have been worth hearing. The pig, incidentally, was confiscated and sold. At the other end of the social scale women suffered most, many sacrificing their meagre rations for their starving children. As a result, female mortality from 'natural causes' rose by 51 per cent.

Post-war estimates of the effects of the British naval blockade are that it cost the lives of almost 800,000 civilians and prevented a further million births. Moreover, deaths among the starving German population were 250 per cent higher during the influenza epidemic than in Britain. It is not surprising to hear that in March 1919, the commander of the

British Army of Occupation, General Sir Herbert Plumer, wrote that British soldiers who were occupying Germany could no longer bear the sight of 'hordes of skinny and bloated children pawing over the offal from British cantonments'.[14] Plumer, a soldier of the 'old school', could not understand this war against civilians. He wrote that many British soldiers were going short of food themselves to feed the starving children. Suicides among German women and children were widespread and everywhere was the smell of rotting flesh on living bodies, the result of malnutrition.

Although Britain and the United States favoured restoring food supplies to the German people, the French were adamant that the blockade should continue until the Germans had finally signed the Versailles treaty. Only then, on 28 June 1919 – nine months after the fighting stopped on the Western Front – were normal food supplies allowed to reach Germany. During this period France and Belgium had seized Germany's dairy cows, which meant that German children had no milk. Hundreds of thousands of German civilians were being killed by Allied statesmen after the war had ended.

In *The Politics of Hunger*, Vincent maintains that the victimised children of 1915–19 became some of the most active and radical members of the Nazi Party in the inter-war period, an irony hopefully not lost on British politicians of the period.[15] While Wilson, Lloyd George and Clemenceau were revising the geography of Europe at Versailles, the British 'hunger blockade' was preparing a response that was to destroy all their efforts and the next generation with it.

The Director of Berlin's Juvenile Justice Department noted ominously that the usually law-abiding Germans were turning to crime:

> It is astonishing, but even among apprentices and university students, the spread of criminality is increasing . . . Only the most severe need, called forth by England's hunger blockade, could have obliterated the vigorous right-consciousness of Germany's youth.[16]

In simple terms, the human self-preservation urge overcame any cultural imperatives like law and property rights. The moral foundations of Germany as a nation were breaking down. And it was the Allies who had caused this dangerous development in a society already made desperate by economic and social changes.

Vincent suggests that it was the blockade and its consequences which tilted some of Germany's most influential thinkers towards a belief that their nation's future lay in expansion to the east where hegemony over Russia and the smaller eastern states could provide them with grain and animal fodder for their livestock, while the Balkans and the Caucasian regions could supply oil, metals and cotton. Trade and political links with the West, meaning Britain, France and the United States, were seen as ill-advised as their naval power would always be able to hold Germany to ransom in a crisis. Thus, although Germany's policy of *Drang nach Osten* (Striving towards the East) was part of the country's traditional aims, it received new stimulus from the starvation policy of 1915–19.

Germany's introduction to democracy at the end of the war was forever tainted by the fact that her fellow democracies – Britain, France and America – still ostracised her for a system she had rejected. The Weimar Republic was doomed from the start because poverty and inflation 'de-classed' many Germans, notably the wealthier working class and the lower middle class who found themselves reduced to the level from which they had struggled to rise. In Vincent's words:

> Many of these people would seek simplistic formulas to overcome a difficult and sad situation. A warped economic and foreign policy proved the logical capstone for a people whose bodies and minds had been enfeebled by the blockade policy of the Allies.[17]

## Victory in the Air 1940–5 (Please take off your gas mask)

*Washington Post*, 3 September 1939: 'Both sides agree not to bomb civilians.'

If the Court of History were available, I should like to address three questions to prime ministers Neville Chamberlain and Winston Churchill. I am informed, however, that they are still enjoying the Christmas recess. I'll pose the questions, nevertheless, though they will, for the moment, remain unanswered:

- Is a democratically elected government entitled to commit its people to a war they do not have the capacity to fight?
- Was Britain's decision to declare war on Germany in 1939 based entirely on confidence in the strength of the French army?
- Was Britain's decision to continue the war in 1940 after the

fall of France based entirely on the hope that the United States
of America would enter the war against Germany?

It was not just the number of casualties suffered by the armies on the
Western Front during 1914–18 that dominated the politics of the 1920s,
it was the nature of the killing: the butchering of herds of men, mostly
from civilian backgrounds, who walked willingly to a blind,
unreasoning death in the mud. The dead were not professional soldiers
who had chosen the way of war. They were civilians in khaki. Their
martyrdom represented the moment when civilians became the true
targets of modern warfare. Britain's first mass armies contained few
with a military background. Instead, they were the shopkeepers that
Napoleon had scorned, the men who tilled the soil, dug the coal, caught
the fish and staffed offices and factories. There were teachers, poets,
composers and sportsmen. They had succumbed to the lies of the
politicians to fight for 'King and Country'.

When the war ended in 1918, politicians were willing to accept any
solution, however unrealistic, to avoid a return to such slaughter. The
Gotha and Zeppelin raids on London had combined with the fiction of
H.G. Wells in *Things to Come* to create the myth that aerial
bombardment pointed the way for future warfare. No power on earth, it
was claimed, could stop the bomber from getting through and delivering
its deadly payload on a helpless civilian population. So the choice was
now a stark one – either avoid war by appeasing your enemy or suffer
destruction. In Britain, the Treasury supported the argument that money
spent on large land armies or expensive new warships was wasted. The
bomber deterrent would keep everyone safe by promising any enemy
that as they sowed, so should they reap. In a bomber war, both sides
would be destroyed.

However, the British people were being lied to by their leaders. The
three main protagonists on the Western Front had drawn different
lessons from their terrible experiences there. The French, forced from
Napoleonic attack in 1914 to mere survival through dogged defence by
1916, opted to invest their funds in the future by building the immense
Maginot Line running between the Belgian and Swiss frontiers, hoping
to thereby gain security from German attack. The Germans learned from
defeat in 1918 that the future rested with Britain's combination of tanks
and planes as used at Amiens, a form of blitzkrieg on the ground and in
the air. Britain alone swallowed the bomber myth, relying on the four-
engined bomber to carry the war to the heart of Germany and to leave

the army and navy to get involved in as much or as little of the war as they wanted.

Thus the prime objective of the Royal Air Force in the inter-war period was to develop a bombing potential that would attack German industrial capacity, communications and war factories accurately. As a result, there developed a belief that the airmen could deliver victory without the country paying the terrible price that was inherent in head-on confrontation between massed armies. The RAF would carry the war to the German homeland so that, just as in the First World War when the navy's blockade had strangled the German people, this time British bombers would destroy German homes and reduce morale to such a degree that the tortured German masses would rise up to overthrow Hitler. But, as the Germans were believed to be able to blot out the sun with their own bomber force, once war started, would London not swiftly be reduced to a giant ashtray? Of course. Thus, with both sides facing mutually assured destruction (MAD), war was better avoided at all costs. And this is where 'appeasement' came in.

'Appeasement' has joined the vocabulary of abuse prepared, since 1945, by American and British politicians. Its widespread use during the approach of the 2003 war in Iraq was just another example of the misuse of history. Out of context, 'appeasement' can become a pejorative description of diplomacy. It implies 'giving in' or 'conceding'. Yet, sometimes it is right to appease an opponent rather than confront or fight him or her. Diplomacy is all about making concessions to secure an agreement that may not give 100 per cent to any side in a dispute but gives enough to everyone so that the dispute is settled without violence. It is the demand for 100 per cent solutions that fuels many of the world's intractable problems today, like those in Palestine and Ulster.

Since 1945, America has been the land of 100 per centery, of white versus black, good versus evil, Free versus Communist, and so on. Compromise, once a vital element in the development of America stretching back to colonial times – one thinks of the Connecticut Compromise, the Missouri Compromise, the 1850 Compromise, the Crittenden Compromise – now seems a dead art. The 'third way' or 'third party' is no longer popular in the United States. Even 'draws' in sporting events – so typical of the British way of sport in which the stronger may be pegged back by the weaker, or the amateur inspired to lift his game to match the professional in the glorious equality of sporting competition – are non-existent for the American. For them there must be a winner, glory and triumph to him, and a loser, oozing shame and failure, in every competition. Where the scores are level, instead of a handshake and a drink at the bar, there must be a 'shoot-out', dramatic and deadly, with only the strongest left standing.

Those modern politicians who use the description 'appeaser' to describe Neville Chamberlain in 1938 miss one vital point. As a democratically elected leader he was reflecting the preferences of the British people. Only Churchillian propaganda, both in Britain and, latterly, from Republican sources in America, has condemned Chamberlain for appeasement. Chamberlain's image is so far from the American ideal that he makes an easy target for modern American politicians. Thin, weedy-looking, besuited and carrying that sign of effete Britishness, a furled umbrella, Chamberlain had 'loser' written all over him. If, however, he had had the build of Arnold Schwarzenegger with the chin of Desperate Dan and carried a 'chick' under each arm, who would be the first to splash puddles up his leg? Then, might appeasement have a different source.

But, was the argument true, that the bomber would always get through?

- Could anything stop the bomber? Yes. The modern fighter.
- Did Germany have a large long-range bomber fleet? No. She had no four-engined bombers at all or plans for them. Her strength was in ground support aircraft – Stukas – and fast, modern fighters – Me-109s – to use against British bombers.
- If Germany did stop Britain's bombers, how could Britain pursue a war against Germany with such a small and poorly equipped army? Only by relying on the French army.
- But if the French army was mainly committed to the Maginot Line how would Britain be able to defeat the German army? Only by killing German civilians through bombing.
- Britain would use 'weapons of mass destruction' against civilian targets? Yes.
- So, Britain's leaders knew their only hope of victory over Germany was by resorting to 'war crimes'? Ummmmmm . . .

By 1941, Churchill's main adviser, Lord Cherwell, had convinced the Prime Minister that just as German morale had cracked in 1918 it would crack again if the German frontline soldiers heard of the destruction of their families and homes. So great was Cherwell's influence that there were few willing to remind him of the need for Britain to maintain herself on the moral high ground. In the depths of wartime, and with British cities – notably London – having suffered heavy and indiscriminate bombing of civilian areas, few people were willing to voice the moral argument. In a sense, there was a more effective argument available. The morale of the British people had stood up well to the bombing, why did Cherwell assume it would be any different in Germany?

Churchill was grasping at straws and grabbed this offer of a cheap way of winning the war. At that time Britain was manufacturing a large fleet of four-engine bombers. If these were not used to raid Germany, what were they to be used for? And why had they been built in preference to the hundreds of escort vessels that were needed in the Atlantic against the U-boats, or the heavy warships needed in the Mediterranean, or the tanks that would one day be needed if Europe was ever to be liberated? Cherwell had used 'lies, damned lies and statistics' to win the argument. The figures he proposed for German casualties as a result of a bombing campaign were, according to the later US Strategic Bombing Survey, exaggerated tenfold.

Precision bombing of German military targets was an oxymoron worthy of the British sense of irony. The Butt Report of 1941 showed that the much-vaunted RAF bombers hardly ever got near designated targets as a result of inaccurate navigation and bombsights. Butt's findings were alarming to say the least. Of British aircraft attacking French ports only two out of three reached their target (according to Butt, 'reaching' the target meant being within a five-mile radius of it). This became one in four for targets in Germany as a whole and for the Ruhr it was an incredible one in ten. Having reached the target, those plucky air crews then had only the slightest chance of hitting what they were aiming at. Precision bombing was a thing of the future.

Although Britain wished to hold the moral high ground, victory over evil could not be achieved without employing some of the weapons that were used by the other side. This was an inevitable moral dilemma for those involved in any 'just war'. To Winston Churchill, as well as to the vast numbers of ordinary people who supported him, the greater immorality for Britain was to risk defeat by Germany or to be forced into a negotiated peace with Nazism. This was certainly the view of the Church, as well as most politicians. However, how far could one get drawn into the evil of war before becoming tainted with the very qualities one had set out to destroy? Britain's professed aim to liberate the oppressed peoples of Europe was a thoroughly laudable one, but wasn't a strategy of civilian bombing, aimed specifically against the lives and property of the German people rather than the military potential of Nazi Germany, running very close to genocide?

At the Yalta Conference of 4–11 February 1945, Churchill was eager to be seen to be helping the Russian advance on the ground and called on Bomber Command to hit the cities to which retreating German troops were heading. These included Leipzig, Chemnitz and Dresden. In fact, it was understood that Dresden was already crammed with refugees who had fled before the Russian advance. This did not, however, change its status as an 'especially attractive target', in the Prime Minister's own words.

Bomber Command's briefing notes on Dresden referred to the city as being the largest un-bombed area left in Germany. Its population of 600,000 had probably been doubled by refugees and prisoners of war. Sir Arthur Harris scornfully referred to the 'sentimental views' of Dresden prevalent among some senior RAF commanders, 'The feeling, such as there is, over Dresden, could be easily explained by any psychiatrist. It is connected with German bands and Dresden shepherdesses. Actually, Dresden was a mass of munition works.' Harris was exaggerating. The later American assessment of the raid on Dresden was that it had 'caused serious damage to the cigar and cigarette industry'.[18]

What do you tell professional airmen about a target when your intention is to massacre women, children and refugees? Do you expect them to obey their orders without question? If so, why do you need to tell them anything? Bomber Command's leaders must have regarded the Dresden raid as something unusual because they chose to lie to their men. The various group leaders explained the purpose of the raid with these canards. In No. 1 Group, aircrew were told that Dresden was being bombed because it was a vital railway centre. No. 3 Group were led to believe that Dresden was a German army headquarters. No. 6 Group learned that Dresden was an important industrial area, producing electric motors, precision instruments, chemicals and munitions (strange that it had not been attacked before then!). It got worse at squadron level. Dresden soon became the hub of all German resistance – indeed a 'fortress city' – and a production centre for poison gas. Incidentally, in passing, it was also Gestapo headquarters. These were simply lies. Dresden was, in fact, one of the architectural jewels of eastern Europe, which had suffered few raids up to that point in the whole war. It was presumed by the inhabitants that – like Florence and

Venice – it was being spared because even in wartime men do not stoop so low as to destroy beauty for its own sake.

German 'war crimes' that had taken place earlier in the conflict, like deliberately bombing civilians and hospitals and mistreating prisoners of war, were 'trumped' in one night as Bomber Command destroyed all 19 permanent hospitals in Dresden, killed so many civilians that nobody will ever know the true number and slaughtered their own prisoners of war and prisoners from other nations at war with Germany. How many died? It should matter. Individual lives should not lose their meaning by absorption into a mountain of statistics. But nobody knows for certain and to quantify is to diminish each individual tragedy.

Ironically, at the end of the war the Soviet Union wanted the bombing of civilian populations to be made a war crime at the Nuremberg trials. They were successfully blocked by the British. In May 1943, the Nazis published a list of 1,100 schools, 600 churches and 300 hospitals, not to mention innumerable sites of architectural or historical importance, that had been destroyed by the RAF. The world would not listen. The Germans had done as much themselves. Were they not reaping the whirlwind? Moreover, Air Secretary Sir Archibald Sinclair claimed at the same time, 'the targets of Bomber Command are always military, but night-bombing of military objectives necessarily involves bombing in the area in which they are situated'. Who did one believe? A British air chief or the head of Nazi propaganda?

By 1944, Winston Churchill must have felt that, with the United States and the Soviet Union as his allies against Germany, his fears for the British Empire were probably over. It was at this moment, however, that the Germans forced the British Prime Minister to experience again the fraught situation that he had faced in 1940 when it seemed that Britain might actually be defeated. Germany's use of flying bombs and V2 missiles seemed to presage the sort of destruction that London had feared but had never seen. It was at this time that Churchill revealed a willingness to go to any lengths to avoid defeat in war. His thoughts on the subject of chemical and biological weapons go beyond anything we know from other democratic politicians in wartime.

Sir Winston Churchill was recently voted the greatest Briton of the millennium. As a Nobel Prize winner for literature and Britain's inspiring war leader during the Second World War, this was not entirely surprising. To what extent, then, should Churchill's use of state terror in both world wars affect his place in history?

Nazi leaders were tried and some executed at Nuremberg in 1945 for war crimes, some not directly connected with the Holocaust. But the war crimes of all national leaders between 1939 and 1945 were presumably undertaken in the context of the most terrible war in human history. They were means, often very unpleasant means, to achieve a necessary end. However, as Stalin or Hitler might have pointed out, even though Churchill was a democratically elected politician, a student of history, a master of literature, an orator of genius, a painter, a bricklayer, a treasured raconteur, a bon viveur, he was above everything else the hardest and the most ruthless of all leaders in the war.

Only Roosevelt ran him close. Hitler was a delusional pervert; Stalin a criminal butcher; Mussolini half operatic tenor, half pantomime horse; but Churchill was that most terrible thing of all, a pragmatist down to his leather soles. There was an answer to every problem if you dug deep enough for it and never let your conscience be your guide.

In any present-day discussion on the threat of weapons of mass destruction possessed by Iraq, Iran or North Korea, it is important that Churchill's thoughts on the subject be borne in mind. Despite the horrors of the First World War, when Churchill was Secretary of State for the Royal Air Force in 1919 he strongly advocated that gas should be retained as a potential weapon and that Britain should oppose any international ban on its use. As he said in one of his memos:

> I do not understand this squeamishness about the use of gas. It is
> sheer affectation to lacerate a man with the poisonous fragment
> of a bursting shell and then to boggle at making his eyes water
> by means of a lachrymatory [*sic*] gas. I am strongly in favour of
> using poison gas against uncivilised tribes where it could spread
> a lively terror.[19]

Churchill's common sense makes the flesh creep. Judged like this he is, of course, quite right. Death in war is not a glorious thing. It is a functional thing as seen through the cold, calculating eyes of the politician. Clausewitz, a Prussian soldier and military theorist, explains in his terms that if war is an extension of politics, then the way it is conducted is less important than the aim which is achieved. Before the political aim can be achieved, the human factor – armies, civilians and so on – which opposes you must be reduced to the point that it can no longer hinder the achievement of your aim. How you reduce the threat from the human factor – elegant executions conducted by French swordsmen may be one way, or soaking enemy citizens in seas of fire, clouds of poison gas or anthrax spores may be far more hideous alternatives – is only important in terms of cost effectiveness. The concept of describing deaths in wartime as 'crimes', consequently, is in Churchill's own terms 'sheer affectation'.

It comes as no surprise that it was Churchill who ordered the manufacture of five million anthrax cattle cakes which could be dropped on six designated German cities in 1944, should Germany escalate the V-weapons attacks on London with chemical warheads. The aim of what would have been entitled Operation Vegetarian would have been to wipe out the German beef and dairy herds and then wait for the bacterium to spread to the human population. With people then having no access to appropriate medical treatment, this would have caused many thousands – perhaps even millions – of German men, women and children to suffer awful deaths.

As neither Britain nor Germany used biological and chemical weapons in the remainder of the war, there can be no certainty that Churchill would have given the British operation the go-ahead and so arguments about the morality of such an action are pointless. Nevertheless, enough evidence exists to show that Churchill was prepared to consider the use of anthrax and/or poison gas and that he would have brooked no criticism from what he referred to as 'that particular set of psalm-singing uniformed defeatists'. In a memorandum to General Ismay, Churchill pointed out that he was not deterred from making tough decisions on poison gas, 'I do not see why we should have the disadvantages of being the gentleman while they have all the advantages of being the cad.' Emotion would clearly have played no part in his decision. As he said to Ismay:

> It may be several weeks or even months before I shall ask you to drench Germany with poison gas, and if we do it, let us do it 100 per cent. In the meanwhile, I want the matter studied in cold blood by sensible people.

In preparation for Operation Vegetarian, the anthrax cakes were tested on Gruinard Island, located off the coast of Wester Ross. (It was so thoroughly contaminated through these experiments that it was not habitable until cleared in 1990.) The operation was planned for the summer of 1944 but was abandoned as the Allies' Normandy invasion progressed successfully. Nevertheless, it presents a truly horrible 'What if?' situation. It was estimated that a single Lancaster bomber would have been able to scatter 4,000 anthrax-infected cakes over a 60-mile area in less than 20 minutes. Just a dozen aircraft would have been enough to litter much of the north German countryside with anthrax spores.[20]

## The Morgenthau Plan

It has been observed that a democratic nation at war can be as guilty of terrorism as any other state in an age of total war. The atrocities of recent war criminals, like Saddam Hussein or Slobodan Milosovic, must be considered in proportion to the actions of the main participants in both world wars. What makes democratic warfare more frightening is that the strategies of conflict which are adopted do not come from the minds of perverted individuals like the war criminals who have been able to flourish since the United Nations ostensibly became the world's conscience and the United States its policeman. Some terrible crimes are based on decisions taken by democratically elected representatives of the people, often made on a 'means-and-end' basis, totally divorced from morality.

As the Second World War drew to a close, the problem of what to do with a defeated Germany weighed heavily on the minds of the Allied leaders, notably Churchill and Roosevelt. In comparison with the American politicians, some of them increasingly influenced by the extreme views of Stalin, Churchill can be viewed in a more positive light. His behaviour during the Teheran Conference of 1943 seems almost life asserting in comparison with his memorandum above on poison gas.

At a dinner hosted by Stalin at the Russian Embassy in Teheran, the Soviet leader made a toast:

> At least 50,000 – and perhaps 100,000 – of the German command staff must be physically liquidated. I propose a toast to the swiftest possible justice for all Germany's war criminals – justice before a firing squad! I drink to our unity in killing them as quickly as we capture them. All of them! There must be at least 50,000.

Churchill, obviously shocked, replied:

The British people will never stand for such mass murder . . . I
will not be a party to any butchery in cold blood. I would rather
be taken out in the garden, here and now, and shot myself than
sully my country's honour by such infamy.

Roosevelt chipped in, 'As usual, it seems to be my function to mediate
the dispute. Why don't we say 49,500?'

The President's son, Elliott, who was a guest at the meal, added, 'I
hope that those 50,000 war criminals will be taken care of – but many
hundreds of thousands more Nazis as well!'[21] Stalin clinked glasses with
him and gave him a bear hug.

Churchill was incensed. 'I cannot forgive you for making such a
dastardly statement,' he said to the younger Roosevelt before storming
out of the room. Stalin followed him saying that it was only a joke, but
later Churchill went into one of his deepest depressions, reflecting that
one day there might have to be a terrible war with Russia. As he said, 'I
want to sleep for billions of years.'[22]

Churchill never forgave the young Elliott Roosevelt. Soon, however,
he found he had even more to worry about with the President himself,
who was under the influence of the Jewish Secretary of the Treasury,
Henry Morgenthau Jr. Morgenthau had a plan for settling the German
problem once and for all. There was to be no repeat of 1918, when
German troops marched home giving the impression that they had not
been beaten but 'stabbed in the back' by their political leaders. This time
America and Russia must remove the German threat forever by de-
industrialising Germany and reducing it to an agricultural or pastoral
state. It was anticipated that this would cause starvation and might cost
tens of millions of lives but it was felt to be justifiable in terms of
putting an end to Germany's record of three aggressive wars in seventy
years. But Morgenthau was out on a limb. Secretary of State Cordell
Hull said to Roosevelt:

Morgenthau's plan was out of all reason. Its net results . . . would
be that nothing would be left to Germany but land and only 60
per cent of the German people could live on the land. This meant
that the other 40 per cent would die.

Herbert Hoover also strongly opposed the plan, saying it would lead to
'a considerable part of the German people being "liquidated" through

disease, malnutrition and slow starvation'.[23]

The plan which was being considered by the American leaders would have even overshadowed the Jewish Holocaust. The ruthlessness of the Americans might have taken Hitler's breath away. I am aware that this statement seems almost too ridiculous to print, yet the Morgenthau Plan envisaged a move into the world of genocide on a scale that was truly astounding. W. Friedman, a historian of the time, commented, 'Extermination need not proceed dramatically, through gas chambers and mass executions, it can be no less effective through the gradual sapping of vitality.'[24] Roosevelt actually discussed plans to exterminate the German people, through castration or sterilisation, with the Secretary for the Interior Harold Ickes. Speaking to Morgenthau, Roosevelt said:

> We have got to be tough with Germany, and I mean the German people, not just the Nazis. We either have to castrate the German people or you have to treat them in such a manner that they can't just go on reproducing people who want to continue the way they have in the past.[25]

In fact, when parts of the Morgenthau Plan became known, it was naturally exploited by Goebbels and served to stiffen German resistance. According to the US generals, it was actually worth ten divisions to the German High Command.

When confronted with Morgenthau's ideas at the Quebec Conference, Churchill refused to agree, calling the plan 'unnatural, unchristian and unnecessary', even though it was presented to him as a way to boost Britain's trading opportunities after the war. As he said, 'You cannot indict a whole nation.'[26] Eventually, Roosevelt, however, used Churchill's senior adviser, Lord Cherwell, to pressure Churchill into changing his mind. Cherwell was successful and Roosevelt and Churchill both agreed to a memorandum to convert Germany 'into a country primarily agricultural and pastoral in its character'.[27] Both leaders initialled the document. When he heard, the British Foreign Secretary, Anthony Eden, lost his temper and had a blazing row with Churchill. When US Secretary for War Henry Stimson questioned the President about the memorandum, Roosevelt replied, 'Henry, I have not the faintest recollection of this at all.'[28]

During the last few days of the fighting in 1945, vast numbers of German prisoners were taken, many of whom were turned over to the

Russians by General Eisenhower as slave labour, which contradicts Roosevelt's absolute denial that the German people would be enslaved. Interestingly, Russia was not a signatory of the Geneva Convention and was not covered by its rules. By handing over prisoners to a non-signatory of the convention, Eisenhower was himself committing a war crime for which he could have been indicted.

America's 'treat 'em rough' policy towards Germany worried novelist John Dos Passos. As he shrewdly observed, 'All these directives about "don't coddle the Germans" have thrown open the gates for every criminal tendency we've got in us.'[29]

In the inevitable chaos that followed the conclusion of so vast a war, many terrible events passed almost unnoticed or unrecorded by history. No reliable figures remain for the German lives lost during the immense movement of the population from German territories east of the Oder-Neisse line. It is believed as many as 18 million Germans were driven out of their homes and sent westwards by the Russians, of which millions died during the operation: US Forces European Theatre (USFET) estimated a figure of three million women and children. Bertrand Russell wrote in *The Times* on 19 October 1945:

> In eastern Europe now mass deportations are being carried out by our allies on an unprecedented scale, and an apparently deliberate attempt is being made to exterminate many millions of Germans, not by gas but by depriving them of their homes and of food, leaving them to die by slow and agonising starvation. This is not done as an act of war, but as a part of a deliberate policy of 'peace'.

It was one of the greatest examples of 'ethnic cleansing' in human history.

In conclusion, one finds oneself left with the books of James Bacque, which allege that a million German prisoners of war died of starvation and neglect in the camps administered by American troops in Germany. One newspaper suggests that in his book *Other Losses* Bacque is stirring up 'a hornet's nest', but the 'hornet's nest' referred to is not so much the furore caused by the subject matter, as the reaction of other historians to Bacque's allegations. The late Stephen Ambrose convened a conference on this subject at the University of Florida. He and many other historians, both American and German, were highly critical of Bacque's statistical methods and felt that his findings on casualty figures could not be substantiated. However, even Bacque's harshest critics concede that there is evidence to support his description of the conditions of the German prisoners of war. I have confined my attention to this 'lesser' charge and, as a result, have found use for Bacque's revelations about the appalling treatment accorded to German POWs by the Americans which, to my mind, was in keeping with policies recommended by Morgenthau, but which were never implemented in their entirety. Nevertheless, the American treatment of Germany during the period 1945–7 must be viewed as a crime against humanity just as were the far greater German crimes towards the Jews. Nobody will gain from a comparison of figures, nor does any American politician or soldier deserve the accusing finger that was rightly pointed at Adolf Hitler and his henchmen. Nevertheless, historians owe it to the profession they follow to make the truth of this terrible period available to the world. And American politicians should not try to conceal such damaging evidence if they aspire to world leadership.

## Who Uses Chemical Weapons and Who Uses Sanitised Warfare?

Why is it considered acceptable for some parties in a war (i.e. the USA) to use weapons of mass destruction, but not acceptable for certain other parties (i.e. the other side) to use such weapons? America's use of Agent Orange during the Vietnam War was the most widespread use of chemicals by any nation in the history of warfare. Does anyone remember Agent Orange, other than those currently suffering from cancer as a result of its use?

Operation Ranch Hand was the harmless-sounding name given to America's herbicidal warfare in Vietnam. By 1963, the Americans had conceived a plan to employ technology and air power to help their troops in the Vietnam jungle by spraying it with a weed killer known as 'Agent Orange'. Huge quantities were dropped in order to destroy the jungles of Vietnam thereby exposing enemy troops and making the conventional bombing of targets easier.

Defoliants had been briefly used in warfare before, by the British in the Malayan Emergency for example, but no power had ever previously possessed America's potential to use defoliants as weapons. At first, defoliation was introduced carefully, to avoid harming friendly peasants, but mistakes soon proliferated as defoliant spread in the wind.

The Pentagon had assured all the commanders that Agent Orange was non-carcinogenic to humans and caused no ill-effects. The army had been using it for three years and had noted some skin problems but these they thought were of a minor nature. In 1967 – by which time 1.7 million acres had been sprayed – public disquiet began to reach epidemic proportions as the Communists demonstrated that the defoliant was not only poisonous, but was affecting human genetics and could, in fact, be a biological time bomb.

Agent Orange was a mixture of two herbicides: 24D and 245T and was given its name because there was an orange stripe around the barrels in which it was kept. The dioxin contaminant in Agent Orange was what created the most concern for human health, as it caused cancers, immune deficiency, reproductive and developmental problems, endocrine disruption and nervous system damage amongst many other health defects. Even though the two herbicides were domestically used in the United States, the type of Agent Orange used in Vietnam was high in the most toxic dioxin. Dioxins are among the most toxic chemicals ever made by man, molecule by molecule, and are very persistent, so they bioaccumulate. More than 30 years after their first use, doctors report elevated dioxin levels from Agent Orange in Vietnamese blood.

There is no doubt about the military advantages that initially flowed from Operation Ranch Hand, yet having failed to research its own weapons adequately, the United States later found that American soldiers on the ground were beginning to succumb to their own chemicals. The chemical companies had apparently known of these dioxins but said nothing because their removal would have increased the cost of production. The fact that Agent Orange would harm both 'friendly' and enemy soldiers who encountered it was conveniently overlooked. When the American military discovered in the late 1960s that laboratory animals had developed cancer in tests when exposed to Agent Orange, they stopped its use in Vietnam. But it was already far too late. Agent Orange had become one of the world's most devastating examples of state terrorism.

In an age of total war, modern states, even democracies, have been prepared to go to any lengths to secure victory. As no totalitarian state has yet won a total victory over a democratic nation, no democratic politicians have faced the consequences of resorting to terror weapons. British and American military commanders were quite aware that if they had been defeated in 1945 they would have had to answer for their crimes as the Nazis had at Nuremberg. It would have been interesting to hear how their moral justification for the terror bombing of German and Japanese civilians differed from the 'genocidal' policies of their enemies. After all, the winners always write the histories and so 'terror bombing' in the name of democracy has always been euphemised by terms like 'area bombing' or 'strategic bombing'. The ruthless German bombing of the industrial city of Coventry, during which 554 died and 865 were injured, is often used to balance the bombing of Dresden, during which uncounted thousands died. As Gandhi said, the victim of such terror bombing does not care who is behind it, democrat, fascist or terrorist. The effect is just as terrible.

Western politicians would do well to remember this. There is no friendly bullet nor well-intentioned bomb.

# CHAPTER 2

## *Homo Hostilis*

The mention of the name Adolf Hitler in any debate about historical dictators is generally sufficient to bring it to an abrupt end. Hitler is so closely linked with the concept of 'absolute evil' that it seems pointless to continue discussing the very worst acts of Idi Amin, Pol Pot or the Emperor Bokassa of the Central African Empire when bringing up Hitler's name can trump them all. This demonisation of a human being is a far from helpful process as it dehumanises the historical Hitler and, in a sense, makes him less responsible for what he did than if he were judged on the basis of evidence rather than prejudice.

Politicians use Hitler as a symbol rather than as a figure from the past, unconcerned with what can be proved from history. No positive statement of Hitler's achievements can be made without being challenged as an apology for the Nazi leader. It is seemingly impermissible to apply objectivity to the actions of Hitler – or indeed to those of his nearest modern equivalent, Saddam Hussein. This moves both figures beyond history and closer to mythology. Here they meet evil itself, manifested in the figure of Satan.

(Ironically, however, an investigation of Satan's origin shows evidence of an earlier demonisation – the treatment of the relatively harmless Greek demigod Pan at the hands of early Christian polemicists.[1])

### Metamorphosis

In order to discredit or even destroy opponents, politicians have learned to demonise them, reducing their humanity and making it easier to treat them in a less than human way. In *Faces of the Enemy,* psychologist and writer Sam Keen described demonisation through the idea of 'Homo Hostilis', in a sense 'mankind the enemy maker'. In his masterful story *Metamorphosis*, Franz Kafka demonstrates this process through the terrifying experience of a man named Gregor Samsa.

> One morning, as Gregor Samsa was waking up from anxious dreams, he discovered that overnight he had been changed into a monstrous, verminous bug. He lay on his armour-hard back and saw, as he lifted his head a little, his brown, arched abdomen divided into rigid bow-like sections. From that height, the blanket, just about ready to slide off completely, could hardly stay in place. His numerous legs, pitifully thin in comparison to the rest of his circumference, flickered helplessly before his eyes.

What follows not only concerns the way that Samsa adjusts to his own metamorphosis but, more importantly, the way that others – his family, friends and colleagues – adjust to their own transformation of feelings towards Samsa and how their inability to empathise with him leads them through stages of disgust and contempt to ultimate neglect. Their reactions may begin like the instinctive reactions of animals to something unlike themselves but eventually develop according to human rationalisation. In this process one observes the small distance that separates the honest and dutiful servant from the 'Homo Hostilis', who can commit the worst atrocities and human rights abuses often with the feeling that he is following orders and only doing what is necessary.

The dehumanisation process as practised by politicians is concerned with social control and manipulation of the masses for political ends, and is responsible for much of the so-called 'evil' in human history. In 1914, for example, how did the political leaders of the Great Powers convince their massed armies, in Britain mainly a civilian force, to overcome a lifetime of Christian upbringing and fight fellow Christians in a terrible and bloody war in which all their values would be challenged?

1. How do you teach people to tread on spiders, pull the wings off flies or attach fireworks to puppies' tails?
2. How do you teach people to plunge bayonets into the stomachs of strangers and twist the blade to extract it?
3. How do you persuade pilots to bomb civilian areas where their victims will be mainly women and children?

# PICKING THE BONES

Answers:

1. You teach the child that the insects or animals are disgusting and dirty, and carry diseases that may be harmful to them and their loved ones.

2. You teach the recruits that the enemy has ceased to deserve any human pity. He is a heartless barbarian who has raped helpless women, crucified British soldiers and bayoneted babies. The only way of preventing him from coming to Britain to do the same to your loved ones is to kill him without mercy in France. (One army recruitment poster from the United States made exactly this point. In it, Germany was personified as a crazed gorilla wearing a *pickelhaube* (German spiked helmet), holding a bloodstained club in one hand and a semi-clothed woman in the other, and arriving at the coast of America. The caption read, 'Destroy this Mad Brute'.[2])

3. There are no civilians in modern war. The only way to make your own loved ones safe is to bring the war to an end. The enemy will not hesitate to bomb your cities so you must bomb their cities twice as hard. When you bring the war to an end, there will be no more bombing and no more civilians will die on either side. So you are bombing these civilians today to save their lives in the long run.

The task of transforming members of the public into soldiers in essentially civilian societies like Britain was immensely difficult and could only be achieved by political lies on a massive scale. Propaganda and hate training were needed to convert 'good citizens' into 'hardened and ruthless killers' and what had always been seen as 'an act of murder' into a 'positive good'. Few of the men of 1914 were natural killers and their metamorphosis was a process by which it was not their 'animal' natures that were unleashed but their capacity to cultivate ideas that led to hate. The propaganda used against conscientious objectors was typical of the depths to which the politicians would stoop, particularly in a democracy. The usual trick employed at tribunals when dealing with a conchie (conscientious objector) was to ask the man whether his conscience would prevent him from taking action if a fierce Hun was about to ravish and murder his mother or sister. The objector would usually reply that he would try to save his mother or sister but not if it meant taking the life of the German, whereupon everyone present would virtually spit contemptuously at him, saying that he did not deserve to live. These wretched men were often imprisoned and treated so badly that many took their own lives.


## 'To a Louse'

It has been observed by many commentators that one of the main problems faced by modern America is its inability to see itself as others see it. The political commentator Chalmers Johnson has referred to the 'reservoirs of resentment against Americans for their arrogance and hegemony' that most Americans do not even seem aware of.[3] Robert Burns, of course, examined this theme in his poem 'To a Louse', which contains these famous lines:

> O wad some Pow'r the giftie gie us
> To see oursels as others see us!
> It wad frae mony a blunder free us,
> And foolish notion.

America's crusade against terrorism, launched by President George W. Bush after the terrorist attacks of 11 September 2001, appears to most Americans as an entirely appropriate response to a great crime and an act of war. However, the crusade that they are following seems more like terrorism itself to the Muslim world, as its brunt is being borne by Afghani and Iraqi civilians, not those responsible for the terrorist attacks themselves.

The choice of Afghanistan for America's first war against terrorism seemed understandable to Muslims throughout the world. If the Taliban had maintained Osama bin Laden and al-Qaeda then it seemed no more than a 'police response' by the Americans to pursue the criminals of 9/11. However, the choice of Saddam Hussein and Iraq for America's second war seemed totally unjustified to Muslims, if terrorists were truly America's targets. Nobody denied the existence of fundamentalism within the Muslim world, or that of many terrorist groups and circles. Saddam Hussein, however, represented a totally different type of threat. Most Muslims would have thought that Saddam's day was done and that his capacity to harm his neighbours through the use of weapons of mass destruction had been extinguished by the 1991 Gulf War and the subsequent inspections and sanction policies of the United Nations.

# PICKING THE BONES

I'M FIGHTING SADDAM IN THE MORNING
(to the tune of 'I'm Getting Married in the Morning')

I'm fighting Saddam in the morning,
Bang, crash, the guns will end his crime,
Maybe we're barmy,
But send in the army,
And get me to the war on time.

We gotta be there in the mornin',
Tanked up and smilin' fit to kill,
George Bush will kiss me,
Cherie will miss me,
But we'll never pay the butcher's bill.

If I am bombin' stay on the floor,
If I am firin' shoot me out the door!

For I'm fightin' Saddam in the mornin',
Whizz, bang! The guns are in their prime,
Long live pre-emption, UN don't mention,
And get me to the war, get me to the war,
For Gawd's sake, get me to the war on time!

Saddam was no longer a big player in the Arab world and in terms of terrorism he was a non-player. To attack him, using 9/11 as a justification, seemed to weaken the whole American case for their war on terror. It diverted resources that should have been used to pursue existing terrorists and undermine the roots of terrorism itself in the Muslim world.

No statistics are available and so these estimates are based on my impressions of what has taken place. I would suspect that, in proportion to Muslim terrorists in Afghanistan and Iraq, innocent civilians have died in a ratio at least 10–1, and non-terrorist military personnel in an even greater proportion than that – perhaps 20–1 or 50–1 – simply defending their country against foreign invaders.

## The Lone Ranger

The official doctrine of pre-emptive war was adopted by the US on 20 September 2002, as a direct response to the terrorist strikes on New York and Washington. In accordance with this, America will not hesitate to act alone, if necessary, to exercise her right of self-defence by acting pre-emptively against a real or imminent threat. With a Bible in one hand and a pistol in the other, the 'Lone Ranger' will ride out to combat the ills of the world.

President Bush announced that the struggle against global terrorism would be a different kind of war to anything hitherto seen in history. The United States has been 'called as a blessed country' to preserve God's gift to humanity from evil. The terrorists are men who threatened to destroy freedom, liberty and civilisation with 'weapons of mass destruction' and America, 'God bless her', is putting on the 'armour of light' to fight against the demonic enemy – by which America seemed undecided whether she meant Osama bin Laden, Saddam Hussein, Ayatollah Khomeini (who died in 1989) or indeed members past and present of a world Axis of Evil, including any dictator who people could be convinced was similar in actions or opinions to the daddy of them all – Adolf Hitler.

# PICKING THE BONES

Overstatement, overreacting, over-thereism, over-the-topism, over-and-over-againism were all in the ascendant – and understandable from a paranoid nation in shock. What was needed was a period of calm reflection and a Prozac the size of the Grand Canyon. The Republic of Fear was girding its loins to save the world again, just as it had when the Martians came in *Independence Day* and Bill Pullman and Will Smith 'kicked ass'. But what about the earlier time the Martians came? Then it had been different.

On 30 October 1938, Orson Welles broadcast a radio adaptation of a science fiction novel about a Martian invasion of the earth called *The War of the Worlds*. Welles's broadcast gave the impression that it was a news programme about a real invasion from Mars and millions of Americans panicked. Gathered around their radios, Americans learned a Martian had emerged from a large metallic cylinder at the New Jersey crash site. 'Good heavens,' the actor/reporter declared, 'something's wriggling out of the shadow like a grey snake. Now here's another and another one and another one.' By the time it was reported that similar Martian cylinders had landed in Chicago and St Louis, the panic had begun. An Indianapolis woman ran into a church screaming, 'New York has been destroyed! It's the end of the world! Go home and prepare to die!'

Dorothy Thompson reported in the *New York Tribune* that people abandoned their houses and took to the roads, hid in cellars, loaded guns, even wrapped their heads in wet towels as protection from the Martians' poisonous gas, in an attempt to defend themselves against aliens, oblivious to the fact that they were acting out the role of the panic-stricken public that actually belonged in a radio play.

In the article 'War of the Worlds, Orson Welles and the Invasion from Mars', Thompson foresaw that the broadcast revealed the way politicians could use the power of mass communications to create theatrical illusions and to manipulate the public:

> Hitler managed to scare all of Europe to its knees a month ago, but he at least had an army and an air force to back up his shrieking words. But Mr Welles scared thousands into demoralisation with nothing at all.

**Gone to the Devil**

Saddam was not a terrorist, that is true, nor had he been involved in 9/11, but he was the founder member of the Axis of Evil. He was the new Hitler, thoroughly evil, and, as in the case of the German dictator, nobody would complain if somebody put a 'slug' between his eyes. In fact, irrespective of 9/11 and the threat – imminent or otherwise – from Saddam's weapons of mass destruction, the Bush administration had been planning to overthrow the Iraqi leader since they took up power in the White House. They only needed an excuse and perhaps 9/11 was what they had been waiting for?

Yet was it enough to claim that Saddam Hussein was a loathsome tyrant who deserved to be overthrown? Had he not been the same loathsome tyrant during the 1980s when he was a friend of America? Was he any better to his people in the 1980s than he was in the 1990s or even 2002? Unlikely, since the gassing of over 5,000 Kurds in Halabja occurred in 1988. Why, then, had he not been overthrown earlier?

Moreover, why had so many states joined the 1991 coalition against Saddam and so few the 2003 coalition of the willing? Had he improved rather than got worse? Or was it something to do with any of the following:

- The fact that in 1991 he had actually invaded Kuwait, and the world, acting through the United Nations, insisted that he should be forced to leave?
- Or the fact that in 2003 he had not invaded any of his neighbours, had allowed UN weapons inspectors to look for WMD and that the United Nations had not supported his overthrow by military action?
- The fact that most of the world did not trust American and British motives – while they claimed to wish to overthrow Saddam Hussein for the benefit of the Iraqi people, they were prepared to subject these same people to Shock and Awe, and made the capture of the Iraqi oilfields their absolute first priority on entering Iraqi territory, not the water and power supplies for the Iraqi people.
- Maybe the fact that the performances of Colin Powell and Jack Straw in the Security Council were unconvincing. Their arguments followed the line that so great was the threat which Saddam posed that only immediate military action could prevent the Iraqi dictator using his weapons of mass destruction. Nobody believed this, particularly after Hans Blix had shown that he and his inspectors were unconvinced that Saddam posed such a threat.
- Or the fact that when the Security Council was offered a choice of arguments, which should prevail? The one that preferred a peaceful option of extending the time available to the weapons inspectors to see if war could be avoided? Or the one that insisted on immediate war because Saddam Hussein was fundamentally 'evil'?

If evil dictators were always to be overthrown, then numerous countries, notably many in South America, Central America and the Far East, would have been virtually leaderless during the Reagan administration of the 1980s. Had American policy towards loathsome tyrants changed since that time?

In an essay entitled 'Evil Enemy Versus Agonistic Other', rhetorician Robert Ivie examines an interesting issue that arises from the diplomacy that led to the second Gulf War in 2003. At what point does a political opponent become an enemy? No state can agree with every other state on every issue – disagreement is why diplomacy is needed. An enemy, however, is not just somebody who disagrees with you. It is someone who threatens to harm you or those close to you. During the months leading to the 2003 Gulf War, the United States found herself at odds with many countries, notably France and Germany. She did not, however, refer to these countries as 'enemies'. In contrast, she did refer to Saddam Hussein as the enemy with whom, by the fact of his acknowledged evil, no compromise was possible and no cost too high to eliminate.[4]

The demonisation of Saddam Hussein, by comparison with Adolf Hitler, was carried out by politicians, not historians. No self-respecting historian would have used such an unhistorical and unhelpful method of describing a leading political figure. Without becoming too pedantic, one must point out that comparisons between Saddam Hussein and Adolf Hitler, Saddam's Iraq and Hitler's Germany, and George W. Bush and, say, Winston Churchill, are totally invalid and the lowest form of intellectual tomfoolery. It hardly requires a high intellect to see that comparisons between people in different historical periods are about as valid as children imagining matches between the Real Madrid of Puskas and Di Stefano and the Liverpool of Dalglish and Souness, or Dennis Lillee bowling to Sir Jack Hobbs, or Jesse Owens taking on Linford Christie. There is no harm in this whatsoever unless one begins to claim it is the truth. Thus, it is barking mad for American politicians, notably the two Bushes, to claim that experiences learned from dealing with Adolf Hitler in the 1930s could help us deal with a dictator like Saddam Hussein in 2003.

Adolf Hitler was a pseudo-intellectual with a second-rate mind but he combined these qualities with first-rate energy. He was, furthermore, backed up by men of ability and armed services of the highest calibre. The German people were three or four times more numerous than the Iraqis. They constituted some of the best educated in the world, with one of the highest literacy rates, coupled with university research by some of the world's leading authorities in all branches of learning. Comparisons with Iraq, at any stage since the ancient Babylonian, would be misleading.

Saddam Hussein was a small-minded gangster who, though ruthless, possessed few of the qualities needed to lead a nation through at least three major wars against stronger foes. He was an unprincipled opportunist trying to survive in a world dominated by bigger thugs than himself. He knew his limitations and would have been content to lick the hand of the Americans or the Soviets if it meant that he could get from them something that would make him the biggest fish in his little pond. Iraq was a small Third World country blessed with nothing other than its oil. It had an uneducated, unskilled population and a large but weak peasant army that had been so heavily defeated in the 1991 Gulf War that its capacity was minimal by 2003.

The idea that he could ever really threaten the United States of America would not have been a serious consideration for Saddam Hussein. It was American paranoia that elevated him to the position that he occupied in the minds of George W. Bush and Tony Blair during the latter part of 2002.

The clinching difference between Adolf Hitler and Saddam Hussein is, however, a very surprising one. So much vitriol has been poured upon Hitler's rise to power that a simple fact has been obscured: Hitler came to power democratically, within a democratic system. Saddam Hussein simply seized power by the force of the gun. Now, before an avalanche of academics try to sweep away my description of Hitler's accession to power we must remember that even those democracies that take themselves most seriously have deficiencies that others might like to point out.

The 2000 presidential election in the United States, for example, was conducted in a way that would have earned criticism in any modern democracy, even that of Weimar Germany. Failing to count votes that were definitely cast is a damning indictment of an undemocratic system, and having a politically appointed judiciary decide the result of a public vote to the advantage of the dominant party's candidate is just about as obvious an undemocratic action as one can find. If one can joke about Ronald Reagan as the 'acting President', one can surely refer to George W. Bush as the 'appointed President'.

When the Weimar constitution was established in 1919, it was probably the most democratic in the world. At a time when universal female suffrage still did not exist in Britain and the United States, Reichstag representatives in Weimar Germany were elected by the universal, equal, direct and secret suffrage of all men and women over 20 years of age, in accordance with the principle of proportional representation.

From the mid-1920s, the National Socialist German Workers' Party (NSDAP) took part in all national elections and won seats in the Reichstag. Only after 1929 did the Nazis win a substantial number of seats so that Hitler became a prominent national figure in a parliamentary sense. As such he came to the attention of President Hindenburg, whose responsibility it was as Head of State to appoint the

Chancellor as head of the government. In 1933, when Hindenburg appointed Hitler as Germany's Chancellor, the NSDAP was the largest party in the Reichstag with 288 seats, although they could only hold power as part of a coalition with the Nationalists. Nevertheless, up until the Reichstag fire in 1933, Hitler had operated within a democratic system. It would be foolish to pretend that German elections during the inter-war period were as peaceful as in some democracies, nevertheless, the Communists were no less violent in the streets than the Nazis and the control of the press by the Nazis was far less stringent than is currently the case in some more apparently democratic countries.

Hitler's aggressive foreign policy was very much in the German tradition. As far back as the eighteenth century, Frederick the Great of Prussia had invaded Silesia, an important territory of the Austrian Empire that Prussia coveted for its raw materials. Frederick's action was based on the simplest principle of national aggrandisement. He had no intention of negotiating with the Austrian ruler, the Empress Maria Theresa, but relied instead on the superiority of the Prussian army. His victory at Mollwitz in 1741 ushered in more than 20 years of intermittent warfare until by 1763, with Prussia on the verge of collapse, his hold on Silesia was finally agreed. During the nineteenth century, German unification was achieved through Bismarck's use of superior German military strength aggressively employed against Austria, culminating in the great Prussian victory at Königgrätz, and against France, ending in the German victory at Sedan. Bismarck's wars were Clausewitzian, designed to further political aims by military means.

By 1914, however, it can be argued that Germany's policy was different. Facing a war on two fronts, her assault upon France was more pre-emptive than simply aggressive.

Are you listening, George W. Bush? Kick the Clausewitz habit and remember, 'Diplomacy can be the continuation of politics by other means.'

The Schlieffen Plan, in as far as there ever was a real Schlieffen Plan, served several purposes at once. Facing the danger of a war on two fronts, against two enemies who were likely to go onto the offensive immediately – France towards Alsace and Lorraine, and Russia into east Prussia – the Germans reasoned that a swingeing attack through Belgium and then into northern France would either succeed in knocking France out of the war quickly or at least keep the French from attacking into Alsace. Meanwhile, they would have more time to confront the slowly advancing Russians in the east. As we now know, the Germans had made no allowances for British troops on the Belgian frontier, and it was the British Expeditionary Force, combined with the hastily transferred Paris garrison under Gallieni, which stopped the German assault on the Marne.

The aggressive warfare of the Kaiser, therefore, was actually a pre-emptive response resulting from a defensive fear. However, if George W. Bush examines German pre-emption he will notice one major difference between Germany's situation in 1914 and that of the United States in 2003 – Germany's fear was real. America's fear, George, was totally contrived.

Hitler's early acts of territorial 'aggression' in Europe, from 1935 to 1939, were initially geared towards recovering lands inhabited by Germans which had been removed by the treaties of Versailles and Saint Germain. Their restoration to the Reich was, in his opinion, justified by Woodrow Wilson's own principle of self-determination. Thus the acquisition of the Rhineland, the *Anschluss* with Austria, the occupation of the Sudetenland and the taking of the Polish Corridor, Danzig and Memel were not acts of aggression at all but the restoration to Germany of land or people that were naturally German.

It is as a mass murderer that Hitler has qualified for his special designation as the epitome of evil. The Holocaust of the Jews, during which six million were murdered by the Germans, must never be allowed to be taken beyond the bounds of humanity and mythologised. On any level it was an atrocity that takes the breath away by the sheer efficiency with which human beings can carry out such a task. Yet, stripped of the natural emotional repugnance that it calls forth, it must be seen in context as the greatest of a series of mass killings and acts of genocide committed at intervals throughout recent centuries. It otherwise loses its impact as a real event.

Josef Stalin's eradication of the kulaks in the 1930s accounted for vast numbers – millions – of deaths of these rich peasants, although precise figures are impossible to obtain. Who mourns for them? Nobody. Instead, by 1941 Stalin had become the jovial 'Uncle Joe' figure, an ally of Britain and the United States during the Second World War.

The earliest genocide of the twentieth century is still denied by its perpetrators – the Turks, currently close allies of the United States. Between 1915 and 1916, one and a half million Armenians within the Ottoman Empire were massacred. At the time, the genocide was condemned by representatives of the American, British, French,

Russian, German and Austrian governments. In the late 1970s, the Killing Fields of Pol Pot's Khmer Rouge accounted for the deaths of two to three million Cambodians, though again precise figures are quite impossible to collect. The massacre of Tutsis by Hutu tribesmen in Rwanda in the mid-1990s accounted for a further million or more lives.

So what makes Hitler different, except for the number of innocent lives he took during his reign? Surely the killing of any one human being is evil? The killing of two human beings, however, is intrinsically no more evil, it is merely the 'evil' of killing a human being, committed twice. To argue otherwise is to diminish the integrity of individual human life. This would be a triumph for statistics.

A historical character cannot usefully be described as the epitome of anything, except as a very generalised way of bringing him or her to life as an aide-memoire. Evil is an adjective with no independent existence beyond the action it describes. Even used like this it lacks precision, depending as it does on the ethical standards of the reader or listener. Evil as a noun cannot be defined as it refers to an absolute condition of which no human concept exists. Nor can Saddam Hussein be compared with Hitler, except in practical terms of height, weight, shoe size and so on. Comparisons in terms of personality or intellectual achievements are meaningless and, when used for political purposes, very misleading.

A question for all American presidents since George Washington: are all despots tyrants by definition, who deserve to be overthrown? Was the Emperor Joseph II of Austria a tyrant?

- He forced Austrian nuns to stop wearing corsets.
- He ordered Austrians to be buried in hardboard coffins to save wood.
- He told Mozart to change one of his works because it had too many notes.

## Playing the Devil

In the mythology of ancient Greece there was no representation of absolute evil. Certainly, some of the gods and goddesses got up to some fairly nasty activities – Cronos, for example, ate his own children – but these deeds, which might be viewed as 'evil' in the Christian world, pass for allegorical demonstrations of the misuse of absolute power.

Once upon a time, in the sylvan glades of Arcady lived the demigod

Pan. In those days – the days when mythological figures knew the roles allotted to them by those humans who had invented them – Pan, goat-footed shepherd as he was, spent most of his time either playing his pipes or chasing the wood nymphs. Pan was so thoroughly natural in his pleasures – wine, women and song – that he grew to be the most popular deity of the ancient Greeks and, as such, one of the most powerful, if harmless, of pagan gods.

Such natural behaviour, however, did not fit in with the dualistic morality of the new Christianity, in which sexual activity was specifically geared towards childbirth and not for physical pleasure. Pan, therefore, was increasingly seen as a manifestation of amorality within the Christian moral absolutes of 'good' and 'evil'. Moreover, images of Pan simply reeked of rampant masculine physicality quite at odds with the ascetic ideals and celibacy of the early Christianity. Pan was literally a beast, a phallic deity with rippling muscles and a face carved out of solid testosterone.

When Roman Christianity was established after the Council of Nicea in 325, the struggle against paganism involved the demonisation of Pan into the great 'Adversary', the personification of evil. During Europe's conversion to Christianity, missionaries needed to defame the pastoral gods, with their sexuality symbolising the reproductive cycle of animals and crops. In the fourth century, Christian thinkers like Eusebius and St Augustine of Hippo associated the pagan gods with demons, and the ugliness and power shown in representations of Pan became associated with the image of the single, all-powerful Devil himself.

The continuing struggle between Christianity and paganism, notably in the first millennium of the Christian era, saw the adaptation of the image of the Devil in Christianity into the terrible monster of the medieval Church. The relatively neutral figure of Satan represented in a sixth-century mosaic at Ravenna was a blue angel, seated at the left-hand side of Christ, and almost identical to the red angel, seated at Christ's right-hand side. Satan and the angel are separating the sheep from the goats. Yet this representation was distorted for political purposes into a far more terrifying depiction of monstrous evil. Western Christianity aimed at social control of the Christian masses by the established Church, as well as encouraging resistance to the external threats to Christianity posed between the eighth and tenth centuries by pagan Vikings, Magyars and the Muslim Arabs.

Stressing the physical attributes of the demigod Pan, the Western Devil is associated with depraved women. The Satan depicted in medieval stained glass is much closer to the Pan character with a strong, ugly face, horns and cloven hoofs.

The demonisation of Pan is simply the use of symbol to achieve political ends and is typical of the actions of what Sam Keen called 'Homo Hostilis'. When today's politicians compare Saddam Hussein or others to Adolf Hitler, they have created a modern demon in the German dictator through whom they can dehumanise their political opponents with a view to winning popular support for their destruction. The demonised Hitler or Saddam that one is left with often bears no more relation to the historical personality than a fictional depiction in a Hollywood film. It is most important that voters in a democracy maintain their demand for evidence before supporting unscrupulous character assassinations.

# CHAPTER 3

# *The Noble Art of Dying*

## The *Wehrmacht* in Waitrose

While the *Wehrmacht* is queuing in Waitrose to pay for its weekly shopping and there is no room in the car park because of all their Panzer tanks, you don't need to be told that you are at war . . . and that you are losing.

In 1944, Dutch women pulled back their net curtains and watched as stormtroopers trod clumsily through their flowerbeds and passing tanks cracked the road surface where their children played. Those who have seen the film *A Bridge Too Far* may remember British troops taking over a four-storey building near the bridge at Arnhem, wounded men being laid bleeding on the best carpets, windows being knocked out and booted soldiers clumping up and down the stairs, apologising to the Dutch family who lived there for any inconvenience. An old lady setting out to go shopping is cut to pieces by German gunfire. War has returned to Arnhem and while the soldiers go through the rigmarole of war, firing this or that weapon of minor destruction at each other, and tanks take out their frustration like Godzilla biting chunks out of the buildings and spitting them down on the heads of scurrying, troglodytic humanity, life goes on as normal.

Women get the children up and washed and fed and ready for school and . . . then they remember . . . the school was struck by bombs yesterday . . . and there has been no milk for days, only vegetables to eat . . . and there has been no running water in the taps since the mains were bombed . . . and the children are dead, buried under the rubble of the collapsed building over the road. The hands on the clock go backwards

. . . soon it will stop, they tell themselves. The war, that is. They once had tears; now all that is past since the Allies came to liberate them.

In Britain, war is declared on the radio at eleven o'clock, after the chimes of Big Ben, all very civilised. This is different. This is *Hope and Glory*. If the Germans are coming, there will be a siren so everyone will know and go to their places: the troops to man the guns, the firemen to their engines, the women and children to their Anderson shelters. And when the raid is over there will be another siren and everyone will return to the places they left before the alarm went off. In those houses still standing, tea will be made and taken to the people sitting in the rubble of those houses no longer standing. The milkman, meanwhile, will pick his way through the streets covered in rubble and the occasional corpse, and deliver milk to the survivors. The British are at war.

There has been no serious foreign invasion of England since 1066, when both William of Normandy and King Harald Hardrada of Norway arrived almost simultaneously. (I am excluding the Jacobites, William of Orange, Monmouth and Louis VIII as they offered no threat of a foreign occupation.) As a result, no Briton for centuries had seen foreign troops in British streets.

What is true of England is also true of the United States, where, since 1815, no foreign troops have been seen. As a result, it has been unknown for either an American, or indeed a British, civilian to have experienced war at first hand except as a resident of a foreign land. This has emboldened Anglo-American politicians to use war more willingly as a threat in their rhetorical armaments than the politicians of less happy lands.

One might almost accuse such politicians of treating war more lightly – as the first port of call after a diplomatic rebuff rather than the last – when they know that the destruction caused will take place in someone else's backyard.

NIMBY

In Flanders Fields the poppies blow,
Not in my backyard, you know!

G.B. Regan

After the Battle of Fredericksburg in December 1862, Confederate General Robert E. Lee said, 'It is as well that war is so terrible. We should grow too fond of it.' Generals like Lee understood the horrors of war and generally wished for peace. To them the rhetoric of war was simple: war to win peace. In a pre-Orwellian age, Lee would have been puzzled at the double-think that goes into modern wars. What would he and his contemporaries have understood from the rhetoric of modern politicians like George W. Bush and Tony Blair who managed to keep a straight face while telling their people that war was peace and designed to save life? Lee might just have shrugged his shoulders and reminded us that 'Hell hath no fury like a non-combatant' and pointed out that some of America's most warlike politicians had been those most happy to evade the draft themselves as young men. It is sometimes easier to 'talk a good war' rather than to have to fight one.

In fairness to one of the greatest of rhetoricians of war, Winston Churchill, I should remind people that Winston actually fought at the Battle of Omdurman in 1898 and took part in the last cavalry charge of the British army by the 21st Lancers against the Dervishers. More often, however, politicians far away from the battlefield or danger zones have the most unhealthy affection for something that settles political problems so decisively. Yet nobody has the right to play at war or ignore civilian casualties without knowing the pain and suffering that war can bring. Konrad Lorenz reminds people that, 'the crooking of the finger to release a shot tears the entrails of another man'.[1] However sanitised the war, there are consequences for someone. Politicians should stop trying to benefit from the 'feel-good factor' on television, having arranged for limbless children to have medical treatment in the West as if they had no part to play in mutilating them in the first place.


### All Whose Yesterdays?

In a memorable phrase, Ed Murrow wrote that Winston Churchill 'mobilised the English language and sent it into battle'.[2] A less well-known expression (which I am just preparing to type) notes Winston Churchill 'transformed history into myth and therefore ennobled the acts of common men'. And in a final noble reflection (that I am going to crib from Shakespeare), Winston Churchill used his oratory to 'light fools the way to dusty death'.

Through Churchill, the myth of war as a noble human pursuit was used to justify the horrors of war as a reality. Those who had lived through the First World War knew the importance of 'mythic reality' compared with the 'sensory reality' on which people usually rely. The sights, sounds and smells of a battlefield will always overwhelm the uninitiated. Better by far that they will never know 'the Hell where Youth and Laughter go', as Wilfred Owen wrote. As the politicians of all nations knew after 1918, if the people had only known what had transpired on those far-flung fields of conflict, the war could never have continued. The people must never know or else war would no longer be a viable weapon for a democratic state.

In the early days of the 1939–45 war, the English language seemed to undergo a transformation to the style of high-Victorianism, with Arthurian imagery and a vocabulary that would have satisfied such writers as William Morris, Rider Haggard and G.A. Henty. It was a poetic language closer to Tolkien than reality, a feudal language full of high diction, matching the escapism of neo-Gothic literature, art and history. Suddenly comrades rode steeds or chargers against the foe, facing peril in their efforts to vanquish the enemy. Gallant warriors and their plucky squires and staunch yeomen revealed previously unsuspected valour in battle. Those who died were the fallen in glorious strife and perished full of deeds of great heroism.[3]

In metaphorical terms, Sir Winston Churchill, armoured like Lancelot or Galahad, entered the lists against the Black Knight, aka Adolf Hitler, and fought him rhetorically and oratorically from 1940 to 1945. In Churchill's own words, he gave the 'roar' on behalf of a nation of lionhearts. Yet the rhetoric was more appropriate to a kind of medieval pageant, beloved of English villages in their halcyon days, whimsical and amateurish yet stirring for the patriot inside. It was not the language of the city folk – the poor evacuated from their urban fastnesses and expected to instantly absorb a lifetime's rural idyll. Much of what Churchill said was fanciful and by no means represented the true feelings of the British people. Churchill's 'roar' was sometimes less than a true reflection of what the British people were thinking.

George Lakoff has said, 'metaphors can kill, especially when they are followed by bombs.'[4] In 1940, there were plenty of bombs, but they were falling on British heads, helmeted or otherwise. In the absence of our own bombs, and indeed most of the rest of the nation's military equipment which had been abandoned at Dunkirk, Churchill chose to continue the war against Hitler with metaphor.

Nature sometimes equips animals with a natural propaganda vital to their survival, in the shape of a resemblance to a fiercer species or a size or strength exaggerated by false markings. Yet in Churchill's case one is entitled to ask whose survival depended on the propaganda of his rhetoric – that of the British people and state, or that of himself and his vision of Britain? Did Churchill speak for the British in 1940 or for the British in his vivid historical imagination? The novelist Evelyn Waugh was a harsh critic of Churchill, commenting 'How we despised his orations', while a Scottish soldier rationalised Churchill's appeal in these words:

> If Churchill, instead of his blood, sweat and tears thing had said, 'Any man or woman in the forces who would like to give it all up and go home, can', he wouldn't have got the microphone out of his mouth before he'd have been trampled to death in the rush.[5]

Cynical, certainly, but closer to what many people were really thinking.

How many people were really experiencing their 'finest hour' in 1940, sitting amidst the rubble of their houses and hearing Churchill speaking on next door's radio? Or soldiers marching home in their socks from Dunkirk, having lost everything but their rifles, which many of them threw away as they travelled inland from the coast? Some 'finest hour' for the British army! When Churchill made his great speech in parliament:

> We shall go on to the end, we shall fight in France, we shall fight on the seas and oceans, we shall fight with growing confidence and growing strength in the air, we shall defend our Island, whatever the cost may be, we shall fight on the beaches, we shall fight on the landing grounds, we shall fight in the fields and in the streets, we shall fight in the hills; we shall never surrender . . .[6]

. . . it is said that Churchill's own sense of the ridiculous caused him to whisper that 'we shall hit them on the head with beer bottles' when that was all we had left to fight with after Dunkirk. Stirring stuff. In reality it was empty rhetoric for two reasons:

1. Hitler had nothing to gain from invading Britain. His real enemy was Soviet Russia and time spent overcoming Britain would be time wasted. Even victory over Britain would not make war against the Soviet Union any easier for him. German losses in men, machines and aircraft would weaken

him militarily and in order to keep both France and Britain quiet he would need to use vast armies of occupation. Once Stalin saw how fully occupied Hitler was in the west there was every chance that he would try to take the territory in Poland and the Balkans that Hitler had earmarked for his *Lebensraum* (living space). Hitler knew that his defeat of the British army had been a relatively easy achievement. Britain's strength lay in her air force and navy. It would be absurd for German planners to risk very heavy losses in the air and at sea in order to secure a secondary strategic target like Britain.

2. Britain could not possibly win the war on her own. To continue the fight against Germany was merely a symbolic gesture. The Royal Navy could probably ensure the safety of the British mainland from invasion, while the Royal Air Force could make any German victory in the air counter-productive. Defensively, Britain was fairly secure and a German invasion in 1940 was most unlikely. However, although Britain was probably secure from defeat, there was no likelihood whatsoever that Britain would be able to invade France and liberate the continent. Offensively, therefore, Britain could only conduct an extended bombing campaign against the Fatherland, provoking the Germans into likely retaliation. Only the entry of the United States into the war on Britain's side offered her any chance of ultimate victory.

Churchill's rhetorical tactics were designed to remind the British people of the proud heritage most of them had never possessed except in dreams or stories. Yet, if being British meant losing everything you had but your life so the politicians could play the power game with Hitler and Mussolini, was it too high a price to pay? Could Britain – meaning the millions of ordinary people who made up the class that suffered in war – really afford to continue the fight for Poland or France or the Empire or King and Country or Drake on the bowling green or Raleigh with his cloak or a thousand silly reasons, none of which could put food on the table, shoes on your children's feet or a roof over your head? And was Churchill right to ask it of them? It was men of his class who had taken them into a life and death struggle with the Nazis in the first place and for what? Honour and love of country? It was empty patriotism all over again, the same as in 1914.

In 1940, Churchill faced the problem of whether Britain should have a policy suited to its armed strength or an army suited to its policy. Under Appeasement it had had an appropriate army, but for war under Chamberlain and Churchill it had not. The fatal mistake was to muddle this up and employ over-ambitious policies without the army to back them up or, like the French, to have a powerful army without the policies capable of using it.

Oh, Professor Charmley, what are you saying when you suggest Britain would have been better off ending the war against Hitler in 1940?[7]

What? Us? 'Beef-eating surrender monkeys'? Better off?

Pull the other one!

## Your Country Needs You

Martyrs are powerful political weapons even in a democracy. Where the murdered brownshirt Horst Wessel became a strong but transient symbol of Nazi Germany, the men and women who had died for Britain in previous wars have come to represent everything that was fine and noble in our country. As such, they are brought into the public domain by politicians who need examples of selfless sacrifice. Related to the people by politicians, such stories were designed to kill all debate and express an elemental truth about Britain.

The British troops of 1914 signed up under the gaze of Kitchener's famous poster and, since then, every true-blooded Briton supports the descendants of these loyal and patriotic warriors in British conflicts. Public support for British troops is assumed to be automatic and unthinking.

The noble motives of the men of 1914 were encapsulated in *the* war poster – 'Your country needs you' – one of the most effective and yet cynical propaganda exercises ever undertaken. The lie of why men fought in 1914 has lain heavy on generations of Britons who followed in the footsteps of the men who fought for 'King and Country'.

The truth, of course, was very different. The men of 1914 were patriotic – what passed for an education in those days stressed the Pax Brittanica above all and glorified the deeds of imperial warriors like Drake, Raleigh, Hawkins, Frobisher, Clive, Wolfe, Moore and Wellington who had served their country with absolute conviction, many of them – like Wolfe at Quebec, Sir John Moore at Corunna and Nelson at Trafalgar – giving their lives in the service of the country they loved. But the reason the men of 1914 flocked to join up was not as simple and certainly not as glorious as the propagandists claimed. Britons were no more patriotic than the people of France, Russia or Germany.

In the late nineteenth century, all populations were misled in the same way by their leaders. While some men who volunteered for war had a romanticised vision of England that few had experienced, these were very much the exception. For every poet and scholar who yearned for the dreaming spires of Oxford or the beauty of the English countryside there were dozens who joined up because their friends did or, more prosaically, to get away from the wife, to escape the police, to enjoy three square meals a day, to escape the misery of unemployment, or to get a uniform which would help them 'pull the birds'. This latter motive, for young men, was one of the strongest reasons for taking the King's Shilling, yet one of the least acknowledged by those who stressed the patriotic agenda. Truth is rarely patriotic, of course, because patriotism is built on *lies*.

Patriotism is merely a form of social control based on the most primitive territoriality that is part of all humans' animal nature. Reduced to its crudest essentials it consists of identifying with something (nation, race, religion, cult, school, club, team, society ad nauseam) for the simple reason that you 'belong' to it. In a national sense, the mere fact that you were born in a certain place makes that place seem important to you. The steps that take you from that point to the final outpost of 'My country right or wrong' vary from individual to individual. Ultimately, it is the sheer fact of belonging to something larger than yourself that seems to matter. You feel able to 'share' the achievements of others who belong to your group or nation. Naturally, the military heroes or sporting champions exert the strongest appeal to patriots. You may feel uplifted morally or even strengthened physically by the actions of past heroes, especially when their achievements are presented through the inspiring words of a master rhetorician like Winston Churchill. It is an art wonderfully conveyed by Sir John Gielgud as the headmaster in Alan Bennett's *Forty Years On* and though now perhaps a dying one, it was once used to great effect in public schools the length and breadth of Victorian Britain.

Stories, like that of the young lieutenants Melvill and Coghill dying amidst a horde of Zulus to save the regimental colours at Isandhlwana, were used by parents and teachers alike to point the way for Victorian teenagers. 'Die hard, 57th, die hard,' shouted the dying Colonel Inglis at Albuera in 1811, showing that regimental loyalty, like team spirit, never fails to bring out the best in a person. 'Play up and play the game,' calls a voice as cricket match and bloody battle are merged together in Newbolt's famous poem 'Vitai Lampada'. Suppress the snigger and breathe in the scent of the sea spray as you look back towards the white cliffs of Dover with the eyes of Drake's sailors sailing out towards the Armada anchored at Calais, preparing to send in the fireships. Or listen to the drum roll as Nelson's body is returned to England after his great victory at Trafalgar . . . and exult, if you dare, in one of these anecdotes:

A British soldier, awaiting treatment in a British field hospital was angry at the screams of a French casualty lying alongside him. As soon as the Frenchman's arm had been amputated, the British soldier seized the severed limb by the wrist and hit the Frenchman a sharp blow with it, saying, 'Here, take that, and stuff it down your throat and stop your damned bellowing.'[8]

Or, at the battle of Waterloo the spirit of the French soldiers was not broken by defeat. One soldier in the French ranks was seen, when his arm was shattered by a cannon ball, to wrench it off with the other; and, throwing it up in the air, he exclaimed to his comrades, '*Vive L'Empereur jusqu'à la mort!*'[9]

**True Patriotism**

Patriotism makes people do funny things, like giving up their civil rights so that their leaders (frequently acting on behalf of powerful business interests) can use their support for military action against foreign rivals. The reaction of the American people to the shocking events of 9/11 demonstrated the dangers of mindless support for one's country.

Americans' terrifying knee-jerk patriotism showed how thin the veneer of civilisation is, even in the twenty-first century. The lynch-mob mentality surfaced in the media. Steve Dunleavy headed his column in the *New York Post* 'SIMPLY KILL THESE BASTARDS'. It went on:

> No, I don't mean hunt them, arrest them, extradite them and prosecute them in a court of law. I mean a far quicker and neater form of retribution for this cabal of cowards. A gunshot between the eyes, blow them to smithereens, poison them if you have to.

Journalist Ann Coulter of the *National Review* was even more succinct: 'We should invade their countries, kill their leaders and convert them to Christianity.' Enough said.

## The Nobility of War

Barbara Tuchman has written of the British 'way of war' that:

> No nation has ever produced a military history of such verbal nobility as the British. Retreat or advance, win or lose, blunder or bravery, murderous folly or unyielding resolution, all emerge alike clothed in dignity and touched with glory . . . Everyone is splendid, soldiers are staunch, commanders cool, the fighting magnificent. Whatever the fiasco, aplomb is unbroken. Mistakes, failures, stupidities or other causes of disaster mysteriously vanish. Disasters are recorded with care and pride and become transmuted into things of beauty . . .[10]

According to an edition of the *Daily Mirror* in 1916, reporting from the Somme battlefield, the moral superiority of the British soldier could be seen in death, 'Even as he lies on the field he looks more quietly faithful, more simply steadfast than the others.'[11]

Wow! The British even die better than everyone else. The unfortunate foreigner curses his fate and envies the Briton his heritage. 'If only I could die like that,' he sadly reflects.

# PICKING THE BONES

The idea that there is nobility in war is sentimental nonsense. Nobody has ever thought to ask the dead and dying about their experiences, particularly their feelings as their living bodies were destroyed. Was death in battle better by the sword or by the bayonet, bullet, bomb or depleted uranium shell? Why don't people compare entry wounds? How did they feel as somebody plunged a sword into their chest? Was it a nice sword, made of fine Toledo steel with runnels down which their blood could run? Or was it filthy with caked blood upon it and a serrated edge which hit against their ribs as it was plunged into them? Or did they notice none of these things, only the blackened fingernails of the hand that held it?

Quick, Winston, come to our aid to lift us from the blood and shit of reality into your world of historical fantasy.

The language of war should be closer to the lavatorial than the poetic. Battlefields are places of blood and body parts, of terror, pain, horror and the lowest forms of instinctive behaviour, but shit mainly – and bullshit. The dying lose control of their muscles. The poets lose control of their imaginations. In truth, every left boot at Waterloo was caked in human and animal excrement. Every right one was caked in blood and guts.

John Ellis, the historian of modern warfare, revealed that in 1944 one American unit questioned admitted that over 20 per cent of their men vomited before action in the Pacific. The same number lost control of their bowels before action began or urinated in their pants when an enemy was encountered.[12] And in case anyone thinks that this was unusual, Thucydides wrote of the same thing during the Peloponnesian wars, with lines of Greek hoplites urinating unconsciously as they faced up to a cavalry charge. Presumably, only the modern uniform's capacity to absorb and conceal such natural reactions to fear allows the statistics to remain as low as 20 per cent.

For all the golden rhetoric of the poets and the politicians, war is as messy a business as humanity ever gets involved in. Few casualties wait patiently for their death or lie at the correct angles so that their corpses can be stacked or stored in an orderly fashion. For most soldiers, death is very violent, unexpected and indiscriminate. Death by artillery shell leaves the victim with little self-respect. It is quite unlike its reflection in Hollywood films, where bodies fly comfortably through the air like stuntmen from *Peter Pan*. An American captain reported its effects on five of his sleeping men:

> At the bottom and down one side of the gulley there was a pile of gray shredded fabric. It had no shape and it was not very big. The whole bottom of the gulley was coated evenly with a gray powder and you would not have noticed the pile of gray shredded fabric except for a foot and a shoe with no body attached to it. This object lay by the edge of the pile. There was no blood whatever. All the blood had been blown out of the man who wore the shoe.[13]

During the wars of the twentieth century, the folks at home sometimes have the comfort of having something to bury and grieve over as their loved ones are returned to them in a body bag wrapped in a flag. The problem comes when their loved one returns in a bag big enough for a paperback novel.

Hollywood never gets the ending right. The extended death of Tom Hanks in *Saving Private Ryan* was closer to a death scene from a grand opera, like Mimi dying of consumption in *La Bohème*. Instead, when the guns fall silent the battlefield is temporarily alive, according to General Frank Richardson, with the cries of dying men calling for their mothers. Richardson records that he has heard them do so in five languages.[14] This is the true language of war. The rhetoric is gone, and dying men from Homeric Greece to Bushite Iraq seek maternal consolation as they once did for a grazed knee.

But it's worth it, isn't it? I mean, all that nobility, all that glory? All that . . . all that . . . waste. History sometimes tells a different story from the one politicians use to sell their policies.

In the absence of a tin opener, the average modern citizen is puzzled as to how to prise open a container and release its steaming contents of meat or pudding. Imagine, then, the task of the servants of the French nobleman Louis de la Trémoille, Prince de Talmont and Marshal of France. Charging at the Battle of Pavia in 1525, the Frenchman was unhorsed by a lowly German or Spanish *arquebusier*, who found on the ground at his feet a foe armoured against every spiked instrument ever devised. Forced to improvise, the arquebusier pulled up one of the armoured plates on the fallen knight's thigh and thrust his firearm against it, blowing La Trémoille to pieces inside his iron container. After the battle, the friends of the Marshal could not prise his body free of his armour and had to pull pieces out one at a time with a hook.[15] It was perhaps a sad end for one of the flowers of French chivalry but a triumph for the democracy of warfare.

On the other hand, the cost of La Trémoille's armour alone would have fed the arquebusier and his family for life. Instead, the man got no ransom for the life of one of France's richest nobles, no price for the ruined suit of finest Milanese armour and probably no wages from his notably mean master, the emperor Charles V.

After the bloody Spanish siege of Ostend in 1602, the fields around the city were covered with the remains of 2,000 dead Spaniards and Italians. The surgeons of the time, believing that human fat was an efficacious salve for wounds, went out after dark to scrape the fat from the bodies and bring it back in bags.[16]

Yet, hush . . . while some crinolined lady lifts her veil momentarily as she stands guard over the corner of a foreign field that is forever England and sweeps the battlefield with her beauteous gaze . . .

Napoleonic battlefields, in fact, were swept for human bones, which were imported through the port of Hull to a Yorkshire bone grinders, who reduced them to bone meal which farmers used to manure their lands.[17] Yet in some yew-shaded church in an English shire, a bronze plaque records the sacrifice of farmer's son and squire's boy, joined in the glorious equality of death, shovelled with the horseshit back onto the farmland.

Winston Churchill wrote about such heroes in his books, spoke to them with his golden tongue and pointed them towards glory. Marching with A.E. Housman's soldier down English lanes, shaded from the summer sun or dancing with spring blossoms above the hedges. Whatever happened it was all worth it, eh? For King and Country, eh?

In 1900, during the disastrous British defeat at Spion Kop during the second Boer War, a British soldier was shot in the face by a piece of shell that carried away his left eye and upper jaw, with the corresponding part of his cheek, and left a hideous cavity through the bottom of which his tongue was exposed. He had been lying in agony for hours on the hill. He was unable to speak and as soon as he arrived at the hospital he made signs that he wanted to write. Pencil and paper were given him and it was supposed he wished to ask for something, but he merely wrote, 'Did we win?' None of the doctors had the heart to tell him the truth. I wonder what the Prime Minister would have told him.[18]

Come, Tony Blair, and reflect on these thoughts of a great leader.

## THE NOBLE ART OF DYING

After the Battle of Eylau in 1807, Napoleon walked amidst the French dead on the field, and all he could think about at the sight of so much death was, 'Small change, small change. One Parisian night will replace these losses.'[19]

And what is it all for?

During the First World War, a British regiment was marching through a Belgian town where a steam-saw was working continuously. As they passed the wood mill, the men could see that the front of the building was piled high with recently made wooden crosses. Through a window, the men could see further rooms and a garden behind with stacks more of the crosses, awaiting distribution. Some men smiled, others joked, while still more would not look. But they had all seen and understood.[20]

The unknown soldier is a potent myth in every culture. He is everyman and as such symbolic of the noble sacrifice of war. Yet this 'unknown' figure can also be given the tongue of any politician who cares to speak for him and be given any lines devised by patriotic poet or playwright. As a result, he becomes a tool of the powerful, not a symbol of the causes for which he once may have fought.

A young Walloon soldier in the Austrian service was killed near Breslau in 1757. His father wanted the body returned to him and the

**The Old Lie**

Austrian authorities faced the problem of finding it among the grave pits into which corpses had been thrown thousands at a time. The father was 600 miles away and the request was made some 2 months after the battle was fought. As fate would have it the Austrians were encamped not far from the battlefield and the officer entrusted with the task took the first body he came upon, which happened to be the corpse of an enemy soldier – a Prussian. The body was duly sent to Namur where a thousand masses were offered uselessly for its benefit. A splendid marble tomb was erected – for the wrong man.[21]

# CHAPTER 4

## *History in Black and White*

Racism and white supremacy have been dominant issues in American history since the time of the Declaration of Independence. Modern Americans have ignored the basic incongruity built into their independence as a nation: claiming for themselves a love of freedom and yet maintaining slavery. The problem is that white supremacy has made America what it is today. It has created an underclass of poor blacks and an arrogant white population that is not prepared to find common ground with cultures it regards as inferior.

National myths are the raw material of creative politicians. Their value is that everybody knows them and they never need to be proved or even attributed. Any politician can feel assured of his reception when he 'myth-informs' his audience. Everyone knows, for example, that the British believe in fair play and that America is the 'Land of the Free'.

Along with her sense of 'irony', Britain's sense of 'fair play' singles her out in the family of nations. At the Battle of Inkermann in 1854, during the Crimean War, a British soldier was engaged in desperate hand-to-hand fighting with the Russians. Having knocked a Russian soldier to the ground, he prepared to kick his adversary, only to hear the solemn voice of his sergeant nearby, reprimanding him, 'What did I tell you about kickin' a man when 'e's down?'

'Sorry, sarge,' replied the soldier, 'I forgot.' The soldier then brought the butt of his rifle down on the Russian's head with shattering force.

Like most battles of the Victorian era, the Battle of Inkermann was won on the grimy streets of Britain's industrial cities, not on the playing fields of Eton. Yet still the idea survives as a national myth. *Floreat Etona*!

America's love of freedom, liberty, democracy and the rights of the common man are part of the powerful 'foundation myth' taught to all American children. At any table of prominent nations it entitles the USA, 'Land of the Free', to occupy at least six chairs by right. It is odd that nobody has asked American politicians why they think they are the guardians of 'freedom', particularly when they refused it to Native Americans and African–Americans for most of their history. Britain, demonised by Americans for 200 years, on the other hand, earned the thanks of both Greece and Italy for helping them towards freedom and independence during the nineteenth century. In fact, in spite of his poetry, Lord Byron stands as high in the ranks of freedom fighters as any single American.

In what passed for the US presidental election of 2000, both candidates drew on the bank of American myths. Democrat Al Gore observed:

> From the beginning, our leadership of the world community has been based on much more than military and economic strength. The American drive to correct injustice – from the abolition of slavery to the granting of women's suffrage – has constantly renewed our moral authority to lead.

Nobody – not even Gore's wife – dared to raise the awkward point that the word 'abolition' presupposed the existence of slavery just as 'granting' presupposed the prior absence of a woman's right to vote. Blissfully unaware of such subtleties, Republican candidate George W. Bush announced, 'The United States is the best and fairest and most decent nation on the face of the earth.' He knew nobody would question him on something that all American schoolchildren are taught from the first bell. In fact, Lynne Cheney, wife of vice-president Dick, with her book *A Patriotic Primer*, has ensured that even pre-school children are never told the truth about American history.[1]

But why do men like Bush and Gore assume that politicians have a divine right to mislead the American people? For the answer to that we need look no further than the 'foundation myth' that rules all others, contained in the Declaration of Independence.

## The Court of History v. Thomas Jefferson[2]

'Thomas Jefferson, according to one of your biographers, James Parton, you are a man of many talents who can "calculate an eclipse, survey an estate, tie an artery, plan an edifice, try a cause, break a horse, dance a minuet and play the violin".[3] Is this true?'

'It is, your honour.'

'In that case, Mr Jefferson, can you also identify the truth if it strikes you upon the head?'

'I certainly can.'

'If, as you clearly believe, you can do almost anything, why did you fail to detect the hypocrisy in your position on the subject of slavery? When you said that all men had a right to "life, liberty and the pursuit of happiness" you did not mean black slaves, did you? No, I see you did not. You meant white, propertied free men, did you not? So, "freedom" was never intended to be universal in your United States? There were exceptions right from the start? American exceptionalism, I suppose you might call it.

'Did you not write in 1785, in your *Notes on the State of Virginia*, that black slaves lacked "the capacity for self control, rational forethought and devotion to a larger community" and that they were incapable of freedom?'

'I believe so.'

'That seems rather convenient, does it not, in view of the fact that the 187 slaves you owned formed the major part of your wealth and it was their labour that allowed you to indulge your superior interests? Correct me if I am wrong, but if these slaves had been capable of freedom would it not have ruined you financially, along with at least half of your fellow Founding Fathers?

'In 1776 Mr Jefferson, you were asked to prepare a – *the* – Declaration of Independence, which would call into existence the United States of America, and at the same time excuse what to some observers might appear treason on the part of the American colonists. I cannot resist quoting John Harington, godson to Queen Elizabeth I and – if I may presume upon the court's time – also the inventor of the first flushing water closet. Anyway, Harington observes:

> Treason doth never prosper, what's the reason?
> For if it prosper, none dare call it treason.[4]

'Yes, I can see you approve of that and I think I speak for us all in saying that we are very appreciative of the work of young Harington as a plumber.

'Allow me to say, Mr Jefferson, that, unlike most works of popular American fiction, the Declaration of Independence does show signs of talent. In fact, it seems to be worthy of a much better cause than the replacement of a fat and foolish German monarch by an oligarchy of wealthy landowners. The Founding Fathers were not democrats at all and seem to have been even more contemptuous of the rights of the lower orders than "Farmer George" himself.

'Yet the Declaration of Independence contains an idea so splendid that any nation built upon such a rock would have a very fortunate birth indeed. Unfortunately, a founding father never knows how his children are going to grow up. And your choice of the words, "All men are created equal", has had the most mischievous effect, if I may say so. It has given rise to unrealistic expectations in the United States ever since.

'My sources tell me that there was a first draught of this declaration, which is now known as the *Rough Draft*. In this it is apparent that you were at a loss about how to relate the ideal of "liberty and equality" as every man's right, to the reality of slavery, which was the lot of 20 per cent of the population? Clearly, Mr Jefferson, you thought you had better blame somebody else for this conundrum. After all, you had already accused the British of trying to turn white Americans into slaves by taxing them . . . (stretching the truth a bit there, I feel, even for a disciple of the French philosopher Montesquieu). As about half of the colonists thought King George was a thoroughly bad lot – a German and not a true-born English king – then you thought you could probably get away with blaming him.

'And so, in the *Rough Draft*, you claimed that slavery was all King George's fault. George III, you wrote:

> . . . has waged cruel war against human nature itself, violating its most sacred rights of life and liberty in the persons of a distant people who never offended him, captivating and carrying them into slavery in another hemisphere, or to incur miserable death in their transportation thither. This piratical warfare, the opprobrium of infidel powers, is the warfare of the Christian king of Great Britain. Determined to keep open a market where men should be bought and sold . . .

'Blah, blah, blah . . . and so on.

'Your pen had clearly run away with you and, if I may say so, your imagination as well.

'In view of the fact that slavery had existed in the American colonies for over a century it is a mite unfair to blame George III, who only ascended the throne in 1760. It also seems a bit rich to make Britain solely responsible for the existence and continuance of the institution that allowed your class of wealthy plantation owners to live in luxury and you, meanwhile, to indulge your interests in the arts and sciences.

'It comes as no great surprise that more experienced politicians in South Carolina prevailed upon you to scrap this part of the *Rough Draft*. Nevertheless, one thing is crystal clear: the fine principles of your Declaration of Independence did not survive a threat to your pocket, eh, Mr Jefferson, or to the interests of the American establishment?

'In passing, I would like to point out that in 1772, four years before you wrote your script, the Somerset case confirmed that slavery was not legal in Britain whatever accusations you may like to make against the king.

'At the time the American colonies declared their independence from Britain, one in five of their inhabitants was a black slave. Furthermore, of the 55 men who signed your Declaration of Independence and were therefore known as the "Founding Fathers", half of them were slave owners. Now, these men were not Fausts. They had not suddenly "sold their souls" for the wealth that accrued from denying freedom to their fellow men. They and their families had owned slaves for generations.

Slaves comprised their property, on which their wealth and social standing depended. Slaves were power and gave their owners control over those who owned none. Am I not right?

'It was only when you tried to justify severing the link with Britain that slave owners found themselves trying to balance freedom and equality with slavery. Freedom and equality were battle cries for the masses, not for the plantation owners, were they not? Men like you could buy as much freedom as you liked and how many of your 54 friends would have paid a penny for equality? Yet without battle cries like that how would the "haves" succeed in persuading the "have-nots" to lay down their lives in battle? It was "jam tomorrow", of course, but perhaps I do you an injustice, Mr Jefferson. Perhaps you did really mean that everyone should be free. Just not "free" in America. If the slaves were to be free they should go back where they belonged, to Africa or to the Caribbean. They had made you rich already and so their task was done. Now sentiment could make you mellow and soften your greed.

'If you feel that this intellectual burden was yours alone, you are wrong, Mr Jefferson. Many other colonists recognised that the question of slavery challenged the assumptions of the Founding Fathers. In 1785, one Richard Price questioned whether slavery did not undermine the integrity of the entire revolution. "Had it been right," Price asked, "if the people who have been struggling so earnestly to save themselves from slavery are very ready to enslave others?" Price had hit the nail on the head exactly, had he not? In order to justify what had been treason against your king, you, Madison, Franklin and George Washington had been rather imprecise in using phrases like "slavery" and "tyranny" to describe the struggle against Britain.

'Your use of rhetoric cheapened the whole fight for independence. How could a wealthy man like you describe yourself as a "slave" of George III? That was simply a lie and an insult to the real slaves who worked on the plantations, were bought and sold, whipped and brutalised. And what was the extent of this taxation that was enslaving you? A paltry one shilling a year for the average American. In England, the average was 26 shillings a year from a comparable income.[5] Some slavery!

'The example set by the Founding Fathers breathed not freedom into the American nation but racism and white supremacy. The domination of blacks by whites has been *the* dominant theme of American history for 200 years. When John Jay, the first Chief Justice, described slavery as a "relic of a barbarous past",[6] he was wrong. It was the barbarous future that was the problem. In the 200 or so years since your declaration was written, Mr Jefferson, American whites have committed atrocities in the name of "freedom and equality" that would have singed that good judge's wig. Your freedom has been the black man's tragedy.

'Freedom in America may have an assured place in books of quotations. However, if I may offer you my own opinion, freedom in the United States has often meant little more than "those who are fortunate in life must be free to exercise their advantage over those who are less fortunate". It is the American Way and owes nothing to justice or to morality. In simple terms it may be summed up as "might is right". If you are on top, you will do anything to keep it that way. That, of course, was the way the framers of your constitution saw it.

'The constitution upon which the new republic was based depended not on a series of compromises as the textbooks proclaim with such optimism, but on a built-in guarantee that slavery would dominate the United States for all time. Congress was not allowed to abolish the slave trade for 20 years. During this time, the slave population of the South increased by more than a third. All the northern states had abolished slavery by this stage, but they were still required to return runaway slaves to states where slavery still existed, thus tying the whole country in to the practice of slavery. Furthermore, control of the new legislature by the South was aided by the arrangement that though slaves were granted no civil rights, like freedom or suffrage, they counted as three-fifths of a person in terms of determining a state's representation in Congress or in the Electoral College. Forgive me if I am going too fast for you, Mr Jefferson, but was it not a strange decision that slaves were viewed as property rather than as human beings, but when it came to determining how many representatives there should be from each state, the same "piece of property" was somehow allowed to count as three-fifths of a free man. I will have you know that owners of property in northern states, rich in horses, cattle and grandfather clocks, have raised this with me. Pray tell me, as a philosopher yourself, why Connecticut, for example, won no extra seats in Congress on account of her famous collection of antique firearms?

'Now tell me, Mr Jefferson – Thomas, if you like – there are some who have claimed, in fact, that you never would have been President of the United States had slavery been abolished. Is that true? Take your time; think about it. I admit that the title 'Negro President' may seem a little highly flavoured but it does contain an element of truth, does it not? Take a drink of water, why don't you?

'As one Boston newspaper phrased it in 1801, the Sage of Monticello ... yes, I like that, sage ... had ridden "into the temple of Liberty on the shoulders of slaves". They can be cruel, can't they, the gentlemen of the press?

'The point they are making, however, is a good one. As a result of the Three-Fifth Compromise, although you received eight more votes than President Adams in the Electoral College, at least twelve of your votes were not based on citizen voters who could express their will but on the property owned by Southern masters, namely slaves. If real votes alone had been counted, John Adams would have been returned to office.

'Your very own Gouvernor Morris summed it up very well, I think. The admission of slaves into the representation basically comes down to this:

> That the inhabitant of Georgia and South Carolina who goes to the coast of Africa and, in defiance of the most sacred laws of humanity, tears away his fellow creatures from their dearest connections and damns them to the most cruel bondage shall have more votes in a government instituted for protection of the rights of mankind than the citizen of Pennsylvania or New Jersey who views with a laudable horror so nefarious a practice.

'Oh, yes, very good.

'Now I have heard it whispered that two of your most important projects – the Louisiana Purchase in 1803 and the Embargo Act of 1807 – amounted to little more than a means to extend the economic power of slave states.

'Furthermore, is it not true to say that most of the territorial expansion undertaken by the United States in the following 60 years was designed to allow slavery to expand into new lands, thus guaranteeing a virtual stranglehold by the slave-owning states on the federal government?

'What liberties are taken in the name of freedom.

'Now, Mr Jefferson, it strikes me that from the start you have been rather loose in your choice of vocabulary. You, and those who claim you as spokesman for the new nation, have encouraged Americans to believe they were spreading freedom and democracy around the world when they were doing nothing of the sort. You cannot have your own definition of words in everyday use, Mr Jefferson, otherwise nobody will understand you. Or was that the idea? For "freedom" to include "slavery", and for "equality" to represent "inequality", and for "democracy" to mean that civil rights were denied to substantial parts of the population? You were not communicating to the world in any language they could understand. Saving people by killing them, liberating towns by destroying them, showing unfortunate natives that the benefits of American civilisation were that you had the big guns and they had the small sticks – these were just some of the odd characteristics of the freedom you exported.

'While at home in the United States, women, Native Americans, African–Americans, unpropertied whites and so on could admire the democratic values of the Founding Fathers with their noses pressed to the window. I put it to you, Mr Jefferson, that for a century or more your democracy was a sham.'

'Are you listening at the back Colin Powell, Secretary of State in the administration of President George W. Bush?

'Well, Mr Powell, if you have been listening, which personally I doubt, tell me where exactly black slaves were to fit into this war of American Independence and Mr Jefferson's new democracy?

'When you claimed, during a recent UN Security Council debate on Iraq, that the USA was the oldest of all democracies, did you consider that in 1776 your ancestors – if indeed they were in America at all – would have been:

a) slaves
b) NOT free
c) NOT "Americans" nor even "African–Americans"
d) NOT citizens
e) NOT considered human beings at all but articles of property
f) NOT any part of a democracy
g) more likely to receive freedom and fair treatment from the
    British invaders than from their owners

'While the British freed the slaves who deserted to them, a Virginia law of 1780 rewarded war veterans with 300 acres of land and a slave. Matters could not be much clearer than that. Which side was really fighting for freedom? Faced with the choice of slavery under the new republic or freedom under the British, who can blame slaves like one Gabriel [Prosser] (Gabriel had adopted his owner's surname, as he lost his own when he became a slave) who gave his name to a slave revolt in 1800, when he said, "we have as much right to fight for our liberty as any men".[7] White America did not agree and Gabriel was hanged the next day for insurrection.

'Incidentally, Mr Powell, it did not go unnoticed in 1776 that Thomas Jefferson's good idea was less suited to the new American republic than to almost any other country on earth. For those who know him, and I haven't personally had the pleasure, Doctor Samuel Johnson in England simply snorted at the news, "How is it that we hear the loudest yelps for liberty from the drivers of the Negroes?" A man of Johnson's literary skills might have set a hare running by renaming the recent War of Independence as the War of Black Independence. By an irony which, presumably, would not have been appreciated in the tea shops of Boston, 100,000 American slaves deserted their owners and won their freedom at the hands of the British who supposedly were taking the freedom away from their owners. Patrick Henry, ready to accept "liberty or death" from the British, was at the same time organising patrols to catch any slaves trying to gain their liberty from the same British. They certainly would have gained none from Henry himself who, even at his death, I gather, freed none of his slaves.

'Montesquieu had always been aware of the contradictory nature of Jefferson's position on slavery. The Frenchman realised that Thomas had worked himself into an awkward position and in an attempt to help suggested that blacks should not be regarded as humans, otherwise no Christian could justify owning them.[8]

'Jefferson picked this up and ran with it for a while, paving the way for future eugenicists when he alleged in the *Notes on the State of Virginia* that the blacks were inferior in both beauty, intellect and character. As he observed, "The circumstance of superior beauty is thought worthy of attention in the propagation of our horses, dogs and other domestic animals; why not in that of man?" Miscegenation was what he feared, was it not – mixed marriages and the pollution of the purity of the white race? And yet he did not fear it too much. The supposed ugliness of the black race did not stop him from keeping a black mistress, Sally Hemmings, and having a son, perhaps two, by this woman.

'So what, you might say? If we understand that historical figures are products of their own age, then why is it surprising that a slave owner like Jefferson should have fathered a child by a slave? It was a common occurrence of the time, so that it is thought that many American blacks of today have "white blood" in their ancestors. The answer is simple. Until recently, American textbooks did not mention that George

Washington and Thomas Jefferson were slave owners at all. Neither that the fourth president, James Madison, was a slave owner nor that of the first 16 presidential elections 12 returned a slave owner to the White House. This is irrefutable. As such, why has the United States denied any knowledge of this historical truth to successive generations of its citizens? Is there shame in the past? Not if it is taught properly. What we cannot do is eradicate it by doctoring photographs or letters or records. This is not the democratic way. On the other hand, historical openness should teach us to be more cautious in building our contemporary lives on what men experienced centuries ago.

'Thomas Jefferson was not perfect. He made serious mistakes. The truths he expressed were worthy of our attention but the weaknesses he showed were part of the same picture. To build a future on Jefferson's fudge on slavery, freedom and equality in the Declaration of Independence was fraught with danger. If future generations then carefully air-brushed Jefferson's image to remove imperfections, they failed to acknowledge the dangerous racism that became a part of every corner of America in the two centuries since Jefferson's time.

'Between 1830 and 1860 slave owners became more aggressive in their defence of slavery, building on Jefferson's doubts to insist that "slavery was of a positive value to the slaves themselves". In a sense they were revealing that in some ways – even more dangerous ways – slavery was affecting the white population even more than the blacks. The whites were no longer simply racist, they were white supremacists.

'The infant prodigy "Honest" Abe Lincoln had the answer as usual. Born in a log cabin that he built with his own hands, Lincoln debated this very issue with Stephen Douglas in Illinois in 1858. As Abe observed:

> I should like to know if taking this old Declaration of Independence, which declares that all men are created equal upon principle, and making exceptions to it – where will it stop? If one man says it does not mean a Negro, why does not another say it does not mean some other man? If that Declaration is not . . . true, let us tear it out! [Shouts of No! No!] Let us stick to it then, let us stand formally by it then.[9]

'Great oratory, Abe, but where did it get everyone? You got the presidency in 1860, the slaves got their freedom in 1863, you were shot dead in 1865, the African–Americans became citizens in 1870. But everything you and the boys in blue had died for, Abe, was lost in the next generation. It was the South that won the Civil War and African–Americans were going to find that freedom came at a price!'

Many people have the impression that after the emancipation of the slaves by Lincoln, the problems caused by that peculiar institution ended. But they were wrong. The end of slavery and the freeing of the African–Americans opened the door to what had always lain just below the floorboards – the fear of a threat to white supremacy. While the African–Americans had been enslaved they seemed to offer no threat to the whites. Once freed, however, they were in competition for jobs and had to be suppressed.

Reconstruction after the Civil War failed to integrate the ex-Confederacy into the nation as a whole and the period 1890–1920 saw the nadir of race relations in the United States, culminating in racial massacres that bear comparison with the worst racial violence in India after Partition and Yugoslavia in the 1990s. Between 1890 and 1920, every Southern or border state disenfranchised the vast majority of African–American voters, by imposing tests for potential voters with questions like, 'How many windows are there in the White House?' African–Americans were forced back into the position of second-class citizens which gave the lie to 'freedom, liberty, democracy' and all the other rhetorical terms that politicians and media men use to cover their tracks. Thousands were lynched, some for crimes as simple as trying to vote.

For modern politicians to blandly overlook these atrocities, while preaching the values of 'Americanism', is deeply offensive and dishonest. And for Colin Powell to claim Thomas Jefferson was a supporter of democracy and equal rights is an irony even the British might find hard to accept.

Only recently, the family of Strom Thurmond, the former United States senator, dropped decades of denials and acknowledged that Mr Thurmond, who recently passed away at the age of 100, had fathered a daughter by a black maid in the family household in 1925.[10] The daughter, a retired teacher named Essie Mae Washington-Williams, 78, had periodically denied Mr Thurmond's paternity for the public record but had passed on the truth to her children, who pressured her to come forward. How could Strom Thurmond, who sought the presidency on a segregationist platform in 1948, have lived publicly as a racist while secretly helping to support a black daughter?

If this is the 'American Way', it is just another phrase for *hypocrisy*.

# CHAPTER 5

# *Selling the USA*

A poll taken in 1962 revealed that most Americans believed that if a fifth face were to be carved at Mount Rushmore, it should belong to Woodrow Wilson.[1] This shows how little the real achievements of Wilson are known or understood in his own country. Heroification has distorted history and the real Wilson remains left behind in the archives while another Wilson rules the history texts.

For most Americans, the author of the Fourteen Points is renowned for the vision and idealism that he brought to the peace conference in Paris after the First World War.[2] Modern American politicians cite Wilson's idealism as evidence of how much good America has done in the world and this emboldens them to continue their own policies of Wilsonian idealism.

The truth is very different. Helen Keller referred to Wilson as 'the greatest individual disappointment the world has ever known'.[3]

## A Nation of Cupboards and Skeletons

American school-history textbooks can be dangerously emotive and unbalanced: patriotic but unhistorical in starting with a conclusion and then working relentlessly towards its glorious denouement in today's American superpower. The titles give it away: 'The Great Republic', 'The American Way', 'The Land of Promise', 'The Triumph of the American Nation'. Even *A Patriotic Primer* starts off every tiny American child with the belief that America is 'an inspiration to the world'. This is not teaching history, it is indoctrination.

# PICKING THE BONES

In a land that sets its standards by democratic fundamentalism, controlling the minds of its people is the most profoundly undemocratic act possible. Americans are told that criticism of the government is incompatible with good citizenship and so they are taught from their earliest years that there is nothing to criticise in American history. Yet for teachers to discourage criticism in their pupils is to make them live in the dark. Passivity in such new minds, and servility in the minds of their parents, is the new slavery. And the mind controllers of the American media and education system are the new slave owners.

Paul Gagnon commented on Americans' lack of empathy in an article entitled 'Why Study History?': 'To study foreign affairs without putting ourselves into others' shoes is to deal in illusion and to prepare our students for a lifelong misunderstanding of our place in the world.' Is it any surprise that the Americans cannot understand other nations and cultures when they show so little understanding of themselves? Their own history has been hidden from them and they therefore reject any criticism from outside as either liberal or communist propaganda.

When educated Americans claim that their modern foreign policy contains elements of Wilsonian idealism, it bewilders this foreigner – at least – who can see little in Woodrow Wilson but a racist and a white supremacist, whose foreign policy was not idealistic at all but based on hegemony rather than democracy. The dishonesty of a white supremacist like Wilson was partly concealed by the self-righteousness of a religious bigot who felt that he was superior to the perfidious and corrupt Europeans he met at Paris in 1919. Wilson was a hypocrite who joined the Allied intervention in Russia in total defiance of his own theory of self-determination in order to destroy a popular movement fighting for its freedom against an autocratic regime and foreign invaders.

According to Frances FitzGerald, American school textbooks present their country as 'a kind of Salvation Army to the rest of the world',[4] whose policies are part of a morality play in which the USA typically acts on behalf of human rights, democracy and the 'American Way'. Thus American children grow up believing their country is a kind of international 'good guy' when it should be obvious to anyone that the rest of the world is more worried about the supposed 'good intentions' of the Americans than they are about the 'bad intentions' of many other states. This kind of educational brainwashing has never occurred before in a democratic country and is far more typical of a totalitarian society. One US textbook claims, 'The US has done more than any other nation in history to provide equal rights for all.' This is nothing more than what Loewen refers to as 'ethnocentric cheerleading'.[5] Making white racism invisible to young Americans is preventing anybody today from really dealing with a problem that is at the root of many of modern America's problems. This should be very worrying for any free-thinking American.

Politicians have transformed history to make it palatable to the voters of the present. It is a tool in their contemporary armoury to guarantee control of the future. Political control of the education system, notably what American children learn of their past, is at the root of Americans' distorted view of their own history and that of the rest of the world.

American politicians assert almost ritualistically – as did Madeleine Albright in Columbus, Ohio, in February 1998, whilst being heckled about her Iraq policy – 'We are the greatest country in the world!'[6] It was almost like an incantation to her tribal spirit, which had to be made or else the crops would fail. On 11 September 2001, congressmen standing on the steps of the Capitol in Washington sang 'God Bless America', like the soldiers on the sinking troopship *Birkenhead* singing 'Auld Lang Syne' as the waves broke over their heads. If God really was blessing America on 9/11 as the land of his chosen people, he was choosing an odd way of showing it.

From colonial days, America has been driven by the belief that she is divinely inspired to make the world a better place. In 1775, the British commented that the colonists they encountered behaved as if they possessed, 'some superior sanctity, some peculiar privilege, by which those things are lawful to them, which are unlawful to all the world besides'. This has resulted in Americans according every action they take a slant that makes it unrecognisable to the rest of the world. Every military conquest becomes a 'regenerative intervention' or, as with the 1898 war against Spain, a 'crusade for Cuban liberation'. Even when they commit atrocities – for example in the Philippines – it is 'benevolent assimilation' and returning soldiers seemed scarcely aware of the incongruity of liberators also being oppressors. As one said of the Filipino Revolt, 'The country won't be pacified until the niggers are killed off like the Indians.' Corporal Moses Smith put it better: 'Now I don't believe that there is a soldier or an American but believes the Filipinos must be whipped thoroughly. After that we can give them their independence under an American protectorate.'[7]

Many American 'crusades' or 'regenerative interventions' in Central and South America had an underlying theme which, stripped of American cant, was clear to everyone else. Writing in 1931 and reflecting on a lifetime's career in the US Marines, Marine Corps General Smedley Butler said:

> I helped make Mexico safe for American oil interests in 1914. I helped make Haiti and Cuba a decent place for the National City Bank boys to collect revenue in. I helped purify Nicaragua for the international banking house of Brown Brothers . . . I brought light to the Dominican Republic for American sugar interests in 1916. I helped make Honduras 'right' for American fruit companies in 1903. Looking back on it, I might have given Al Capone a few hints.[8]

The 'ideals' that drove the foreign policy of the United States, notably that of Woodrow Wilson, were fourfold:

- The creation of 'free market' economies welcoming exports and foreign investment
- The privatisation of local resources, thus allowing the USA to acquire them
- The free flow of Christian and Western ideas like 'freedom' and 'democracy'
- The intervention in 'failed states' by American troops to ensure 'freedom' for the sort of people that America felt would maintain the 'American Way'

In Hawaii, from the mid-nineteenth century, American missionaries had 'hit the beaches first', followed by American sugar and pineapple planters, with the Marines keeping up the rear. It was observed cynically that, 'In the beginning the missionaries had the Bible, and the people had the land; now the people have the Bible, and the missionaries, the land.' In Hawaii, God's work involved dispossessing the indigenous population of land tenure that had ensured that commoners could engage in subsistence agriculture and replacing it with a system of private property that soon dispossessed the majority of Hawaiians. King Kamehameha III was persuaded by the missionaries and the planters to allow resident foreigners to vote in elections for the newly formed legislature, thus guaranteeing American economic interests a virtual stranglehold.

Tragedy for Hawaii took place when Queen Lili'uokalani tried to turn back the tide of American cultural and economic domination. Then the other side of America's crusade became apparent. Their actions had been divinely inspired and whoever resisted America resisted God. The American business community now plotted the annexation of Hawaii. Thirteen American capitalists, naming themselves the 'Committee of Public Safety', organised a coup while Marines aboard the USS *Boston* in Honolulu harbour were 'ready to land at any moment' to assist. On 17 January 1893, the Committee of Public Safety dethroned Queen Lili'uokalani on the grounds that she was attempting 'with armed force and threats of bloodshed' to impose a new constitution. The American sugar producers called for help and soon the Marines charged ashore to restore order. Sanford B. Dole, sugar magnate and Supreme Court Justice, proclaimed a provisional republic and the queen was arrested when arms, including 21 coconut bombs, were found at her residence.

Queen Lili'uokalani was charged with treason and placed under house arrest. After she agreed to abdicate she was sentenced to five years in prison and fined $5,000. In an attempt to destroy her reputation, she was also accused of witchcraft and making sacrifices to the native volcano goddess, Pele, as well as promoting the lascivious hula dance against the wishes of US missionaries. It was a thoroughly unedifying action by the United States for which a full apology was made under President Clinton in 1993:

> The Congress – apologises to Native Hawaiians on behalf of the people of the United States for the overthrow of the Kingdom of Hawaii on January 17, 1893 . . . and the deprivation of the rights of Native Hawaiians to self-determination;[9]

In the words of Gary Leupp, 'It was an early instance of US imperialism, supported ideologically by religious fundamentalism and racism, and justified by bald-faced lies.'[10]

## White Man Speaks with Forked Tongue

'White man speaks with forked tongue' was all the Native Americans were ever allowed to say before the cowboys or cavalry shot them. In the films of my youth, often watched at Saturday morning pictures visits, there were many such scenes, portraying the good guys with forked tongues but straight rifles and the bad guys with bullets in them. Disputes between Native Americans and white settlers over tribal hunting lands often ended with someone speaking on behalf of the Great White Father in the East. The Native Americans never learned. They always trusted the Great White Father whose soldiers betrayed them, sold them liquor and then shot them down. And out of these scenes, to an impressionable child, emerged the thought that perhaps the Native Americans were right after all. Perhaps white man did speak with forked tongue.

At school I studied the First World War and the subsequent Peace of Paris. It was then that I learned about the Treaty of Versailles, where the same men who had lied to the Native Americans and – I learned later – the African–Americans, came across the Atlantic to show the Europeans how to conduct their affairs. Woodrow Wilson was their leader and he was touting his Fourteen Points, while French Prime Minister Georges Clemenceau quipped glumly, 'God himself only needed ten.' None of us laughed, although we were supposed to.

And yet there was a hidden flaw in all this that a ten year old watching cowboy films would never have noticed, nor a sixteen year old, grubbing through facts for O level history, would have had time to consider, and it was this: Woodrow Wilson was an idealist, we were told, and the Americans thought themselves better than the Europeans they were coming to liberate. Yet these were the same Americans who had lied to the Native Americans and kept the African–Americans as slaves, and they were coming to lecture us! Just who was this Woodrow Wilson and where on earth had he picked up his ideals? The mystery deepened.

When he spoke of self-determination for virtually unknown European states, was Woodrow Wilson really thinking of the Saar or Bohemia and Moravia or Memel, or was he instead really pining for 'Dixie', his beloved 'Old South' which had been denied self-determination in 1861 and had been prepared to fight to be free?

When the first 'doughboys' arrived in France in 1917 to 'liberate' Europe, were they carrying an extra pair of sheets in their knapsacks? Did General Pershing himself or his aide, Colonel Charles Stanton, really say 'Lafayette, we are here'?[11] What were the ideals that these tall, fresh-faced Americans were bringing from the New World 'to redress the problems of the Old'?

The United States that Woodrow Wilson's soldiers were leaving behind them was at the darkest hour of its struggle with racism and had its most racist government ever. Many of the soldiers would have seen D.W. Griffith's film *The Birth of a Nation* in the 12 months before they left for France and some might even have echoed the views of one man who, on leaving the cinema, announced, 'It makes me want to go out and kill the first Negro I see.' This was the America that was to be the example for the Old World – the America of the Ku Klux Klan and the burning cross, the land of racial intolerance and white supremacy.

Historians seem to have created a dual personality for Woodrow Wilson. The word 'idealism' has been used to depict Wilson so that European historians have a vision of an 'ivory tower' called Princeton, inhabited by a handsome, schoolmasterly gentleman with good intentions. Like something out of *Goodbye, Mr Chips*, Wilson visits a Europe inhabited by creatures that need to be shown there is a better way – the American Way. This is a total misrepresentation of a man who may have claimed to have 'ideals' but was a religious bigot of the same school as Oliver Cromwell and a white supremacist who had as little to teach the future as Kurtz from Conrad's *Heart of Darkness*.

To call Wilson an unreconstructed Confederate might seem severe, yet his persistent romanticising of the Old South was nothing less than the 'Magnolia Myth' writ large.[12] In his view, slavery was a positive good that had brought cohesion and stability to Southern life. 'Great gangs of cheery Negroes' shouldered their hoes and spades and walked the dusty paths singing 'Swing Low Sweet Chariot'. Or, for those fond of musical theatre, 'Old Man River' floated across the cotton fields with the steamboats on the Mississippi in the background. All the whites were called Ravenell or Rhett and in an earlier age these cavaliers would have been at King Charles's or Prince Rupert's service against the roundheads instead of against Northern carpetbaggers or 'uppity niggers'.

It was sentimental nonsense yet, to the first Southern President since reconstruction, it was where he belonged, in an independent, unreformed South where blacks were minstrels who played banjos and slept in the barn. Wilson appears to have seen his presidency as an opportunity to correct history and to restore white Americans to unchallenged supremacy. He was convinced that Southern campaigns to disenfranchise African–Americans had helped to 'undo the mischief of reconstruction'. But the basic problem remained unsolved: Southern blacks had forgotten they were naturally and properly a servile race. Until they recognised that they had taken the wrong path, the wonders of ante-bellum Southern society would never return.

As president of Princeton in the first years of the new century, Woodrow Wilson had discovered that blacks were trying to enrol as students. Such effrontery outraged him because higher education for the servile race was 'unprecedented' and 'unwarranted'. Nevertheless, this racism was at the root of Wilson's political philosophy and made him a popular politician in the first decade of the new century. On lighter occasions, Wilson revealed that he had a skill for mimicry and entertained his dinner guests with funny voices, his favourites being those of the black slaves he had known in his youth.

With the Republican Party split in 1912, Wilson won the election for the Democrats, becoming the only ever Ph.D. graduate to sit in the White House. However, no sooner had he taken up the reins of power in Washington than he began a rigorous campaign to turn back the clock on race relations. Wilson was of the opinion that whites represented high ideas like civilisation, wisdom and moral feeling, pride and responsibility. Blacks, on the other hand, stood for the opposite: wildness, ignorance and barbaric aggression, because he saw them as basically savages.

If anyone had any doubts about what the American people had voted for in 1912, these doubts cannot have outlasted Wilson's inauguration. Against a background of 'Rebel Yells' and bands blaring 'Dixie', Edward Douglass White, ex-Confederate, ex-Ku Klux Klansman, and Chief Justice of the United States Supreme Court, administered the oath of office to Woodrow Wilson. In keeping with Southern tradition, an anonymous donor sent a possum to the new president, while an unidentified associate of the new Chief Executive announced to the American people that since the South now ran the nation, African–Americans should expect to be treated as a servile race.

It may not generally be known that while Wilson was president of Princeton, that university was the only such institution in the North that would not admit blacks. Even at the Peace of Paris, during discussions about the formation of the new League of Nations, Wilson vetoed a clause on racial equality. If racism was America's disease, Wilson was looking to spread it worldwide. In other remarks, it has been noted that he charged that slavery had disciplined African–Americans to defer to the 'superior' race.

The word most associated with Woodrow Wilson is 'idealism' and it is said that all subsequent American foreign policy contains at least some of that idealism. So, the question should be asked: what were the ideals that motivated a man like Woodrow Wilson? Should we look at the Fourteen Points that he wrote to make the world a better place or should we instead look at how he ran his own home before he presumed to run others' homes for them?

The period between 1890 and 1920 was worse than the last days of slavery had been for the black community in America. Discrimination was widespread and violence common, with lynchings reaching the level of a national epidemic. As Leon Litwak has shown in *Without Sanctuary: Lynching Photography in America,* many lynchings were filmed and were public events, attended by the whole white community, including women and children. In fact, children were often given time off school to attend. In April 1899 a black man named Sam Hose was accused of murdering his employer in self-defence, but was executed without trial. First stripped and tied to a tree, Hose had his ears, fingers and genitals cut off and his face skinned. He was then burned alive before his heart and liver were cut out. A slice of his heart was then delivered to the Governor of Georgia. One Atlanta newspaper commented, 'The people of Georgia are orderly and conservative, the descendants of ancestors who have been trained in America for 150 years. They are a people intensely religious, homeloving and just. There is among them no foreign or lawless element.'

Even in the North, hostility to blacks was widespread. No black could even buy a house in Minneapolis nor could he work in the construction industry in Philadelphia or as an assistant in a shop in Chicago. Throughout the North, no blacks could belong to Labour unions.

The segregationist policy of the Wilson administration after 1912 was primarily inspired by two claims from white Americans: that blacks carried contagious diseases and that blacks had become disrespectful to their white superiors. Among some administration officials, these two apprehensions may have blurred into one – the insolent African–American was also the diseased African–American. Yet even before 'uppity niggers' were reprimanded, administration officials felt that toilets and lunchrooms would have to be segregated. If they were to prevent a mass epidemic, no time should be lost.

For such a well-educated man, Wilson revealed little evidence of the benefits of schooling when dealing with race relations: most black American diplomats were replaced by whites; numerous black federal officials in the South were removed from their posts; the local Washington police force and fire department stopped hiring blacks; the President himself showed his sympathy for the prevailing racism by dismissing 15 of the 17 African–Americans that the previous administration had appointed. Wilson persuaded Atlanta's postmaster to discharge 35 black employees to help them find themselves again. Georgia's Collector of Internal Revenue said that there were no Government positions for Negroes in the South, suggesting a Negro's place was in the cornfield.

In November 1914, when the black journalist Monroe Trotter met the president to denounce federal racial policies, Wilson became so infuriated with his 'uppityness' that he had him forcibly ejected. 'Your manner offends me,' was his explanation.[13]

Even for those who regard Wilson as an idealist whose fine sentiments supposedly underpinned the Peace of Paris, his welcoming of Griffith's epic film *The Birth of a Nation* is surely hard to stomach. Griffith had designed a film to make people feel, but not to think. At a time when the British propaganda services, both in Europe and America, were twisting the truth to blacken the Germans with images of bayoneted babies and stories of crucified Canadians, Griffith was using the same methods to damage race relations in America. At Wilson's request, the film was first screened in the East Room of the White House for himself and his Cabinet. The next night it was shown to the Supreme Court and members of Congress with the consent of Chief Justice Edward White. Wilson was deeply impressed by the propaganda of the film. 'It is like writing history with lightning,' he said.[14]

At the first public performance, opponents of the movie appealed to the city magistrate to close down the theatre and they got their way. But with the President's prestige behind it, Griffith was bound to win. A national advertising campaign was launched with the theme that the film was 'federally endorsed' with the President and the Chief Justice approving of it personally. After just six months, two million people had seen the movie. It was turning the entire population of the North and West into future supporters of Dixie. It was also teaching the entire nation the wisdom of Wilson's racial policies. Most people who saw the film were deeply and emotionally touched by the story, which showed barbaric black men threatening the virtue of the South's white women. The Ku Klux Klan were portrayed as chivalric knights who came to the rescue of their womenfolk.

Nevertheless, the film caused race riots. Millions of white Americans cheered hysterically at the Ku Klux Klan's violent suppression of the blacks, transformed by Griffith into a symbolic defence of white civilisation against black savagery. Some spectators left the cinemas so overstimulated by the violence they had witnessed that they headed for 'niggertown' to 'let loose' their frustrations on the black enemy. In Knoxville and in Chicago, in Washington DC and in Omaha, in Elaine, Arkansas, and in East St Louis, Illinois, whites rioted against blacks. White savagery, not black, reigned supreme.

Wilson was indeed writing history with lightning. *The Birth of a Nation* was a direct incitement to racial war and the President of the

United States was encouraging it. What on earth does this tell us about a country where this sort of thing was allowed to happen, and which fails to explain why to its future generations? Is it shame or hubris?

The revival of the Ku Klux Klan during this period was clear from the number of prominent people in American life who supported the organisation. In New York, KKK balls were all the rage for the young and fashionable, while at the University of Chicago a special Klan party attracted 2,000 guests in KKK costumes, carrying burning crosses with the American flag and the Bible. Even the next President, Warren G. Harding, agreed to be sworn in as a member, and a five-man Klan team conducted the initiation in the Green Room of the White House.

In 1919, there were two dozen race riots from Houston to Minnesota, where whites feared African–Americans would take their jobs and deflower their women. Anecdotes of the period reveal a country that has lost its senses. A black boy swimming in Lake Michigan drifted too near a 'whites-only' beach, was stoned by whites and drowned. In Tulsa, Oklahoma, in 1921, a black boy trod on a white girl's toe in a lift and set off the worst race riot in American history. The Tulsa Massacre, as it was later called, was virtually unknown to most modern Americans as a result of a successful cover-up which lasted until the 1980s, when historians finally published the details.[15]

Tulsa was a boomtown after the First World War and the black population had benefited from the general increase in wealth. They lived in a part of the city known as Greenwood, an impressive black township that had earned the sobriquet 'Negro's Wall Street'. Here the fancy cars and smart houses owned by some of the black professionals were considered to be examples of the African–American's 'uppityness' by many of the whites.

A black boy in a lift was accused of assaulting a white girl, who had apparently overreacted as a result of an ingrown toenail. He was taken to jail and the local newspaper, the *Tulsa Tribune*, brought out a special edition with a headline calling whites to attend a lynching of the black boy that night.[16] The sheriff was determined that there would be no lynching but as night fell hundreds of armed whites appeared outside the jailhouse ready to execute the prisoner.

Suddenly, however, groups of armed blacks also began to appear at the jailhouse to defend the prisoner and shooting broke out. The whites called up reinforcements and soon thousands of vigilantes, many of whom had only recently returned from the war in France, armed with a wide range of weapons, joined the fight. Once the armed blacks were driven back, a general race riot broke out throughout the city as mobs of whites carried death and destruction into the black areas.

There was a complete breakdown of law and order as 35 blocks of Greentown were burned to the ground and looted. Vehicles of all kinds, driven by whites, roared through the streets dragging black corpses tied to the bumpers behind them. One old black cripple was dragged alive behind a car.

As the white mob passed through the black areas, white women followed carrying bags which they filled with jewellery, silverware and curtains looted from the black properties. Heavy furniture and pianos were smashed, while cars were wrecked and their tyres stolen. By the next morning most of Greentown was in ruins, with 1,115 houses burned and looted, as well as 5 hotels, 31 restaurants, a school, a hospital, a library and 12 churches.

At one stage in the fighting, six two-seater First World War trainers from the nearby Curtis Field were commandeered by the white vigilantes and used to bomb Greentown from the air with nitroglycerine. When the Fire Department was desperately summoned, it ignored the black houses burning.[17]

According to books written recently, for example Tim Madigan's *The Burning* – and contrary to official figures – possibly 300 African–Americans died in the rioting. So many corpses were disposed of during the cover-up that ensued that accurate estimates of the number of casualties would never be known. The official reaction to the 'massacre' came from Oklahoma's attorney general, who claimed, 'It might have happened anywhere, for the Negro is not the same man he was 30 years ago when he was content to plod along his own road accepting the white man as his benefactor.'[18]

One Klansman interviewed in old age said he would do it all again.

## Self-determination

From his first days in office, Woodrow Wilson was very active in foreign affairs, usually defending American business interests rather than spreading the other benefits of American culture, such as freedom and education, that have occupied the attention of historians until perhaps the last decade or so. In fact, Wilson intervened in Latin American countries more often than any president in American history. American Marines were an ever-present factor in the affairs of Nicaragua, where they enforced the election of a president favourable to

US businessmen, while US troops intervened in Mexico on 11 occasions during Wilson's presidency. They also intervened in Haiti in 1915, the Dominican Republic in 1916, Cuba in 1917 and Panama in 1918.[19] In between, of course, in 1917, they landed in France, bringing American values to the rescue of the Old World, notably Britain and France. In case anyone was feeling overlooked, the idealistic Wilson also sent troops to take the side of the White Army in the Russian Civil War. American expeditionary forces went to Murmansk, Archangel and Vladivostok to help suppress the Russian Revolution. Winston Churchill, of course, had instigated the intervention and British soldiers were there as well, along with French, Japanese and Czech troops.

Wilson's opposition to Bolshevism was based on its aim to create one world – which made it more idealistic than even he was. Instead, he believed in separate nations, and democracy and American values were regarded as correct and universal. One effect of the American intervention in Russia was the start of nearly a century of Russo-American hostility. One writer has observed:

> The immediate effect of the intervention was to prolong a bloody civil war, thereby costing thousands of additional lives and wreaking enormous destruction on an already battered society. And there were longer-range implications. Bolshevik leaders had clear proof ... that the Western powers meant to destroy the Soviet government if given the chance.[20]

During his presidency, Wilson made colonies of Nicaragua, Cuba, the Dominican Republic and Haiti. His occupation/conquest of Haiti is very little known in America. American Marines invaded the country in 1915 and forced the Haitians to select a president favoured by the USA. Next, a referendum was held which supported the American action by 98,225 to 768, even though democracy had been overthrown and replaced by a less representative constitution. Individual ownership of land was abolished in favour of large plantations, as in Hawaii, and US troops shackled Haitian peasants to work on the roads. In 1918, the Haitians rose in revolt against the Americans but were suppressed at the cost of 3,000 lives. George Barnett, a Marine general, admitted that indiscriminate killing of Haitians by American troops was a regular event. He admitted that this was 'the most startling thing of its kind that has ever taken place in the Marine Corps'.[21]

# PICKING THE BONES

## Vive l'Amérique, Vive Wilson

Between January and June 1919, Woodrow Wilson was President of Europe as well as America – at least he thought he was. Before he left America, he addressed Congress in these words: 'It is now my duty to play my full part in making good what they [the troops] gave their life's blood to obtain.' The British attitude towards the first American president to visit Europe was different. Wilson came to Paris, 'as a debutante is entranced by the prospect of her first ball'.[22]

Self-determination was the poisonous gift that America sent the Europeans by the hand of Woodrow Wilson. Instead of a stable future for post-war Europe it produced a feeding frenzy amongst the sprats, who in turn supplied shoals of prey for the sharks. It brought chaos to central Europe in the wake of a terrible, destructive war and played into the hands of demagogues throughout the continent. Emerging fascists had reason to thank Woodrow Wilson and his Fourteen Points, none more so than Adolf Hitler.

Wilson was an egotist who simply would not see the truth if it differed from what he wanted it to be. 'Even established facts were ignored if they did not fit in with this intuitive sense, this semi-divine power to select the right.'[23] Wilson has been overrated by European politicians and historians ever since, who have tended to take the President at his own valuation. His political opponents were not so kind. Theodore Roosevelt thought him 'as insincere and cold-blooded an opportunist as we have ever had in the presidency', while the French ambassador to Washington was even more damning, warning his government that Wilson was 'a man who, had he lived a couple of centuries ago, would have been the greatest tyrant in the world, because he does not seem to have the slightest conception that he can ever be wrong'.[24]

Wilson's tyranny can best be seen in his attacks on civil liberties after America entered the First World War in 1917. Americans did not take to the war in the way Europeans had in 1914. In spite of Wilson's urgings, the call for a million volunteers in 1917 brought forth just 73,000! Congress thereupon voted for conscription and the draft was introduced. Protests against both the draft, and the war as a whole, came from the Socialist Party.

Wilson responded with the Espionage Act in 1917, which threatened opponents of the war with 20 years in jail. The Sedition Act followed the next year, after which the President tried to acquire direct censorship laws for the executive. Next he applied new censorship powers under which the postmaster general could refuse to handle anything socialist, anti-British, anti-war or pro-Irish. Where *The Birth of a Nation* had directly profited from presidential support, the film *The Spirit of '76*, about the American War of Independence, made by Robert Goldstein, was declared anti-British and therefore anti-war, and Goldstein was given ten years in jail! The case was officially listed as US v. The Spirit of '76 and nobody noticed the irony.

The leader of the Socialist Party, Eugene V. Debs, became Wilson's main target and when in June 1918 he gave an anti-war speech in Canton, Ohio, he was arrested and sentenced to ten years in jail. Even as the war ended, Wilson was not prepared to pass an amnesty for political prisoners. After nearly three years and in spite of pressure from within his own administration, the President said that he would *never* pardon Debs. Eventually, Wilson's successor, Warren Harding, freed Debs and 23 other political dissidents on the grounds that 'I couldn't do anything else . . . Those fellows didn't mean any harm. It was a cruel punishment.'[25]

Wilson's constant references to freedom and democracy were as fraudulent as the representation of America during his presidency. He created an atmosphere of fear that assured him of political security at home. His supporters were willing to suppress free speech. Elihu Root, ex-Secretary for War, was quoted by the *New York Times* as saying, 'We must have no criticism now . . . there are men walking the streets of this city tonight who ought to be taken out at sunrise tomorrow and shot for treason.'[26] Vigilantes patrolled the streets suppressing 'anti-draft sentiment'. The American Protective League had a membership of 100,000. Its task was to hunt down un-American activities and it claimed to have found three million cases of disloyalty. The press also joined the witch-hunts.

While in Paris, Wilson's arrogance stemmed from a feeling of superiority that America had assumed in dealing with what he considered the effete diplomats of another, bloodier and more corrupt age. Significantly, when Wilson travelled to Europe for the peace conference, he took his new wife, Edith Bolling, who apparently had a black maid with her. Edith enjoyed her time in Paris but was advised not to take her maid to London when the American delegation crossed to England because the British were inclined to 'treat blacks too well'.[27]

American arrogance stretched history to the point that they saw their intervention in the war as indispensable to the Allied cause and that the Entente was facing defeat when American troops rushed to save them. This is untrue. During the first 12 months after Wilson joined the war, the influence of America was more apparent than real, a psychological factor on the Allied side and a threat of what might happen if the Germans continued fighting beyond 1918. It took the Americans a full year to send just four divisions to France. In the same period it should be pointed out that the defeat of Russia in the east enabled the Germans to transfer 34 divisions to the Western Front to bolster their plan for a decisive offensive against the Allies in March 1918.

Against American claims to have 'won' the First World War it is necessary to point out that, in reality, it was a combination of factors that brought the Germans to accept the armistice on 11 November 1918. These were:

- British tactics and victories during the period August–October 1918. The British combination of 1,900 aircraft, 2,000 artillery pieces and 500 tanks broke the German army once and for all at Amiens on 8 August 1918. Ludendorff admitted it was 'the black day of the German army in the history of the war'.

  The Kaiser accepted, 'We have nearly reached the limit of our powers of resistance. The war must be ended.' And the German official history recorded: 'As the sun set on the battlefield on 8 August the greatest defeat which the German army had suffered since the beginning of the war was an accomplished fact.'[28]

  The British army now won eight consecutive victories over the Germans:

  Bapaume 21 August–1 September
  The Scarpe 26 August–3 September
  Havrincourt and Epéhy 12–18 September
  The Hindenburg Line 27 September–5 October
  Flanders 28 September–14 October
  Le Cateau 6–12 October
  The Selle 17–25 October
  The Sambre 1–11 November

  During these battles, 59 divisions of the British army defeated 99 German divisions, captured 188,700 German prisoners and 2,840 German artillery pieces. In the same period, the Americans took 43,300 German prisoners and 1,421 guns. It was the greatest period of continuous military success in British history and, in the words of J.P. Harris, 'It was . . . the campaign in which ground forces under British command exercised the most influence on the history of the world in the twentieth century.'[29]

- The collapse of the German Home Front through the effects of the naval blockade. The British naval blockade (1914–19) broke resistance on the Home Front, costing the Germans 800,000 lives by the time of the armistice and many more in the nine months before it was lifted, when the Germans agreed to sign the Treaty of Versailles.

## The Fourteen Points

Wilson's 'pitch' at Versailles was that, as the author of the Fourteen Points, America came as arbiter of justice and generosity, and represented the 'only disinterested people at the Peace Conference'. In view of the fact that Wilson worked to create a better world 'for the American system', this was not entirely true. Wilson proclaimed that the USA had not entered the war for selfish reasons. He did not want territory, tribute or revenge – he had always called his country an 'associate' of Britain and France rather than an 'ally'.

But the arrogant and inexperienced men who travelled to Europe with Wilson were insufferable companions. One supposedly educated diplomat revealed the fact that he saw Europe as little different from the states of Latin America whom the Americans were accustomed to bullying. He declared:

> Europe is bankrupt financially and its governments are bankrupt morally. The mere hint of withdrawal by America by reason of opposition to her wishes for justice, for fairness, and for peace would see the fall of every government in Europe without exception, and a revolution in every country in Europe with one possible exception.[30]

Such arrogance would be intolerable if it were not so naive. Wilson felt European states could be led by the nose because of the debts they owed America. But he was wrong. Britain and France had their own agendas and once the future of Germany was settled and Wilson was securely packed off to wherever he had come from, they could get down to carving up the German and Turkish empires between them as they had secretly planned in 1916.

Wilson's Secretary of State Robert Lansing was highly critical of his President's lack of clarity on the subject of self-determination. When Wilson said, 'We say now that all these people have the right to live their own lives under governments which they themselves choose to set up. That is the American principle,' did he really know what he was talking about? What unit had he in mind for this self-determination: town, county, province or country? And who constituted a unit of people who would have the right to choose? Above all, what happened to minorities living within larger groups of different racial or national inclinations? Were they allowed to vote for themselves or must they be swallowed up by a different and perhaps hostile people? It was tribalism rather than nationhood and it should not have been encouraged. Wilson was courting popularity by trying to be all things to all people but he would end by disappointing everybody.

The shallowness of Wilson's appreciation of European affairs was revealed when the nationalist Irish asked for help through self-determination but were told to go to hell by an overstressed Wilson. 'They live in a democracy. Let them use that,' was what he said later.[31] Clearly, he had never encountered the Irish question in British politics.

Lansing was shrewd enough to see that self-determination would cause fighting – and not just amongst the Irish – because 'It will raise hopes which can never be realised. It will, I fear, cost thousands of lives.' Lansing underestimated by many millions. The Sudetenland (Bohemia and Moravia) was to bring on the Czech crisis of 1938 when war was only temporarily avoided at Munich, and Danzig and the Polish Corridor were to be the actual sparks that ignited world war in 1939.

By the end of 1919, Wilson was already fearing defeat on self-determination. 'When I gave utterance to those words, I said them without the knowledge that nationalities existed, which are coming to us day after day.'[32] Essentially, the President was out of his depth and was only just beginning to realise it. The arrogance of the Americans was showing through embarrassingly. One young diplomat had boasted, 'Before we get through with these fellows over here we will teach them how to do things and how to do them quickly.'

It is easy with hindsight to criticise the peace settlement at Paris. Hindsight may be unhistorical but it is almost unavoidable in view of the terrible things that we know grew out of the work of Wilson and the other leaders. Yet Wilson set the agenda and his imposition of un-European answers to European problems was likely to end badly. Failure to deal with the main subject of German nationalism, while encouraging nationalist aspirations in many parts of the continent, was simply obtuse. If self-determination was to be the guiding principle for the future of Europe, how could it be denied to the country most in need of it? Creating German minorities throughout Europe was an invitation to future trouble, and commentators in 1919 saw this even before Hitler had been demobilised from the Germany army.

The threat posed by a nationalist Serbia to the ramshackle Habsburg Empire containing, as it did, a mass of conflicting races, faiths and national groupings, had been one of the main causes of the First World War in the first place. To use self-determination to 'Balkanise' central and south-eastern Europe was merely postponing for a few years the continuing round of wars that had taken place in the first decade of the twentieth century. Self-determination was idealistic nonsense without a supervisory authority and the League of Nations would only be strong enough to supervise the peace settlement with America as a permanent member, committed to overseeing the future of Europe.

When the Americans – notably politicians like George W. Bush – blame Britain and France for their appeasement of Nazi Germany in the 1930s, they overlook the greatest failure of the period: not appeasement by Old Europe, but the blundering policies of Woodrow Wilson and the 'New World' at Paris in 1919 and the failures of the United States to clear up the mess they left behind in Europe. In the end, it was only the old alliance system of the Entente powers that offered any resistance to the fascists. So unhelpful was America's contribution to controlling the aggression of the fascist states that even after the Japanese attack on Pearl Harbor on 7 December 1941, it was uncertain whether the United States would enter the war against Germany.

It should be remembered that Hitler declared war on the United States, not the other way round. America was not doing Britain a favour by joining her in the war against Hitler, she was giving up appeasement herself at last, appeasement of her own isolationists. The Second World War has been called the 'unnecessary war', unnecessary because it was a product of the failures of the Wilson-dominated peace settlement of 1919. With less vision and more practical sense, the war of 1939–45 need not have been inevitable.

# CHAPTER 6

# *The Evil Empire*

The rhetoric of politicians was once the supreme 'weapon of mass distraction' for voters in a democracy. In 1948, the speech by President Harry S Truman that contained the so-called Truman Doctrine created a Cold War mentality among Americans based on emotionally supercharged images of a Soviet threat. Truman described Communism as a plague and 'a great red sea that splashes all around us and whose waves somehow break upon every shore and unless we are vigilant might some day break upon our shores'.[1] In the words of Arthur Vandenburg, the speech was 'designed to scare the hell out of the country'.[2] And it did just that. By playing on the vulnerability of the United States, Truman won political support from Americans for a policy of combating Communism globally and directly pointed the way to US intervention in Korea and Vietnam. America invented the Cold War and sustained an inaccurate image of the Soviet Union for the next half century by a deliberate act of distortion.

## Making Friends

In the immediate aftermath of 9/11 George W. Bush challenged the world to take sides: you were either with America or you weren't, and if you weren't with America, you must be supporting the terrorists. There was no middle ground.

He can be excused for talking like this. He was as shocked as everyone else after so immense a tragedy. The problem is, however, that most people have recovered from the shock, but Bush is still talking in the same way and offering the same choice. What appeared to be a simple and understandable knee-jerk reaction on his part now appears to be part of an agenda.

In order to understand where Bush is coming from with his agenda of fear, it is interesting to look at how American politicians exploited another real but exaggerated threat in foreign affairs 60 years ago for political and economic reasons.

When, in 1917, the Russians had risen against their absolute rulers, the Americans did not applaud the struggle of a people fighting for their freedom. Far from it. They joined the forces of reaction and sent troops to Russia in 1918 to try to stamp out the freedom fighters at birth. Thousands of US troops fought the Communists in probably the least-known war in American history. Until the 1930s, America even refused to recognise the Communist regime in the Soviet Union. Yet in 1941 all that changed, with the invasion of Russia by Hitler's Germany.

Suddenly, being an enemy of America's enemy, Communist Russia had automatically become America's friend and the recipient of America's largesse. However, the friendship lasted only long enough for the Soviets to defeat Hitler before they became the enemy once again. It was like a merry-go-round in foreign affairs, or a diplomatic revolution.

To understand America's basic hatred of Communism, one must examine the fundamental distortion that was built into the American 'foundation myth'. There was nothing democratic about the American War of Independence. This war was not like both the French and Russian revolutions, a struggle between the 'haves' and the 'have nots'. The American Revolution was, instead, a civil war between the 'haves' and the 'haves'. Victory went, eventually, not to the American people but to a wealthy oligarchy who would in future decide how the new country should be ruled, without the assistance of the property-less masses.

The Americans were not revolutionaries. Their main concern over the next two centuries was to strengthen and preserve the status quo so that wealth begot wealth and poverty, poverty, and the only way up was by the skin of your knuckles and somebody else's teeth. Inherited wealth gushed down from one oligarch to another and trickled through cracks in the pipe to poorer Americans who called their good fortune the 'American Dream'. Certainly there were opportunities for 'rags to riches' transformations for some people, but those who climbed successfully were very careful to kick down the ladder so that nobody else could follow them.

## PICKING THE BONES

By the start of the twentieth century, the American nation had no time at all for revolutionary climbers from the masses, particularly any who harboured ideas of 'fair shares for all'. For them, socialism and freedom ran in different directions and their lack of understanding of the history of other countries meant that they feared what they did not understand. News in 1917 that the Bolsheviks in Russia wanted to establish a socialist state seemed like a threat to capitalism throughout the world and for that Americans were told they must be prepared to fight.

For Russians it had seemed inexplicable that a state that they believed had risen by overthrowing a tyrant in George III should, rather than help them, actually join the side of the Whites, who represented the most conservative and reactionary elements in Russia: the army, Church and aristocratic landowners. Even as late as 1959, Premier Nikita Khrushchev spoke with bitterness of his memories of the American troops who came to Russia hoping to stop the revolution.[3]

Counterfactual history has become very popular in the United States and 'What if?' has been a question that has exercised the minds of armchair historians a lot lately. In *Killing Hope*, William Blum raises an intriguing question for all survivors of the Cold War. How might the Soviet Union have developed had it not faced American hostility and threats from its very inception?[4]

There is no easy answer but it is one of the most important questions of the last 50 years, both for Communists and for the so-called Free World. Without a Cold War, the Soviet Union would have been able to use its limited funds for the development of its economy and the living standards of its people, rather than the futile arms race with the United States. As Blum writes:

> From the Red Scare of the 1920s to the McCarthyism of the 1950s to the Reagan crusade against the Evil Empire of the 1980s, the American people have been subjected to a relentless anti-communist indoctrination. It is imbibed with their mother's milk, pictured in their comic books, spelled out in their schoolbooks; their daily papers offer them headlines that tell them all they need to know; ministers find sermons in it; politicians are elected with it, and *Reader's Digest* becomes rich on it.[5]

Blum argues that by 1945, every middle-aged American had already been subjected to a quarter of a century of anti-Communist propaganda and the sheer intensity of this cannot fail to have had a serious effect on the capacity of a voter to reach a balanced opinion on the subject. For Americans, the world had become one simply divided between Communists and anti-Communists. Their reaction was a knee-jerk one. At the mere mention of Communism, American minds conjured up thoughts of Siberian labour camps and salt mines, grim faces and endlessly replicated blocks of flats in an industrial wasteland. Communism meant hell through monotony and dreary poverty. It must not be allowed to spread.

**MEDiaUSA**

## The Cold War
Robert Ivie has studied the rhetorical content of Truman's famous speech on 12 March 1947, which established the Truman Doctrine and unleashed the themes that were to distort perceptions of post-war

Russia.[6] The master metaphor was to cast Communist Russia in terms of disease. This theme was embedded in Truman's speech and emerged at strategic moments to warn of an epidemic that would sweep through the world. Communism was an infestation of the body of nations, a 'malignant parasite', and only the United States, the immune system of the world, could combat it. Without the United States the world would die of Communism.

The basic idea behind Truman's speech was to create a generalised fear in the listener, based on images of danger (red). America must stand tall in a 'feverish world', facing the 'virus of communism' where the 'red fire is burning with a high and livid tongue'. Democracy everywhere was vulnerable to the disease of Communist (red) chaos.

America's national newspapers took up the theme immediately, with the *Washington Daily News* referring to a 'Red tidal wave' and the *New York Times* to a 'Russo-Communist tide'. The same paper stressed that President Truman had called on the nation to take up the 'heroic role of world saviour' and that the world was 'looking to us with hope in their hearts and a prayer upon their lips . . . The United States with a glorious tradition, faces the judgement of history. The United States, the nursery of liberty.' Senator Myers added, 'To resurrect a whole world will take heroism – real heroism' by the 'one potent democratic nation in the world'.[7]

Truman never understood the forces he was letting loose. Whatever he may have believed himself, his words were metaphors followed by bombs. With the dangers of Hitler's own oratorical effect on the German people so fresh in everyone's minds in 1947, it was an irresponsible use of the spoken and written word by the greatest of the capitalist powers. It was brainwashing on an unimaginable scale. The only parallels were with Mussolini's Italy and Hitler's Germany. Capitalism was stealing history from the people and reinventing it. As Louis Halle observed, the Truman Doctrine made everything worse by exaggerating the Communist threat and elevating the differences between the United States and Russia into an ideological conflict that was mythical in origin.[8]

Truman's speech was not without its critics. Senator Pepper showed prescience when, although referring to the 'honest but misguided zeal' of Truman's words, he added that he feared they would:

> . . . sabotage the United Nations, destroy any hope of reconciliation with Russia, launch the United States upon an

unprecedented policy of intervention in remote nations and areas of the world unilaterally, allying us with the corrupt and reactionary regimes of the world.

In fact, the Truman Doctrine paved the way for direct military confrontation with Communist forces in the Korean War, which was aimed at turning back a 'tide of atheistic Communism' that existed only in the minds of American people because their rulers had implanted it there. As Ivie shows, the Truman Doctrine 'compounded the exaggeration of 1945–8 into a guiding metaphor and then into the literal truth'.[9]

Far from emerging from the Second World War as the confident leader of the Free World with visions of a better future, America was weighed down by the fear of losing everything she had gained. The USA felt immensely insecure. It was as if the 'Peter Principle' existed for nations. America had been promoted beyond her capacity, to the level of her own incompetence. With the death of Roosevelt and the reduction of Winston Churchill and the British Empire from parity with the USA, Harry Truman's America emerged on the world stage as undisputed leader. And then got stage fright. The Soviet Union was no real threat to American supremacy in 1947. As the only atomic power, with a vast and vibrant economy, America had a military–industrial sector that was capable of out-producing the rest of the world put together. Only a state of national neurosis can explain America's deliberate elevation of the Soviet Union to a position of equality and enmity. Stalin might have looked the part, with his bushy moustache, but only when compared to the ageing Churchill and the dying Roosevelt. The truth was that behind the triumphant scenes of victory over Germany, the Soviet Union had suffered more than any country in the war. Living conditions inside Russia were at a Third World level and the Soviet economy was geared to nothing but her wartime needs.

As John Charmley has recently shown in *Churchill's Grand Alliance*, the strategic situation in 1945 was misinterpreted by the Americans. Britain, though much diminished, was in no way a weaker member of the 'Big Three' at Yalta than the Soviet Union. Yet, with the removal of defining enemies like Germany and Japan, the Americans needed a new focus for their foreign policy. Truman and the new Labour leader in Britain, Clement Attlee, did not achieve the sort of intense love–hate relationship that Roosevelt and Churchill had endured. Instead, Britain readily accepted her new reduced status in relation to America and the

Americans in turn looked to Communist Russia as the major threat to the future. Russians were no longer the people of heroic allies and fellow warriors in the great struggle against Nazism but once again the Bolsheviks and socialist criminals of 1917 who threatened world capitalism and spoke for the 'have nots'.

America needed a new enemy and Stalin's Russia was made for the job. The problem was that this decision was based merely on rhetorical vision rather than historical reality.

Abraham Lincoln was once criticised for claiming that the people of the Confederacy were human beings. He was told that he should be doing everything he could to destroy them. Lincoln replied, 'Do I not destroy my enemies when I make them my friends?'

Unfortunately, after 1947 nobody in the United States ever tried to make friends with the Soviet Union or even understand them. Lacking a Lincoln, the American people were badly let down by their own political leaders. With narrow-minded bigots like Senator Joe McCarthy in the ascendant, they allowed a dualistic, bipolar world of 'Good and Evil' and 'Free and Communist' to develop with the result that the theoretical alarmist visions and 'rhetoric of yesterday' became the 'reality of today'.

How real was the danger that the Soviet Union would overrun western Europe during the 1950s or 1960s, bearing in mind that both Britain and France had nuclear weapons and the USA had numerous bases in the region with an immense nuclear arsenal? William Blum answers this question from the position of common sense. What on earth had the Soviets to gain from mutually assured destruction (MAD)? Even at the time of the 1962 Cuban Missile Crisis, Khrushchev knew that to try to militarise Cuba was to risk a reaction from the United States that the Soviet Union could not possibly survive. In view of the suffering of the Soviet Union between 1917 and 1945, and the painstaking process of rebuilding the country in the interim years up to 1962, a Cuban 'adventure' could only risk unimaginable destruction. There was brinkmanship, damned brinkmanship and plain madness.

One of the myths that American politicians called on regularly during the Cold War was that Communism was always ready to spread into new regions and was only prevented from doing so by American vigilance. This theory justified big defence budgets and US interference in the affairs of Third World countries in order to save them for democracy. Blum's study of American military interventions throughout the world between 1945 and 1991 suggests that what really motivated the Americans was not the threat of the spread of Communism, which was never as serious as portrayed by the American media, but the threat of self-determination on the part of Third World nations. Whether Woodrow Wilson turned over in his grave at that moment is uncertain, as a stake through the heart tends to limit lateral movement in the grave, even for ex-presidents. Blum believes that what really brought the CIA running was evidence that a Third World state wished to do one of three things: a) free themselves from economic and political subservience to the United States; b) fail to reduce relations with a socialist bloc country when ordered to by the United States; or c) try to replace a government – even democratically – which was already subservient to the United States.[10]

Rather than allow a Third World country to achieve independence from them, America was prepared to ally with the worst tyrannies in the world and support dictators who made George III look like the constitutional monarch he actually was. This awful policy was responsible for the most 'un-American' activities, including genocide and many kinds of human-rights abuses. And it was a policy that was to come ingloriously of age during the Reagan era.

# CHAPTER 7

## *Barefaced Doctorin'*

The Reagan Doctrine of the 1980s was really just a dilution of the original Truman Doctrine – just less of the same. It was more a case of anti-Communist chest-beating than a really coherent foreign policy. It was full of slogans like 'tough-talk, soft-walk', but once again it only faintly resembled the philosophy of an earlier age, when Theodore Roosevelt had spoken of 'talking softly and carrying a big stick'. Ronald Reagan, the actor, believed instead in 'bellowing and yellow-bellying'. The story of his presidency was one of opportunist strikes against feeble opponents who could offer a negligible threat of piling up politically embarrassing flag-draped coffins.

Through his speechwriters, President Reagan used rhetoric to score a series of sweeping and bloodless victories over the Communists, who were portrayed to the American people as:

- Natural menaces who represented 'darkness', 'shadows', 'tyrants', 'grim, grey repressionists'
- Animals who were 'untamed' and who 'preyed on their neighbours'
- Primitives who 'barbarously assault the human spirit'
- Automatons like 'instruments of destruction' and 'machines of war'
- Criminals who resorted to 'cruel extremes' and who, having erected a 'murderous barrier', were prepared 'to commit any crime'

- Mentally disturbed – a 'world power of such deep fears, hostilities and external ambitions'
- Fanatics and ideologues, 'immune to practical reason'
- Satanic and profane, 'totalitarian' and 'evil'[1]

It was like a Hollywood B-movie scripted by Ed Wood in which a mad politician tries to control the people of America with a magic thesaurus. Reagan was in his element and the American people simply swallowed every word he said. It was a triumph for America and her 'acting President'.

## Friends of America in the 1980s

The nation that had been founded 'under God' foundered under Ronald Reagan. The most powerful nation in history was for a decade governed by a team of dangerous, unprincipled men for whom the *end* meant everything, the *means* nothing. To win the game (the Cold War) they were prepared to do almost anything, except to wonder why Communism might appeal to Third World masses living in poverty, squalor and hopelessness. Principles became the playthings of intellectual pygmies whose appreciation of world problems seemed to come from 1950s comics.

During his presidency, Reagan, cast as King Canute, decided to turn back the tide of 'Soviet expansionism'. As a result, the 'shining city' on the hill found itself twinned with some unexpected places. Why did American voters not notice that in their struggle against the 'Evil Empire' of Soviet Communism they had chosen as their allies some of the worst human-rights abusers of the twentieth century?

Under Reagan, the United States sold its national soul to a series of 'devils', like the great anti-Communists – Somoza (Nicaragua), Botha (South Africa), Marcos (Philippines), Pinochet (Chile), Mobutu (Congo), none of whom were democrats – in a way no other great power in history has ever done. It was as if men like Thomas Jefferson, George Washington and Benjamin Franklin had never lived. When Reagan described Nicaraguan anti-Communists as resembling America's Founding Fathers, one critic observed wryly that they were more like the Hessian mercenaries who served with the British troops in the revolutionary war.

How, precisely, was Communism a greater threat to the world than the genocide which was the particular skill of Ronald Reagan's new friends: Saddam Hussein and the Ba'ath Party in Iraq; Pol Pot and the Khmer Rouge in Cambodia; Jonas Savimbi and UNITA in Angola; Osama bin Laden and the Taliban in Afghanistan.

Washington continued to fund and arm counter-revolutionary bandits and terrorists throughout the world and support the apartheid regime in South Africa, as well as dictators in Pakistan, Indonesia and Chile.

Perhaps the most bizarre development was the US government's secret partnership with the Khmer Rouge. While in power, Pol Pot's regime in Cambodia had amassed a record of brutality comparable only with that of the Third Reich or Stalinist Russia. In less than four years, the Khmer Rouge had systematically exterminated one-fifth to one-third of Cambodia's population. When Vietnam intervened in Cambodia and drove the Khmer Rouge from power in 1979, America became alarmed by the shift in the balance of power in the region and quickly developed an anti-Vietnamese, anti-Soviet alliance involving China. Washington found herself supporting the Khmer Rouge as a guerrilla movement and international relief agencies were persuaded to provide humanitarian assistance to the Khmer Rouge guerrillas who fled into Thailand. For more than a decade, the Khmer Rouge used their refugee camps as military bases to wage war against the Marxist government in Cambodia.

'Freedom' may have been the watchword of the Reagan revolution and the President certainly used the word more often than any president before him, but what on earth did he mean by it? While right-wing intellectuals worked behind the scenes designing the future of the world in the American image, the 'acting President' delivered the lines they prepared for him to his American people – blissfully unaware that he was gradually reducing the English language to a form of mind control rather than communication.

It did not seem to matter what Ronald Reagan said, as nobody was prepared to question the strongly patriotic and militaristic approach that he was adopting. It was a thoroughly shameful period for the American people but it was all conducted with a smile and somehow that seemed to be enough. America was content to support those who were waging war against left-wing groups or governments and the motto became 'Support for freedom fighters is self-defense'.[2]

The Iranian Revolution of 1979 had overthrown one of the cornerstones of American strategy in the world, the Shah of Persia. His replacement by the fundamentalist rule of the ayatollahs suddenly threatened America's domination of the strategic oil-rich region. Washington immediately began to seek ways to reverse the outcome of the Iranian Revolution, or replace the lost Shah with someone equally ruthless and amenable to American policy. Saddam Hussein's regime in Iraq seemed heaven-sent. On 22 September 1980, Iraq launched an invasion of Iran. In the bloody eight-year-long war that followed, at least one million lives were lost and Washington found that the Frankenstein's monster it had created in Saddam Hussein grew into as serious a threat to American interests as Iran had ever been.

American diplomats must have known what they were getting when they bought Saddam Hussein as an ally. He was essentially a gangster, the sort who might have flourished in Chicago during Prohibition: totally ruthless and unprincipled. He ruled by fear and had no interest whatsoever in American talk of democracy, freedom and human rights. He was Al Capone on an international stage and would turn on his master if he suspected weakness in the hand that fed him.

Accusing Saddam Hussein of war crimes is utterly absurd as he operated outside international law and was allowed to do so for nearly 30 years. To a man from his background there were no rules in the struggle for survival. Brute force triumphed over principles every time. He was a piranha, yet he knew that he was swimming in a tank of sharks. Only the greatest powers could afford the luxury of rules in warfare. In any case, their rules were not genuine. The imperial powers had not portioned up the world by following rules. Iraq had always been the property of whichever nation triumphed in the fight to own it. The British in 1918 had wrenched Mesopotamia from the Ottoman Turks by using Arab dreams of independence and nationhood to win them the oil wealth of the region. The British exploited the Arabs' help in defeating Turkey, then abandoned them, offering instead a national home in Palestine to the Jews, in the hope of winning American support in the war.

During Iraq's 1980–8 war with Iran, not only did Washington turn a blind eye to Saddam's repeated use of chemical weapons against Iranian soldiers and Iraq's Kurdish minority, but the USA even helped Iraq develop its chemical and biological weapons programmes. Saddam was also always able to point to the fact that each of the Great Powers – Germany, France and Britain – had used poison gas during the First World War and that they would have done so in the Second World War had they not appreciated that strategic advantage through chemical warfare was impossible while most states possessed the air power to retaliate.

Saddam felt no compunction about using poison gas, both as a battlefield weapon against the Iranians and as a counter-insurgency weapon against the Iraqi Kurds whom, although they were geographically situated within his borders, he did not – contrary to most Western reports – regard as his own people. The Kurds had sided with Iran in the war and Saddam was at least consistent in regarding them as his enemies.

The use of these internationally outlawed weapons during Saddam's war against Iran was never important enough for Donald Rumsfeld and his political superiors to consider withdrawing US support for Iraq. The USA ensured that Iraq was kept well supplied throughout the 1980s with the armaments she needed to conduct the war against Iran, and in 1994 a Senate report on the Iraq–Iran War revealed that US companies had been licensed to export biological and chemical materials, including *Bacillus anthracis* (which causes anthrax) and *Clostridium botulinum* (the source of botulism) to Iraq.[3] Corporations in other Western countries like Austria, West Germany, France, Great Britain and Switzerland also supplied Saddam with raw materials, machinery, missile technology and other 'dual-use' items with the approval of their governments.

The public outrage which followed news of the Halabja massacre on 16 March 1988 should have brought down the shutters once and for all on Washington's love affair with the regime in Iraq. Astonishingly, it did not. The Reagan administration reached its nadir when, on 8 September 1988, the Senate passed the Prevention of Genocide Act, which would have imposed sanctions on the Hussein regime. The White House responded by calling the bill 'premature' and trying to stall it in the House of Representatives. Even when Congress eventually passed the bill, the White House did not implement it on the grounds that 'Normal relations between the US and Iraq would serve our long-term interests and promote stability in both the Gulf and the Middle East.'

And then Saddam Hussein bit the hand that fed him by invading Kuwait.

Just as Franklin D. Roosevelt had allied America with one fascist dictator (Stalin) to fight another (Hitler), so Ronald Reagan, blinded by his anti-Communism, opened the Pandora's box of Islamic fundamentalism by financing and training Mujahidin to fight against Soviet troops in Afghanistan. These US-trained and equipped fighters would later form the heart of the Taliban. Worse than that, one of these,

Osama bin Laden, 'born-again' Muslim and founder of al-Qaeda, was an even more terrifying monster than Saddam Hussein had been. Where Saddam might have doubled for the 'Thief of Baghdad', Osama bin Laden seems closer to the Mahdi, whom General Gordon found such a handful in the Sudan in 1885. Even a younger Charlton Heston, with all the power of an imperial NRA, could not contain him.

The unleashing of Islamic fundamentalism against the Soviets was short-termism of the most disastrous kind and constitutes one of the greatest political blunders in American history. The consequences of this miscalculation may be with America, and indeed the world, for many years to come.

Historically, Americans have had little experience of the Arab world. Their diplomats have often revealed a clumsiness and lack of empathy with Islam and an impatience in dealing with an ancient culture every bit as valid as the Christian culture to which Americans believe they belong and, more than that, lead. Without a complete revolution in the education of the Muslim masses, there is no likelihood that Arab states will accept the kind of democratic governments that are favoured by the United States. Britain (for all her reputed 'perfidy' in the realm of diplomacy) and France have enjoyed far better relations with Arab leaders than the Americans ever have.

In the mid-1980s, the Reagan doctrine of arming anti-Soviet insurgents around the world also benefited UNITA in Angola. Its leader Jonas Savimbi appeared to be a success story for the Americans. But did they really know what Jonas Savimbi stood for? Will the real Jonas Savimbi please step forward?

'Were you, Jonas Malheiro Savimbi, licensed in legal and political sciences at the University of Lausanne, hailed by President Reagan as Africa's Abraham Lincoln and in the 1980s described by America's UN representative Jeane J. Kirkpatrick as "one of the few authentic heroes of our time"?[4] Were you the "pro-Western" leader and dedicated "freedom fighter" against the Marxist regime in Luanda as conservatives claim?

'Conversely, were you the "megalomaniac opportunist", opponent of democracy and friend of South Africa's racist government as liberal opponents claim?'

During the Reagan years in America, Jonas Savimbi and his UNITA forces received a covert aid package to finance their battle against the

Cuban-backed Marxist government of Angola. Through Reagan's support of Savimbi, Angola became a battleground between anti-colonialism and anti-apartheid on the one hand and freedom represented by the odd combination of the United States and apartheid South Africa on the other.

With the support of South African troops, Savimbi and UNITA waged a campaign of brutality involving indiscriminate attacks on schools, health centres and food and water supplies. The country was comprehensively ruined. Accusations of witchcraft were prevalent as were public burnings. In one case, Savimbi accused a woman of spying on him by flying over his house at night. It is also reported that Savimbi personally beat to death with a rifle butt a US representative of UNITA, his wife and his children. During the 1980s, about 300,000 people are thought to have died in Angola as a direct result of the war. Landmines were so widespread that, at one point, Angola had the highest amputee rate in the world. The figures for war-related deaths, and child deaths in particular, leapt dramatically during the Reagan years.

Yet through these dictators and so many others America won the Cold War, or so it has been claimed. *Floreat* Reagan!

The Cold War had been an American invention in the first place. As they made the rules and owned the board, they could call an end to the game whenever it was time to go home or go to bed. In fact, the game ended when the Evil Enemy ran out of money and could not pay the rent demanded for landing on Madison Avenue. The Soviet Union collapsed, fragmented by nationalism and Muslim fundamentalism. The huge Soviet arsenal of nuclear weapons is no longer under central control and offers a honey pot to potential terrorists. The Soviet fleet quietly rots on the Baltic shores, polluting the area, while Soviet scientists offer their services to the highest paymasters, often based in the Arab world. Democracy flickers on and off like the light bulbs in the neglected tenements, while the rich criminals live lives of excess and the ordinary people have lost the security and the welfare services which Communism had offered. Dictatorship, backed by the army, seems a more likely future than democracy. It is the Russian Way. The Communist experiment of the twentieth century has failed. Who will be the next tsar?

# CHAPTER 8

## *Stillbirth of a Nation*

This is part of President Ronald Reagan's final presidential address to the American people:

> I have spoken of the shining city all my political life, but I don't know if I ever quite communicated what I saw when I said it. But in my mind it was a tall, proud city built on rocks stronger than oceans, windswept, God-blessed and teeming with people of all kinds living in harmony and peace; a city with free ports that hummed with commerce and creativity. And if there had to be city walls, the walls had doors and the doors were open to anyone with the will and the heart to get there. That's how I saw it and see it still.
>
> And how stands the city on this winter night? More prosperous, more secure and happier than it was eight years ago. But more than that: after 200 years she still stands strong and true on the granite ridge, after two centuries her glow has held steady no matter what storm. And she's still a beacon, still a magnet for all who must have freedom, for all the pilgrims from all the lost places who are hurtling through the darkness towards home.[1]

By planning that the 'shining city' should be protected by a missile defence system, Reagan had allowed Americans to sleep more comfortably in their beds, secure in the knowledge that their President could talk or spend the Soviet Union into collapse. Yet all the while he was controlling the American people by fear. Every housing estate looked for its own 'Star Wars' defence system and although according to the Puritan divine John Winthrop the walls of the shining city had many doors, Reagan's were all heavily guarded. Reagan had conquered Kissinger's 'Vietnam Syndrome' by creating a new America – The Republic of Fear.

**The American Dream**

## The 'Acting President'

By the late 1970s, the accepted view in America was that the Vietnam War had been lost at home rather than in South-east Asia. The battle for 'hearts and minds' was where the Americans had taken most casualties. During the Tet Offensive of 1968 it had been suddenly revealed on prime-time television that the war was not going as well as people had been led to believe. Politicians and generals had been economical with the truth. Far from the peace and security assumed to have been brought to the Vietnamese capital, Saigon, by the American presence, television viewers now saw every sign of war. In full colour, there were scenes of terrible devastation and chaos, smoke-filled skies, bodies of dead and wounded littering the streets and the constant sounds of firing and explosions.

At a press conference, the US commander, General Westmoreland, seemed almost relaxed, though as the *Washington Post* wrote: 'The reporters could hardly believe their ears. Westmoreland was standing in the ruins and saying everything was great.'[2] Of course, history has no access to 'body language', the way that the shoulders tell us more honestly about events than tongues ever can. How did Napoleon look after the Old Guard had finally been turned back at Waterloo, or Haig as night fell on the Somme on 1 July 1916? No one believed Westmoreland any more and his words were clear proof that he had lost the plot. He spoke of enemy 'deceitfulness' in breaking the New Year Truce and that their 'aim had been to create maximum consternation', as if this was a novel departure for an enemy in wartime. Yet, however reassuring his words were meant to be, the visual evidence gave the lie to everything he said. Behind him was chaos and carnage on a grand scale. This was no isolated raid but just a small part of a country-wide offensive by thousands of well-trained and well-led Communist troops. America's claim that the war was under control had been shown to be hollow.

The Tet Offensive had caught the Americans at a period of political irresolution and confronted them with a stark choice – either escalate the conflict in search of victory or look instead for a diplomatic settlement. President Johnson was shocked out of his complacency. He ordered Westmoreland to limit the damage, instructing the press that he had the situation under control. But nobody believed him either. The press put it bluntly: Americans should brace themselves for news that the war was lost.

Vietnamese commander General Giap was clear as to why the Americans had lost in Vietnam. They had become a superpower because of their money and their weapons, not through the justice of their cause. They were trampling down the right of peoples and nations to be independent and have freedom. Giap was right. For all her military technology, the United States was fighting 'the wrong war at the wrong time'. Its anti-Communist perspective had forced the United States to take the side of France, a colonial power trying to suppress an independence movement.

Washington, Jefferson and Lafayette might have shifted in their graves while King George III would have revelled in the irony. Yorktown was avenged. Perhaps the final words should be left to Giap. 'One thing that they cannot understand is the strength of the whole nation, united against the foreign aggressors. We were prepared to sacrifice everything not to become slaves.' It could have been Patrick Henry speaking. Giap had driven a stake into the heart of the American myth.

In 1965, 61 per cent of the American population had been in favour of US involvement in Vietnam. By May 1971, however, the figures were exactly reversed, with 61 per cent of the population opposed to US involvement. To understand this transformation one has only to consider the damage that the war was inflicting on traditional US values. One example should suffice. In 1967, an army doctor at Fort Jackson, South Carolina, refused to teach Special Forces personnel known as Green Berets, accusing them of being 'murderers of women and children'. He was court-martialled for promoting disaffection and imprisoned. At his trial, the judge made the following statement, summing up the dangerous slope down which America was sliding: 'The truth of the statements is not an issue in this case.'[3]

Desertions from the armed forces rocketed, with between 50,000 and 100,000 draftees fleeing to Canada or western Europe. In 1973, the US Pacific Fleet 'purged itself' of 6,000 'undesirables', by which they meant active opponents of the war in Vietnam. In the same year, 20 per cent of all army discharges were 'dishonourable', while 17.7 per cent of all US soldiers were absent without leave for perhaps the third or fourth time. The army was in a state of self-destruction.

In the last days of Jimmy Carter's presidency, the USA witnessed a military debacle every bit as humiliating as the Tet Offensive had been for Johnson and Westmoreland. The Iranian Revolution and the subsequent hostage crisis culminated in the heroic but ill-fated Operation Eagle Claw to rescue American hostages held in Teheran in 1979. Americans from coast to coast viewed on television the grisly sight of Ayatollah Khalkali holding up the charred bones of the eight dead American airmen killed at Desert Base One.

America needed a shot of self-belief. Empty patriotism and hollow tub-thumping had usually worked in the past. After all, who was prepared to question the flag, the oath of allegiance or the symbols of American greatness like the Statue of Liberty? There were demands for 'less individual thought and more collective obedience'. America was beginning the march towards totalitarianism on the back of a defeat in war, like Hitler's Germany, and a fear of the Left, like Mussolini's Italy.

The only thing that could save the nation was a return to the 'feel-good' factor of an earlier age, a simpler time of ice-cream parlours, B-movies at the cinema and white picket-fences, perhaps with Santa Claus as President.

Enter Ronald Reagan in a red coat, with a large white beard on his chin and a sack on his back. Reagan brought a greater sense of confidence to ordinary Americans by projecting an unruffled 1950s-style optimism. It was almost impossible to underestimate Ronald Reagan and that was the problem. This was the President who once addressed Samuel Doe, leader of Liberia, as Chairman Moe and who, on visiting a military cemetery in Bitburg, Germany, where 49 Nazi SS troops were buried, said of the Nazis, 'They were victims just as surely as the victims in the concentration camps.'[4] While British satire *Spitting Image* joked along the lines that 'the President's brain is missing', Reagan continued to smile with the assurance that while voters in the United States had also mislaid their brains he was perfectly safe.

Sometimes Reagan seemed like a joke played upon the American people. Yet it was dangerous to be taken in by his bonhomie. Much truth was spoken in his jests. Once, while preparing to make a broadcast he unwittingly made the following alarming announcement into a microphone he believed was switched off, 'My fellow Americans, I am pleased to tell you I just signed legislation which outlaws Russia forever. The bombing begins in five minutes.' The laughter must have died in the throats of those who heard it. This was, after all, the man whose finger was on the button.

Reagan 'made arguments about history based on movies he half-recalled'.[5] He thought he had liberated a concentration camp. In 1983, Reagan told visiting Israeli Prime Minister Yitzhak Shamir that he had served as a photographer in a US army unit assigned to film Nazi death camps. He repeated the story to Simon Wiesenthal the following February.[6]

In fact, Reagan never went anywhere near a concentration camp, but spent the Second World War in Hollywood, making training films with the First Motion Picture Unit of the army's Air Corps.

Yet Reagan proved to be a master of symbolic leadership and of massaging the media, using emblems of nationhood like the flag and patriotic rhetoric about 'America's divinely appointed mission as beacon of liberty and freedom'. Was this the rhetoric of a Cold Warrior or of a Puritan bigot named John Winthrop? Or perhaps neither, just an 'acting President' playing Santa Claus? And what if the reindeer were helicopter gunships named 'Donner' and 'Blitzen' and even – perhaps – 'Rudolf'? What he said was hokum but comfortable hokum, the sort a father tells his child so that it will fall asleep in confidence.

## The Almighty Dolour

Reagan had brought with him to the White House a group of patriotic neo-conservatives, eager to rewrite US history according to a new agenda. Among them was Norman Podhoretz, who wrote the influential revaluation of the war in Vietnam, *Why We Were in Vietnam*, claiming that American failure was honourable because the worst that could be said of it was that America had shown 'imprudent idealism'. Now it was time for change. America must overcome the 'Vietnam Syndrome', that phrase that implied a 'sickly inhibition against the use of military force'.[7]

Between 1980 and 1985, American defence spending was increased by 34 per cent and the Pentagon was gorged with funds. State-of-the-art military equipment was designed for the army and air force, while John Lehman planned a 600-ship, trillion-dollar navy for the President's bath, the biggest in American history. Reagan's revival of America's armed forces did not come cheap but it was vital if his America was to match up to the Evil Empire. Lehman was planning to 'kick Soviet ass'. Since Vietnam, the defence industry had been going through a slump. With Reagan in the White House, firms like Boeing, General Dynamics, Lockheed, McDonnell Douglas, Rockwell and United Technologies all revived as dollars were thrown at them in a 'fish-feeding frenzy'.[8]

With money for military research and development doubling in five years within university departments, Reagan's main aim was to develop a Star Wars system of defence against strategic nuclear weapons. Weapons contractors were in heaven. As the *Wall Street Journal* wrote, 'For defense contractors across America, President Reagan's Star Wars Program is more than a new strategy for defense. It is a business opportunity of a generation, a chance to cash in on billions in federal contracts.'[9] Paul Warnke cynically described Star Wars in these terms: 'What we see happening today is the rapid conversion of the President's Star Wars proposal from stardust and moonbeams to that great pork barrel in the sky.'[10] Another cynical comment on defence manufacturers conveyed the way in which military spending was ruling American industry: 'Whether or not it would contribute to the security of the nation, [Star Wars] offers them security.'[11]

## Hollywood Strikes Back

History had always been the putty of Hollywood film-makers, mere clay for the moulding. Generally, film directors had no greater motive than to make a better film, suit a favoured actor or salve an individual conscience by altering the facts of history. However, the onset of the Cold War had changed that carefree attitude. What Harry Truman had done with the spoken word in the Truman Doctrine of 1947, Hollywood could do with the visual arts.

By the mid-1970s, the shadow of the devastation of the Vietnam War lay heavy across all sectors of society. It was the task of Hollywood to make people happy again. And if they were miserable because they lost a war, then Hollywood would weave a little of its magic and – hey presto! – everything would change. After all, just look how Errol Flynn and John Wayne had won the Second World War between them. Who was to say that, second time round in Vietnam, America couldn't win this time? All that was needed was a little tinkering with the collective memory and then, when everyone was a bit uncertain as to what really happened – bam! – Hollywood would tell it as it was. Mythmaking Pictures Inc. was in business.

In 1978 the film *The Deer Hunter* started the revision of the Vietnam War for the American people. The propaganda chiefs of Soviet Russia, Nazi Germany and First World War Britain would have envied the expertise and the budget of Mythmaking Pictures. As Bruce Franklin relates:

> The basic technique was to take images of the war that had become deeply embedded in America's consciousness and transform them into their opposite. For example, in the first scene in Vietnam, a uniformed soldier throws a grenade into an underground village shelter harboring women and children, and then with his automatic rifle mows down a woman and her baby. Although the scene resembles *Life*'s pictures of the My Lai massacre, he is not an American soldier but a North Vietnamese. He is then killed by a lone guerrilla, who is not a Viet Cong but our Special Forces hero, Robert De Niro.
>
> When two men plummet from a helicopter, the images replicate a familiar telephotographic sequence showing a Viet Cong prisoner being pushed from a helicopter to make other prisoners talk; but the falling men in the movie are American POWs attempting to escape from their murderous Viet Cong

captors. The central structuring metaphor of the film is the Russian roulette the sadistic Asian Communists force their prisoners to play. POW after POW is shown with a revolver at his right temple, framed to match with precision the sequence seen by tens of millions of Americans in which the chief of the Saigon secret police placed a revolver to the right temple of an NLF [National Liberation Front] prisoner and killed him with a single shot; even the blood spurting out of the temple is exactly replicated.[12]

The brainwashing of the American people had begun.

With the coming to power of Ronald Reagan in 1980, the pace of Hollywood's revisionism increased. Fascist, racist and militaristic films were all the rage in Reagan's first term, led by *Uncommon Valour* in 1983, starring Gene Hackman. Rob Edelman's review in *Cineaste* magazine said it all:

> The Vietnam war is not really over . . . and we – America – can still pass for a touchdown at Ho Chi Minh Stadium and eke out a last-second victory in the Rice Paddy Bowl. Just send a few good boys back there, kick some Asian ass, liberate a few MIAs. The Laotians – or Cambodians or Vietnamese, for they are really all alike – will fall like Indians in a John Wayne movie and America will be proud and regain its honor.[13]

The advent of John Rambo, the almost superhumanly deadly warrior who was reputedly part Indian, part German and, in American minds, combined the fighting qualities of both peoples, was exactly what America had needed in Vietnam. Ronald Reagan was not slow in identifying himself with this character; shortly after the opening of *Rambo: First Blood Part 2*, he declared, 'Boy, I saw *Rambo* last night. Now I know what to do the next time.'[14] Members of the House of Representatives signalled a 'toughening stance' on foreign relations by invoking the name and image of Rambo a dozen times in Congressional debates.

As the *Rambo* trilogy packed cinemas, audiences cheered wildly as Rambo slew more and more Vietnamese and Russian Commies. Commercial spin-offs flooded America with Rambo action-figures, walkie-talkies, watches, water guns and even Rambograms, while one TV cartoon series based on the character of Rambo transformed him into 'Liberty's champion'. Rambo was next given the title, 'The Chosen

One', with its religious connotations, while it was claimed that his task was a 'mission of national importance'.

When Rambo is offered a chance to return to Vietnam on a rescue mission, he replies, famously, 'Do we get to win this time?' In the words of Bruce Franklin:

> Resonating in the question are years of rewritten and re-imaged history that have taught the 1985 audience that we could have won the war if only the politicians, media, liberal establishment, bureaucrats, draft-dodging college students and their pinko professors, hippies, wimps, bleeding-heart housewives and Jane Fonda hadn't tied our boys' hands and stabbed them in the back.[15]

The successful transformation of the Vietnamese into sadistic monsters in films like *The Deer Hunter*, *Uncommon Valour*, *Missing in Action* and the *Rambo* movies provide satisfying explanations as to why the war in Vietnam was lost in spite of the heroism of the American fighting man, embodied in John Rambo.

While Sylvester Stallone as Rambo had been rewriting the history of the Vietnam War, Sigourney Weaver was taking American military values into space in *Alien*, where she encountered and overcame the most potent alien creature in Hollywood history. With state-of-the-art firepower Weaver, or Ripley as she is called in the film, and her 'colonial Marines' were kicking ass on a planet where 'Terraformers', like American settlers of the nineteenth century, were facing danger from the 'Indians' and needed some 'ethnic cleansing'.

By the late 1980s, Hollywood was making films for a more confident America, no longer mired in the depression of its defeat in Vietnam. Now was the time to turn cinematic victories into real ones.


## Thatcher Shows the Way

After the foreign policy humiliations of the Nixon and Carter administrations, Americans longed for a move back towards a more chilly Cold War, where the enemy was identifiable, evil and ready to stand up at high noon for a man-to-man shoot-out. As a result, Republicans like Reagan claimed that a return to greatness would only come when you stood up against the enemy, the Evil Empire. The drawback was that the first round of the Cold War had cost the United States 50,000 lives in Korea and nearly 60,000 in Vietnam. All of these corpses had been voters and plenty of them had voted Republican. The Cold War needed to be cost-effective politically but more than that it needed to be cheap when it came to body bags and flag-draped coffins.

Although not a Cold War struggle, Reagan found that the British operation to regain the Falklands Islands from Argentina in 1982 was the kind of 'splendid little war' that America needed. Like the Spanish–American War of 1898 which had helped Theodore Roosevelt to launch America on its way to world domination, a nice little war would offer America a way back from Vietnam and establish a pattern for numerous American interventions in the next two decades. As a result, to the surprise of many of his Central and South American allies, Ronald Regan chose to support Margaret Thatcher's gunboat diplomacy against the right-wing dictatorship of the Argentinian junta. Reagan and Caspar Weinberger agreed to supply Britain with the latest military equipment, notably the advanced sidewinder missiles. They were even prepared to lend-lease the carrier USS *Guam* if either of the British carriers, *Hermes* and *Invincible*, were sunk or disabled.[16]

The eventual British victory in the war for the Malvinas owed much to American help. The original 20 Harriers that left Britain with the Task Force might have been overwhelmed by the 200-plus aircraft belonging to the Argentinian air force, some of whose planes, like the French Super-Etendards, could fire ship-killing Exocet missiles. However, in dogfights the US sidewinder missiles gave the British aircraft total mastery of the skies and proved the decisive factor in the entire war. The honorary knighthood accorded by Queen Elizabeth II to Caspar Weinberger after the war shows how much Margaret Thatcher realised the value of American help.

Yet Reagan's own foreign policy had started badly. In 1982, a large force of American Marines were deployed in Beirut, not to fight but to help the UN peacekeepers in Lebanon. On 23 October 1983, 241 Marines were killed after a terrorist bomb exploded in a parked vehicle outside the building where they were sleeping. It was the Tet Offensive all over again. It was the Iranian hostages repeated.

Reagan's advisers realised that their man could go down just like Carter unless they could demonstrate to the world that America was nobody's 'Aunt Sally'. First Reagan ordered the remaining Marines in Lebanon to 'redeploy to their ships offshore'. What a phrase! Who would have thought the English language offered such opportunities for insincerity and obscurity? Winston Churchill must have wished he had thought of that one at the time of Dunkirk.

## When the Cubans Tried to Steal Christmas

Ronald Reagan once told a story of a young Marine lieutenant who had taken part in Operation Urgent Fury, an invasion of Grenada in 1983 just two days after the disaster in Beirut. It concerned the fact that Grenada was known as the largest producer of nutmeg in the world. The young officer had noticed that this fact was mentioned in every article about the operation and decided that it was an enemy code and that he was going to break it. Eventually he succeeded and told Reagan his conclusions:

1. Grenada produces more nutmeg than anywhere else in the world.
2. The Soviets and Cubans were trying to take over Grenada.
3. You cannot make good eggnog without nutmeg.
4. You cannot have Christmas without eggnog.
5. The Soviets and Cubans were trying to steal Christmas.
6. America stopped them![17]

This story encapsulates so much about the Americans in Grenada. In military terms the invasion of the 'nutmeg capital of the world' was a close-run thing. It skirted the edge of farce but the wheels just about stayed on the vehicle. It was enough to make the President laugh and put a smile on the face of the whole American nation. Operation Urgent Fury had kicked the Vietnam Syndrome out of the American mentality.

The Americans never understood the irony in much of what was written about this particular military operation, tending to see it as a triumph of American arms. The fact that the rest of the world was laughing behind its hand was apparently lost on Ronald Reagan, who announced that 'Our days of weakness are over. Our forces are back on their feet and standing tall.'[18] One Grenadan soldier, Keith Phillips, put it another way: 'They're just a bunch of bullies.'[19]

In order to ease the army back into the business of winning wars, a simple target had been needed, one where there was no chance of any military setbacks. Grenada seemed to fit the bill. In addition, two birds could be killed with one stone. Washington was uneasy about the development of Grenada as an ally of Cuba and news that an extended runway was being built on the island 'for the tourist trade' fooled nobody. Cuban 'construction workers' were reportedly building the runway and Washington was convinced that these men were simply Cuban regular soldiers in disguise. A successful invasion of Grenada could restore American military prestige, overthrow an illegal regime and clear out a Cuban enclave all in the name of rescuing American medical students.

To Reagan and his advisers it seemed an opportunity to shine light on the shadow of Vietnam but Congress was kept completely in the dark. As one Congressman said, 'You can imagine how silly we felt learning on CNN about an invasion by our country of another country.'[20]

In order to justify the invasion of Grenada, a member of the British Commonwealth, President Reagan made the following claims:

1. Up to 1,000 American medical students who were studying in Grenada were in danger of being held hostage by the new Grenadan People's Republic's army.

2. The British Governor-General, Sir Paul Scoon, had been imprisoned and was in danger. Reagan went further by forging a letter from Sir Paul, calling on the Americans for help. The Americans claimed that Sir Paul had spirited the message out of prison and they were responding to his official request. (Sir Paul did not even have to write the letter himself. The Americans knew what he wanted to say. After they had 'rescued' him and taken him to an aircraft carrier offshore, all he had to do was sign it. President Reagan could then produce the letter signed by Sir Paul and dated before the event.)

3. The island was in the hands of a military force of perhaps 1,000 Cuban troops, pretending to be construction workers building a 10,000-foot runway even though Grenada had no air force. Any fool could see it was for military purposes. President Reagan was that fool. Six members of the Organisation of the East Caribbean States (OECS), as well as Barbados and Jamaica, had asked the USA to intervene in Grenada, fearing aggression from the new ultra-Left regime on the island. Reagan insisted that there was a complete arsenal of weapons and communications equipment, as well as missile silos, that were being built, making it clear a total Cuban occupation was imminent. Reagan declared, 'Grenada was a Soviet–Cuban colony being readied as a major military bastion to export terror and undermine democracy, but we got there just in time.'

4. In February 1983, a defence official in Washington had reported that the Soviet Union had shipped assault

helicopters, hydrofoil-torpedo boats and supersonic Mig fighters to Grenada, which gave the island an air force of 200 modern planes.

The truth was very different:

1. The US Embassy in Barbados reported before the invasion that most of the US students in Grenada did not want to be evacuated as they were too busy with their studies. Grenada, in fact, had offered the USA an opportunity to evacuate their nationals two days before the invasion and some students had already left in one of four charter flights. The Cuban government later issued documents showing that they had already guaranteed the safety of all American citizens.

2. British Foreign Secretary Sir Geoffrey Howe was adamant on 31 October 1983 that Sir Paul Scoon had not sent a request for help to the Americans. Scoon also denied sending the letter when interviewed on British television. Scoon further denied that he had ever been in prison or in danger. When told on television that Scoon had denied being in prison, Caspar Weinberger replied, 'Well, he thought he was.'

3. There were 784 Cubans on the island, of whom 636 were construction workers, employed by the British firm Plessey, who were mainly in their 40s and 50s. The remainder, which included 44 women, were doctors, dentists, nurses, public health workers and teachers. There were just 43 Cuban military personnel. The weapons found were antiquated, including nineteenth-century firearms for the use of the militia. The 10,000-foot runway was for tourist purposes and was no longer than runways in five other Caribbean islands, which also had no air forces. The new airfield was being financed by the World Bank and built by American and British companies using Cuban labour! Plessey later demonstrated that the airport was indeed purely civilian.

4. I doubt that he could have kept a straight face.

Operation Urgent Fury was more an example of cartoon violence than a measured military response to a real threat to America's national interests. The Secretary of State for the Navy set the tone with this surreal citation for the 7,000 gallantry awards that were distributed to the thousands of American servicemen who took part, presumably as mementoes of their Caribbean trip:

> For conspicuous gallantry and intrepid action against a heavily armed rebel force threatening the personal safety of American citizens and the established government of Grenada . . . Through calculated forethought and incisive action by the officers and men of Task Force 124 . . . the lives of hundreds of American civilians were saved, rebel forces were subdued and the government of Grenada restored.[21]

A more realistic account of what happened comes from Congressman Louis Stokes, who visited the island after the fighting had died down:

> We were taken over to the compound where the Cubans were being held as captured military personnel and we observed that all of the personnel there, the men and the women in the compound, were dressed in the same manner that we were dressed, that is they were in casual civilian dress, none of them were in any type of military apparel and so that immediately raised questions in my mind as to what type of military personnel were these persons who were in short-sleeved summer shirts and khaki pants, things of that nature and of course I did later enquire of our authorities who were in charge if this was the manner in which these people had been dressed who were supposedly the opposition and who were fighting them on the runway and they said that these were the Cubans who were offering the resistance to the American personnel as they came in and so I enquired were they dressed in this manner in which they're currently dressed and they said yes, that is the manner in which they were dressed.[22]

It was clearly a victory for battle fatigues over Bermuda shorts.

The operation, which, according to President Reagan, had put the US army 'back on its feet', involved several bizarre events:

- 12 US Navy SEALs parachuted into the sea but were so overloaded they sank straight to the bottom and 4 were drowned.
- A 90-minute parachute drop at Port Salines by 600 rangers

took place in full view of 'enemy troops' who did not massacre them because they had orders from Castro not to fire unless fired upon.

- It took the Americans 33 hours to 'rescue' the medical students because they did not know they were in two different campuses. One was as little as two miles from the US landing point.

- There were 27 Stinger missile anti-aircraft teams landed even though it was known Grenada had no air force.

- American troops were so overloaded – one complained of carrying 120 lb – that most US casualties resulted from heat exhaustion.

- The US had no proper maps of the island and most troops were equipped with Esso maps from garage forecourts.

- Intelligence was so faulty that US soldiers asked the locals which road they should take for Trinidad!

- Many friendly fire incidents took place. The worst error, however, was the bombing of Fort Matthew by mistake. It was a mental asylum known locally as the 'Crazy House' and 21 inmates were killed and hundreds wounded.

When Reagan told Margaret Thatcher that he had invaded Grenada without advising her in advance, she flew into a fury and sent him to bed without any supper. Conservative peer Lord Christopher Soames, however, put the point more starkly in a House of Lords debate a few days after the invasion:

> I hope Her Majesty's government will draw the conclusion from this sorry episode that perhaps the best way for the United Kingdom to bring influence to bear upon the decision-making process of the United States in the middle and latter parts of the 1980s will be off a European base.[23]

Are you listening Tony Blair?

# PICKING THE BONES

## When Did the American People Finally Lose Contact with Reality?

My choice of date would be 3 July 1988 when the cruiser USS *Vincennes*, reputedly the most advanced vessel afloat, wrongly identified an Iranian airbus, Flight 655 from Bandar Abbas to Dubai, as an Iranian F-14 fighter. The airliner carrying 290 passengers across the Persian Gulf was shot down. There were no survivors. It was a direct result of an interaction between technological failure and human error of the kind that was to dominate American military operations for the next 15 years. 'Friendly fire' and 'collateral damage' joined the phrases 'surgical strikes' and 'smart weapons' during a period which saw the abandonment of the English language as a means of communication and its hijacking by the political masters of spin and disinformation. Why was the American public so willing to be misled by a flim-flam artist like Ronald Reagan?

By the 1980s, Americans had moved on from the state of denial over Vietnam to a 'brave new world' where irresponsibility meant 'no responsibility'. Ronald Reagan felt no compunction about lying about virtually anything and everything – one might have felt uneasy asking him the time. Reagan adapted the old joke that diplomats were men sent abroad to lie for their country to suit a new generation. Politicians now stayed at home and lied to their country. In the words of Eric Alterman:

> Ronald Reagan was many things, but most undeniably he was a pathological liar . . . The President's famous cluelessness was so obvious during his years in office that his defenders would attempt to deploy it as a defense of his actions, as if he were a small child or a beloved but retarded uncle. 'The President tended to "build these little worlds and live in them"'. said a senior presidential adviser.'[24]

In view of the later onset of Alzheimer's Disease, we cannot be certain that Reagan's odd relationship with truth and reality was not an early sign of the senility that was eventually to overcome him. Nevertheless, one way or another, it was utterly amazing that a man with such limitations – medical, psychological, intellectual or moral – should ever have held power in any country, let alone the world's strongest nuclear power.

In August 1980, he apparently escaped from whatever little world he was living in to tell the American people that trees cause more pollution than vehicles do. A grateful people responded by making him their President.

By 1988, the American people were ready to accept anything from their President. Thus, in the aftermath of the Flight 655 disaster they were told that the victims (airline passengers) bore the guilt for their own demise and the perpetrators (US navy) were, in fact, heroes for the efficiency with which they made their mistakes. Reagan described the tragedy as an 'understandable accident'.[25] The US media concentrated on the anguish suffered by the captain of the *Vincennes* rather than the passengers in the airliner. When the cruiser docked at San Diego on its return from the Gulf, its captain was welcomed as a hero by cheering crowds. Incredibly, the air warfare coordinator responsible for shooting down the airliner was awarded the Commendation Medal for his 'ability to quickly and precisely complete the firing procedure'. Vice-president George Bush commented, 'I will never apologise for the United States of America! I don't care what the facts are!'[26] That much seems clear from what followed.

**The Cruellest Cut of All**

## The Patriot Missile

In the 'theatre of war', which from time to time seemed an apt description of Reagan's America, size definitely mattered. Like posturing Shakespearean actors comparing codpieces stuffed with straw, Reagan's service leaders competed to spend the military budget on weapons ever larger and more potent than their predecessors. It was like warfare through symbolism and Reagan had left his mark on the Republican presidents who followed him. Wars were no longer about body parts, amputations, eviscerations, obliterations, exterminations and all the sorrows of thousands of years of conflict. Instead, prepare for *MASH* to take over control of the Pentagon.

When the curtain went up on the first Gulf War in 1991, it was George Bush Snr who was occupying the stage. Bush had learned his part well. After years of study under the master, he was every bit the B-movie actor and he was preparing to surgically alter human perceptions of warfare. The truth was that nothing had really changed, but the words 'death' and 'suffering' had been struck out of American editions of the *Oxford English Dictionary*.

The new American way of war was unveiled. Surgical strikes were to keep casualties to a minimum – on both sides – and the advanced technology available would protect American servicemen and make extensive body counts a thing of the past. In fact, according to the Americans, the new smart weapons were so clever that the Iraqis would hardly know that they had been killed at all. Cruise missiles would unlock windows rather than break them, or enter by catflaps, picking out their targets on a 'deserves to die' basis. According to the new Puritan war ethic, Iraqi casualties would have earned their fate.

And it would make such good television with all the video footage of smart weapons homing in on their military targets and not on the homes of America's Third World enemies. Quite unlike that nasty war in Vietnam!

For the soldiers of wars between ancient times and 1980, missiles – latterly bombs, rockets and shells – that were propelled but failed to work were considered duds. However, in the world of Reagan-speak, which came to dominate Pentagon thinking, this was too severe a judgement. In future, if missiles were fired from their launchers they were counted as successful even if they did not hit their target. This ensured a very high success rate and, like small children in non-competitive sport, nobody needed to feel that they had failed. Even if you shot down a civilian airliner instead of an enemy fighter plane you still got a medal! In 1991, the US navy announced a 90 per cent success rate for its Tomahawk cruise missiles in the Gulf War, defining success as where the missile 'actually emerged from the launcher'.[27] Ironically, some of the smart Tomahawks became overeducated, questioning their own programmers, and during operations in Kosovo actually landed in Bulgaria instead of Yugoslavia. During the 2003 war in Iraq, other Tomahawks showed unilateralist tendencies, striking Iran, Syria and Turkey instead of their Iraqi targets.

During the first Gulf War one of the first tests faced by the smart weapons was how to combat their less educated opponents – namely Saddam Hussein's Scud missiles – a variant on the German V-2s of the Second World War. These had a nasty tendency to fall indiscriminately on Israel, threatening to provoke that country into retaliation that might unravel George Bush's coalition against Iraq. The Scuds had to be stopped and, if not destroyed, surgically removed from people's memories. The answer, as Ronald Reagan had often shown in the early 1980s when he didn't know what to do, was to start beating the drum of patriotism. All Americans rally to its sound. And when the emperor appears without any clothes, even the little boys will remain silent. And so the legend of the Patriot missile was born.

In 1991, the Patriot missile represented everything that was good in modern America, notably the 'cutting-edge' 'life-saving' technology that had made warfare clinically accurate, bloodless, intelligent and acceptable for television's millions. Above all, it was evidence, if more was needed, that America was still the pre-eminent technological power in the world. The despatch of the Patriot to Israel was accompanied by a PR exercise to convince everyone in Israel that there was no need for them to worry about Scuds because the anti-missile missile would protect them. But who was fooling whom?

President Bush appears to have believed what the military men told him without understanding what they said, something he had learned from Ronald Reagan. Not quite one giant leap for mankind but certainly a rosy future for the air-defence industry. 'Stormin' Norman' Schwarzkopf was also 'sold a pup' by the arms salesmen. It was he who announced the first ever interception of a ballistic missile by another missile. The problem was that, however it looked on television, it never really happened. Later research showed that there was no Scud in the sky at that moment and that the Patriot battery fired their missile accidentally. The explosion everyone saw was the Patriot detonating itself.

Israel's Defence Minister, Moshe Arens, was not so easily fooled. Like many Israelis he had his doubts about the Patriot and he was not convinced that the Americans knew what they were talking about. He later admitted: 'The Americans said to us that they could promise that within 24 and at most 48 hours they would put an end to the missile threat, that there would be no reason for Israel to retaliate.'[28] Prior to the beginning of Desert Storm they were saying there would be no reason for Israel to take pre-emptive action. It turned out that they were not capable of putting an end to the missile threat in 24 hours, not in 48 hours and not during the entire five weeks of the conflict.

When Arens complained, Bush was astonished and asked his advisers to produce charts showing Moshe Arens how effective the Patriot was. Arens queried the American figures and gave some of his own:

> I told him at the time that the probability of an intercept by a Patriot was no more than 20 per cent, well, by now we know it was close to 0 per cent, and he thought it was close to 100 per cent, so there was a little gap between us.[29]

## Lies, Damned Lies and Defence Contracts

At the end of the 1991 Gulf War, the US army testified to Congress that the Patriot missile had achieved a near perfect 98 per cent 'kill' against Scuds. Yet again, however, the new usage of an old English word was apparent. At a Congressional Enquiry the army was asked to explain what they meant by intercepting a Scud missile. The general testifying said by intercept the army meant that the Patriot and the Scud passed each other in the sky. Intercept did not mean the Patriot actually hit the Scud.

Beaten in scientific argument and forced into a most farcical explanation of 'interception' the army now fell back on emotional blackmail, not only against their scientific critics but against the American people as a whole. First the army refused to let Congress see their reports on the success of the Patriot missile and then they accused their critics of unpatriotic behaviour – a delightfully ironic pun:

> They wrapped themselves in the flag, they challenged the committee members for questioning the patriotism and integrity of General Schwarzkopf.[30]

It was not just a fraud foisted on an ingenuous President and Congress by a corrupt military–industrial clique, it was a highpoint of Reaganism. Any lie was an acceptable *means* to an *end*. With the Cold War over and anti-Communism consigned to the Smithsonian Institute, the manufacturers of advanced weaponry could not simply stand by and watch their market dry up. Market forces demanded a new enemy.

## The New Giant

Right-wing think tanks had already begun to fill this enemy vacuum, even before al-Qaeda's attacks on New York and Washington on 11 September 2001. For conservative America, the war against terrorism has become the new Cold War. The use of 'fear' to bolster support for this policy has taken the form of an exaggeration of the military threat Saddam Hussein posed to the people of the 'Free World'. According to intelligence sources, the politicians told us, Saddam Hussein was a direct and imminent threat to us all because of the 'weapons of mass destruction' that he possessed. The dumbing-down of public debate was symptomatic of the real threat to democratic values in both the United States and Britain by politicians who feel that the tabloid journalism in Britain and the abysmal 24-hour news coverage in America is as much as people need to know about why their government has gone to war yet again. 'Be a good American: don't try to think', might as well be the political advice given to more than 200 million voters in the United States.

'Are you sitting comfortably? Then I'll begin. There once was an ogre named Saddam Hussein who had a big club with which he would grind our bones to make his bread . . .'

It is true that everyone else in the Middle East, notably Israel and Iran, possessed the same sort of club that Saddam possessed, indeed America had sold it to him in the first place. But other ogres kept their clubs under lock and key in the garage and cleaned them on Sundays . . .

The standard of public debate was reduced to just about this level. These weapons, apparently, Saddam alone used for 'nasty' purposes, like killing his own people rather than threatening his neighbours. Israel, for example, was hardly threatened by a potential Iraqi nuclear programme as she already had the fifth largest nuclear stockpile in the world, greater in fact than Britain herself. She possessed this nuclear deterrent to overawe any of her troublesome neighbours. Bush and Blair trumped any serious discussion on the strategic situation in the region by uttering the magic words, 'intelligence information', which essentially meant, 'We have proof of what we say and you haven't.'

President Bush used the State of the Union address on 28 January 2003 to turn up the volume on the 'fear–pressure monitor' with which politicians in the USA have all been equipped since 9/11. Bush described Saddam as 'the dictator who is assembling the world's most dangerous weapons'. By the time of his 'ultimatum address' on 17 March, the President was turning the volume up further with, 'the Iraqi regime continues to possess and conceal some of the most lethal weapons ever devised'. This must have been news to the USA's own weapons designers. Nor was this all. Saddam's hidden weapons were replicating like rabbits: 'In one year, or five years, the power of Iraq to inflict harm on all free nations would be multiplied many times over.' Bush went on to list large quantities of biological and chemical weapons that most independent experts believed Saddam no longer had. Bush concluded, 'A future lived at the mercy of terrible threats is no peace at all.' In his 17 March address, after listing Saddam's alleged WMD, Bush declaimed, 'And this very fact underscores the reason we cannot live under the threat of blackmail.' And then came the lie that did not go unnoticed but which was subsumed by a flow of patriotism, so that few dared to challenge it at the time:

> I would remind you that when the inspectors first went into Iraq and were denied, finally denied access, a report came out of the Atomic — the IAEA [International Atomic Energy Agency] — that they were six months away from developing a weapon. I don't know what more evidence we need.[31]

The truth might have helped.

In fact, the Bush administration did not present any evidence to support this assertion. Mohamed El Baradei, IAEA's director general, never produced the report to which Bush referred. On the contrary, the IAEA informed the UN Security Council that 'there is no indication of resumed nuclear activities' in Iraq.[32]

The statement by President Bush was untrue, made either in error or with the intention to mislead. For once, the issue was a simple 'factual' one: not 'did Saddam Hussein have nuclear weapons?' but 'did the IAEA issue a report that said he had nuclear weapons?' Once the American authorities recognised their 'error' and the fact that this information would give people in the United States and the United Kingdom the impression that Saddam posed a 'nuclear' threat, they were duty-bound as a democratically elected and responsible government to see that the voters were not misled. If they failed, they would take their country into a war on the basis of misplaced fear.

George W. Bush is creating a siege mentality in the United States by presenting the threat from terrorism as a virtual Third World War. Rather than seeking to understand the roots of the problem and to minimise it where possible, he is inflating its dangers and contributing to its own growth. Like politicians before him, he is controlling the American people through fear and thereby threatening core democratic values in the United States and elsewhere.

It was Nazi leader Hermann Göring who gave this technique the seal of approval when speaking to psychologist Gustave Gilbert during the Nuremberg War Trials in 1945. Göring said:

> The people can always be brought to the bidding of the leaders. All you have to do is tell them they are being attacked and denounce the pacifists for lack of patriotism and exposing the country to danger. It works the same way in every country.[33]

Göring's advice, to lie about a potential threat or exaggerate a real one, has a startling relevance to the way George Bush and Tony Blair approached the war against Iraq in March 2003.

Adolf Hitler wrote in *Mein Kampf* that the greater the lie, the greater the chance it would be believed. George W. Bush and Tony Blair's propaganda is in bad company therefore with the media machines of totalitarian states. Both Bush and Blair may have innocently misled their people by using inaccurate intelligence when they stressed the existence of viable Iraqi weapons of mass destruction and the possibility that these could be deployed at short notice and with a trans-continental capability. But they were both using 'fear' as a political weapon to win their argument on both a national and international stage.

In a democracy it should be a requirement for any government that where war is undertaken on behalf of a population that has registered its discontent through marches and public protests, that war can be shown to be based on accurate intelligence made available, as far as possible, to the voters and their representatives. Party-political allegiance should always be secondary to an MP's commitment to the public he serves. Loyalty to individuals, in particular the figure of prime minister, must not supersede loyalty to the people.

I ask the following question of the coalition leaders: should there be any consequences for a president or a prime minister who takes his nation into a war based on inaccurate intelligence?

As Harry Truman always said, 'The buck stops here.'

# CHAPTER 9

# *A History of Cartoon Violence*

Scots groundskeeper Willie, a character in the classic American cartoon series *The Simpsons*, has become an unlikely spokesman for the Republican administration of President George W. Bush. In one episode, his description of the French as 'cheese-eating surrender monkeys' unleashed a 'weapon of mass destruction' much to American taste. The phrase was subsequently exploited by American and British politicians, and by the media, as propaganda against President Chirac's failure to support President George W. Bush's policy towards Iraq. Supporters of Bush accused the French nation of cowardice and of a historical tendency to surrender to its enemies rather than fight for its beliefs. The French surrender in 1940 to Nazi Germany was used as a case in point. Britain, of course, did not surrender in 1940, saved by her fleet and the geographical advantage of a 22-mile moat.

The appropriate response would be to ignore such an accusation. However, the use of racist rhetoric by the anti-French lobby in Washington is yet another example of America's dumbing-down policy towards its own people. One feels forced to remind the American people that cartoon-style diplomacy might suit their current political leader, but it hardly reflects well on American pretensions to world leadership or victory in a clash of civilisations. In fact, if by civilisation one meant the culture that was established by a people over many centuries, there might be some who would prefer to live in a world in which the irresistible rise of the United States had been resisted, rather than in one where the profound and subtle contribution of the French was missing.

Ironically, *The Simpsons* seems to offer a suitable reply to George W.

Bush and his supporters. During an episode where Homer is forced to attend parenting classes after his children are put into a foster home, he is involved in a role-play situation with Cleitus, during which he attempts to strangle the hillbilly. The teacher asks the class if they can suggest a different way for Homer to resolve his differences with Cleitus. Everyone puts up their hands. The teacher then adds, 'Without childish name-calling', at which point all the hands go down. It is the American Way. The nation that missed the 'Age of Reason', by breaking away from Europe at the wrong moment, experienced instead an alternative in the 'Age of Reagan', a period of right-wing violence in which diplomacy was replaced by childish displays of cartoon aggression towards smaller nations, like the world's leading nutmeg producer, Grenada.

For the American media, 2003 was open season on the French. One recent joke asked why the boulevards in Paris are lined with trees. The answer was: so that the German troops can always march in the shade. The *New York Post* ran a doctored photo on its front page in which the heads of the French and German ambassadors to the United Nations had been replaced with the heads of weasels, thus producing an 'Axis of Weasels' headline to go alongside Bush's 'Axis of Evil'. A radio disc jockey in Atlanta offered listeners the chance to smash a Peugeot with a sledgehammer. Two Republican congressmen persuaded cafeterias in the Congress buildings to change 'french fries' on their menus to 'freedom fries'. Something similar had happened in 1917 when everything German was changed to the word 'liberty': hamburgers became 'liberty' steaks; sauerkraut, 'liberty' cabbage; even 'liberty' measles entered the medical textbooks.[1] American wit had hit rock bottom in 1917 and apparently stayed there for 86 years!

Car bumper stickers proclaimed: 'First Iraq, then France'. Sofitel, the French hotel chain, pulled down French flags flying in front of their ten American properties and replaced them with US state or city flags. Now that was a surrender! The owner of Roxy's, a popular restaurant and bar in West Palm Beach, Florida, dragged every case of his French wine and liqueurs into the street and tipped them into the gutter.[2] I would rather have been in the gutter than in his restaurant.

When, however, George Will jokes in a *Newsweek* column, 'How many Frenchmen does it take to defend Paris? No one knows, it's never been tried', one is forced to intervene. Disproving a joke leaves one open to another abusive phrase: 'Get a life.' Taking a joke so seriously that you try to prove it is not true is to double the enjoyment for the joker. But in the tabloid-media world favoured in America and Britain, failure to respond is to allow such a joke to burrow away like a destructive organism into the minds of ordinary people. Those who do not know the past are thus open to the lies of the present, even if they are delivered as apparently harmless acts of humour.

The threat of using the French veto by President Chirac was based on the irrefutable fact that it was not designed to prevent an otherwise united Security Council from acting in a just cause, but to prevent two 'rogue states' from using the Security Council as a cloak for their aggression. France, as one of the Security Council's permanent members, had the right to veto actions of which she disapproved. When Britain and the US indicated they wished the council to support their pre-emptive attack on Iraq, Chirac indicated that France would veto such an action.

There was a clear historical precedent which the United States, of all countries, should have recognised. At the time of the Korean crisis in 1950, the United Nations passed the Uniting for Peace Resolution so that in the event of one of the Great Powers using its veto to hamstring the Security Council, a two-thirds majority in the General Assembly could overrule the veto. If George Bush and Tony Blair believed the French threat of the veto was unreasonable, they should have sought a two-thirds majority in the General Assembly. This would have proved one way or the other whether they truly represented the wishes of the world to be rid of the imminent threat that Saddam posed. If, as seems certain, they had been unable to win such a majority – by negotiation or bribery – the legality that they claimed for their actions would have been revealed as less valid than the so-called 'unreasonable' veto of the French.

French newspapers responded to the Francophobia in the American media by comparing the US decision to send troops into Iraq to Adolf Hitler's claim that his invasions of Czechoslovakia and Poland were preventive measures. And there were many 'cowboy' jokes over aperitifs in Paris, where the cognoscenti boycotted McDonald's restaurants.

On a higher, but no less vitriolic, level, Britain and France – those two ancient adversaries in the art of witty diplomacy – exchanged insults. When the French summed up perfidious Albion's 'special relationship' with the United States in these terms: 'We are part of the continent of Europe not just a balcony overlooking the Atlantic', the British responded with, 'France for centuries blocked our way to Europe. Before the invention of the aeroplane we had to step over it to get anywhere.' Children! children!

Not all Americans sank to cartoon level though. Senator Robert Byrd complained:

# A HISTORY OF CARTOON VIOLENCE

This administration has turned the patient art of diplomacy into threats, labelling and name calling of the sort that reflects quite poorly on the intelligence and sensitivity of our leaders, and which will have consequences for years to come. Calling heads of state pygmies, labelling whole countries as evil, denigrating powerful European Allies as irrelevant – these types of crude insensitivities can do our great nation no good.[3]

Comparisons between nations may indeed be profoundly misleading and totally pointless, but the accusation of national cowardice levelled against France should not go unchallenged. As any student of military history is aware, the military record of the French (in an imaginary league table) is probably unsurpassed. While the British may boast about Crécy, Agincourt, Blenheim and Waterloo, the French might point out that these victories have been massaged by the propaganda services of the British state, which is where the true skills of the British lie. What do the Brits know of Bouvines, Formigny, Marengo or Austerlitz? And what do the Americans know about war at all? Those parvenus achieve their greatest

**The French Connection**

victories in the boardroom, the shipyards and the factories. Their battles are won on celluloid. The enemy falls upon the cutting-room floors.

American national victories like Saratoga or New Orleans are minor affairs when compared to any battle fought in Europe at the time. At Saratoga in 1777, the defeated British under Burgoyne suffered barely 1,000 casualties, while Pakenham's losses at New Orleans in 1815 – Andrew Jackson's greatest victory – were a mere 2,100 casualties. During the Peninsular War, on the other hand, British losses in successive victories were: Talavera 1809, 6,500; Albuera 1811, 7,000; Salamanca 1812, 6,000; Vittoria 1813, 7,000; Toulouse 1814, 5,000. At Waterloo, Wellington's casualties amounted to 15,000 and two days earlier, at Quatre Bras, a further 4,500 casualties were suffered.

France's losses in wars throughout her history have been very heavy and indicate the severity of the fighting in which the French nation has been involved. French casualties in Napoleonic battles are on a far larger scale than any battle involving the British. At Austerlitz in 1805, for example, 9,000 French casualties can be contrasted with Austro-Russian losses of 26,000. At Jena-Auerstadt in 1806, French losses of 8,000 compare with Prussian losses of 25,000. At the bloody battle of Eylau in 1807, the French suffered 18,000 casualties in contrast with 25,000 on the Russian side. During the 1809 campaign against Austria, culminating in the hard-fought battles of Aspern-Essling and Wagram, Austrian losses of 45,000 compare to France's 34,000. The Battle of Borodino in 1812 was one of the toughest fights in history and left the Russians with 40,000 casualties against French losses of 28,000. Finally, at the Battle of Leipzig, nicknamed the 'Battle of the Nations' and the biggest battle ever fought before the First World War, French losses of 60,000 were balanced by the same figure for the victorious Austrian, Prussian and Russian alliance.

During this period, as can be seen, these 'cheese-eating surrender monkeys' were kept very busy dying for their country yet, at the same time, winning their battles. British and American skirmishes of the time hardly compare with the vast European encounters, however much the Anglo-Saxon media machines like to inflate the national ego.[4]

Brigadier-General Marie Joseph, Marquis de Lafayette, when he was not bringing freedom and independence to America, must also therefore be stereotyped as a coward. Yet, it was Lafayette, and the French soldiers who fought with him at Yorktown, who brought the British under Lord Cornwallis to surrender. Americans of George Washington's time had no doubt who their friends were and how much they owed to the French. At Yorktown in 1781, 4,300 British, 2,100 Germans and 1,000 American Loyalists surrendered to the French General Rochambeau's 9,500 soldiers, and to Lafayette and Washington's 3,500 American Continentals and 2,000 Virginia Militia. In addition, 25,000 Frenchmen were present with the French fleet off the mouth of the York River, where 32 French men-of-war had scored a decisive victory over the Royal Navy, thus securing America's independence.[5]

When Cornwallis sent his second-in-command, Major-General Charles O'Hara, to surrender his sword to the Comte de Rochambeau, the French general, no doubt enjoying the joke, indicated that he was not in command and that the British should surrender to George Washington. The American commander, eager to milk the British humiliation, sent out his own second-in-command, Major-General Benjamin Lincoln, to receive the surrender for him. The eighteenth century was like that. Presumably Lord Cornwallis felt ashamed surrendering to Washington himself, a mere ex-colonel (honorary) in the British army. The British army was like that.

Geography has given the United States an advantage over European states. For 200 years, 3,000 miles of the Atlantic and perhaps 6,000 miles of the Pacific have prevented anyone from invading America. France, on the other hand, is situated with three 'powerful' (at various times) neighbours (Spain, England and Germany) on her borders, all of whom have invaded the country on many occasions. In recent history, the Germans invaded France in 1870, 1914 and 1940, each time in massive strength. With only the token strength of the British Expeditionary Force in both 1914 and 1940, France found herself facing the entire force of the world's leading military power. The United States, at no time in her history, has ever faced the full weight of any major nation's military power.

If the Americans had faced the full strength of Nazi Germany between 1939 and 1941 there can be little doubt that they would have experienced the same situation faced by Britain and France. Their leadership, equipment and soldiers could not have matched those fielded by the Wehrmacht in the first part of the war. They would have surrendered because they would have been totally outclassed.

In 1944 and 1945, in spite of the pretensions of men like Bradley and Patton, the Americans and the British combined were facing much less than half of the German military and aerial strength. The brunt of the land fighting against Germany from 1941 to 1945 was carried by the Soviet forces on the Eastern Front. Moreover, although American air, sea and

# PICKING THE BONES

land forces faced the Japanese for the bulk of the war during 1941–5, the biggest defeat ever suffered by a Japanese army happened at Kohima-Imphal in Burma (Myanmar), where in 1944 the Japanese Fifteenth Army was destroyed by the British Fourteenth Army under General Slim.

It is only in the light of a statistical appreciation that one can judge France's surrender in 1940. Without understanding the terrible attritional fighting of 1914–16, notably the epic struggle at Verdun, where the German intention was literally to bleed France dry, one cannot view the national complex that saw the creation of the Maginot Line in true perspective. French casualties in the First World War were far larger than the British and American casualties combined, and the cream of the French army fell in 1914 before Britain was able to give more than token help.

## First World War

| COUNTRY | DURATION IN DAYS | KILLED | WOUNDED | CASUALTIES |
|---|---|---|---|---|
| British Empire | 1,562 | 908,371 | 2,090,000 | 2,998,371 |
| France | 1,563 | 1,357,000 | 4,266,000 | 5,623,000 |
| United States | 582 | 50,585 | 205,690 | 256,275 |

| COUNTRY | KILLED/DAY | WOUNDED/ DAY | CASUALTIES/ DAY |
|---|---|---|---|
| British Empire | 581.0 | 1,337.2 | 1,918 |
| France | 868.2 | 2,729.4 | 3,598 |
| United States | 86.9 | 353.4 | 440 |

## Second World War

| COUNTRY | DURATION IN DAYS | KILLED | WOUNDED | CASUALTIES |
|---|---|---|---|---|
| British Empire | 2,218 | 397,762 | 475,000 | 872,762 |
| France | 298 | 210,671 | 400,000 | 610,671 |
| United States | 1,372 | 292,100 | 571,822 | 863,922 |

| COUNTRY | KILLED/DAY | WOUNDED/ DAY | CASUALTIES/ DAY |
|---|---|---|---|
| British Empire | 179.3 | 214.2 | 393 |
| France | 706.9 | 1,342.3 | 2,049 |
| United States | 212.9 | 416.8 | 630 |

# A HISTORY OF CARTOON VIOLENCE

The casualties suffered by France during the German blitzkrieg campaign of 1940 were probably higher on a daily basis than at any time during the First World War. For most of the 298 days France endured during 1939–40 her troops were uninvolved in fighting. As a result, the true rate of casualties for 1940 would have been very much larger, possibly even more so than during the Battle of Verdun in 1916, which won the French glory for their heroic and stubborn resistance. For the French, the casualty figures for 1914–18 were relatively steady on a daily basis, with occasional peaks in August 1914, 1915 and 1917.

During the 1980s, President Ronald Reagan's missile defence system, Star Wars, was a 'space-age' Maginot Line in all but name. And if history spoke to modern Americans, as it does to all continental Europeans, through the bitter experience of war, they might be less willing to support modern war-hawks like the neo-conservatives who came to prominence in the post-Vietnam period and now dominate American foreign policy. Far back in their history Americans learned that foreign invaders can be the most unwelcome guests for a newly independent and militarily weak nation.

In 1814, during the war against Great Britain (far from the second war of independence as described by some American historians – unless the word 'Canadian' is inserted before 'independence'), a British army captured and burned Washington DC in retaliation for American deprivations across the border in Canada. Nobody would have known how many American soldiers would have been needed to protect the US capital, since nobody stopped running long enough to try. When the British troops reached the White House they found the dining room prepared for dinner with all the tables formally laid. The British commander, Admiral Cochrane, treated himself to President Madison's wine and toasted 'absent friends' in honour of the missing 'Jemmy' Madison. As a memento, Cochrane also took one of the President's hats and one of his wife Dolly's cushions. It was intended as a symbolic humiliation. After they had eaten well, the British left, torching the White House and the rest of the new American capital.

Yet, had they been out of favour, the British could also have proved a target for the kilted groundsman of Springfield Elementary. After he had finished with the French, he might have shifted his target to 'beef-eating surrender monkeys' with the names of Yorktown, Kut and Singapore used to milk the laughs from the audience. Nations with military histories as long as those of Britain and France are easy targets for racist stereotyping. On the other hand, Willie, where were the Scots after Flodden or Culloden? Och, feeding the worms!

Each country has both skeletons and triumphal arches in its cupboards, and the study of history should prepare us for unexpected quantities of either toppling out on us should we carelessly open them. The Swiss, inventors of cuckoo clocks and little else except secure bank vaults for the mega-rich of the world, might otherwise be renowned for their fighting abilities. From the fourteenth to the sixteenth century, the Swiss were some of the most renowned and fierce warriors of European history and were in great demand as mercenaries. So formidable were their military skills that they contributed to many of the decisive battles of the Renaissance period. Their national weapon was the halberd (a long spear with an axe-blade and pick at one end), but their professionalism with the pike and many two-handed weapons like the Lucerne hammer and the double-handed sword made them masters of the battlefield. In the period 1300–1550, only the English longbowmen could match the Swiss in the eyes of European paymasters like Francis I of France and Charles the Bold of Burgundy.

During the sixteenth century, the Spaniards and the Dutch, under commanders like Gonzalo de Cordoba and Maurice of Nassau, reached military prominence in European warfare, and in the next century and a half the Swedes, under dynamic leaders like Gustavus Adolphus and Charles XII, made their nation the greatest power of the North. Even this brief summary hints at the fact that history, by sweeping generalisation, is an extremely inaccurate science.

Racial stereotyping has always been a powerful form of propaganda and, at its lowest level, the basis for jokes. Each country seems to have particular targets, with Irish jokes, or Belgian jokes, or Bavarian jokes fulfilling an apparently harmless function for those needing to reduce enemies to the anti-phobic images of spiders with bowler hats and Charlie Chaplin umbrellas, or rats with spectacles and false moustaches. However, as we know, such jokes can conceal far darker depths. Stereotyping has been one of the forms of propaganda favoured by politicians since the First World War, and even earlier. Satirical magazines throughout the nineteenth century, like *Punch*, were able to win the battles for 'hearts and minds' by using humour, but the 'need to kill' has been facilitated by dehumanising the opposition so that soldiers can kill without having any natural antipathy towards the enemy. Contempt and ridicule have served their own purpose in rendering them worthy of death.

# A HISTORY OF CARTOON VIOLENCE

## 'How Have the Mighty Fled?'

What is the thinnest book in the world? You've heard it before – the Italian book of 'war heroes'? Have you heard of the Italian tank that had one forward gear and four reverse gears? Of course you have. But have you heard of the fighting spirit of the Italians in the Dolomites in 1915? Or the courage of the Italian troops in Eritrea in 1940? Or the skill of six daredevil Italian submariners in Alexandria harbour on 18 December 1941?

Three two-man 'human torpedoes' were launched from an Italian submarine lying in the waters off the coast of Alexandria and these mini-submarines negotiated their way into the heavily guarded harbour and placed mines on the keels of two British battleships, *Valiant* and *Queen Elizabeth*. Both sank and were out of action for months before they could be raised and repaired. All the Italian frogmen were captured, but Admiral Cunningham commented, 'One cannot but admire the cold-blooded bravery of these Italians.' In the 1950s, a film was made commemorating the courage of the Italian submariners. That courage has been forgotten and the general view prevails that Italians are cowards and incompetent in war. At least the Italians showed impeccable manners, as demonstrated in this anecdote:

> A British officer, looking for shelter in the desert, noticed an apparently unoccupied Italian truck. Cautiously opening the door, he jumped in only to find the other seat occupied by a slumbering Italian driver. Pulling out a revolver, he jabbed it in the man's chest and muttered, 'alto in mano', which was the best Italian he could manage at short notice. The startled Italian woke up, sized up the situation and put his hands in the air. Then he gently corrected the officer's grammar, 'mani in alto'.[6]

Sometimes, in the words of Johnny Mercer, you have to 'accentuate the positive, eliminate the negative and latch on to the affirmative'. It is a shame that American politicians do not allow their people to concentrate on what they do best – light entertainment. *Floreat* Steely Dan, Stephen Sondheim and Lisa Simpson! If the French are 'surrender monkeys', why do the Americans want them on their side? Why not leave war to those who are good at it like Vercingetorix, Clovis, Charles Martel, Charlemagne, William of Normandy, Bohemond, Tancred, Boucicault, Du Guesclin, Gaston de Foix, Bayard, Monluc, Henri of Navarre, Turenne, Condé, Luxembourg, Boufflers, Villeroi, Saxe, Montcalm,

Carnot, Hoche, Kellerman, Napoleon Bonaparte, Davout, Berthier, Masséna, Soult, Suchet, Murat, Lannes, Ney, Vandamme, Canrobert, MacMahon, Foch, Gallieni, Lyautey, Franchet d'Esperey, Weygand, Bigeard. Remember this when you consider your allies – if you ever do.

If it comes to stereotyping, who has a good record for 'bravery in battle'? The British? The Germans? The Americans? For an answer it is often wise to go to the best. Frederick the Great of Prussia had an interesting story about courage in battle. To his mind no man was naturally a hero or a coward. On different days he could be either. At the Battle of Mollwitz against the Austrians in 1741, a wounded Prussian grenadier seized a riderless horse, mounted it and rode into the thick of the fighting, returning with even more wounds and with an Austrian officer as a prisoner. Frederick was delighted at the man's bravery, had him promoted and transferred to the cavalry. Now an officer and a member of an elite cavalry regiment, the soldier deserted to the enemy at his first opportunity. What lesson can we learn from that? Do not rely on generalisations.

Frederick the Great found the British the most arrogant of all soldiers. Once he was taking a British officer, Sir Robert Sutton, to inspect Prussia's tallest grenadiers and asked if Sir Robert thought an equal number of Englishmen could beat them. Sir Robert thought for a moment and then replied, 'I am not sure about that, but I know that half that number would try.'

Taking the two anecdotes together one can see that courage and cowardice are not absolutes, but depend on many factors. In 1745, at Prestonpans, the renowned British Redcoats threw down their guns and took to their heels, fleeing with terror at the sight of Highlanders brandishing claymores and charging towards them. They displayed rank cowardice in running away from an undisciplined, but ferocious, enemy. The following year, at Fontenoy in France, however, these same Redcoats showed impeccable fire discipline in routing the French infantry.

Ten years later, in 1755, on the Monongahela River in North America, British Redcoats were at it again, this time led by Braddock and George Washington. Overcome by their fears of the unknown and fighting Native Americans and French in the forests, they were beaten by a much lesser force, many panicking and fleeing from the sheer horror presented by the Native Americans. Four years later, however, at Minden in Germany, the British Redcoats turned the tables again, achieving something against the French which was unparalleled in

154

military history – a single line of unsupported infantry charged three lines of French cavalry off the battlefield at bayonet point.

It was a merry-go-round of military triumphs and disasters that would have inspired an eighteenth-century Kipling to write 'If'. What is clear, though, is that to generalise about these Redcoats is unproductive. They are depicted as some of history's finest fighting men, known to their commanders as the 'scum of the earth' and to their enemies as the 'bloodybacks' (referring to the number of times they were flogged). At Albuera in Spain in 1811, the British infantry suffered 50 per cent casualties in driving the French off the field. Even as fierce an opponent as the French Marshal Soult told Napoleon that at Albuera the British had been beaten, but did not know it and would not run. Yet on a day-by-day basis, who was to know how they would perform?

The same might be said of the American GI. The first time the American troops met Rommel and the Wehrmacht in North Africa in 1942 at the Kasserine Pass, they ran for their lives. One whole reconnaissance unit of 100 men surrendered to the Germans without firing a shot. Soon the panic spread and many other soldiers were looking for the easy way out. They simply abandoned their vehicles, took off their helmets and held up their hands. The lines of the 168th Infantry were virtually swept away by fleeing men shouting 'the Krauts are coming'. Officers, in the tradition of futile gestures the world over, pulled out their pistols and waved them at the fleeing columns. In the words of the British military historian Charles Whiting in his book *First Blood*:

> Here and there an officer tried to stop them, his arms outspread
> as if he were trying to catch his playmates at a childish game of
> Tag. But there was no holding them. Eyes wild and staring with
> fear, the fleeing men struggled on.

No officer, it seemed, had the courage to fire into the deserters and demonstrate to them the consequences of running away in wartime. As a consequence, it fell to Rommel to show these young American soldiers that they were fighting for their own lives in the desert. They could never outrun a bullet.

The US commander heard news of the panic by telephone. 'They're running away, General. Your men are running away.'

'You don't know what you're saying,' he replied. 'They're only shifting position!'

'Shifting position, hell!' he was told, 'I know panic when I see it.'[7]

## PICKING THE BONES

The Americans suffered a stunning defeat. It emphasised that technological superiority, notably in tank manufacture, had given the Germans a material advantage that the Americans had been unable to combat. And the GIs had run rather than confront their fears. They had shown less stomach for fighting the Germans than the Poles had at the outbreak of the war. The difference, of course, was that the Poles knew what they were fighting for – national and personal survival, in that order. In the desert, the Americans could feel no commitment to the cause for which they had been sent to Europe. At that moment of crisis, democracy and the four freedoms of Franklin D. Roosevelt seemed a million miles away. The GIs were fighting for their own self-preservation and if this could be achieved by running away rather than fighting, then flight rather than fight was the option every time. It was not their fault that the Germans were better at war than they were. After all, their tanks were impervious to American fire. Never mind that in Russia peasant soldiers were finding ways to halt the German juggernaut. It took fighting spirit of a different order to lay down your life for a cause other than your own. American GIs felt that they had too much to lose. Comfortable homes, good food and good prospects were too much for a man to sacrifice in defence of something nobody seemed able to define. They were all conscripts anyway. After all, who would volunteer to lose their life in the Tunisian desert? As one German prisoner laughingly told a British Eighth Army soldier who took him captive, 'We have the Italians; you have the Americans.' Yet, it is all too easy to allow stereotypes to develop.

In the final stages of the Battle of Waterloo, General Cambronne, commanding the Old Guard, would not surrender even though the British had him virtually surrounded. When called upon to throw down their arms he replied, memorably, '*Merde*', an example which can hardly have been unknown to the American general, McAuliffe, at Bastogne in 1944, who responded, when the Germans called on him to surrender, with the splendid 'Nuts'. Unfortunately, the Germans, true to form, took the reply literally and could not understand what the American meant.

British soldiers of Gough's Fifth Army ran on 21 March 1918 – between the rivers Oise and Sambre they had been hit by 6,000 German guns in the heaviest barrage in history. Within an hour the Fifth Army had lost 30 per cent of its infantry strength. Norman Gladden described how panic spread:

> Panic took command. In a mad stampede we passed through the
> relieving company. Undoubtedly we had lost our nerve. I saw
> men crying and I would have cried myself had I the tears. The
> company that night was in the grip of a communal terror, 100
> men running like rabbits.[8]

The 'brutal Huns' were not all brutal that day. One British machine
gunner reported that a German officer came up behind him and thrust a
gun in his back, capturing him with the words, 'Come along, Tommy.
You have done enough.'

All armies – large or small – face the fact that surrender is one of the most
civilised aspects of international warfare. Denied the option to cease
fighting in impossible situations, the individual soldier would find that
warfare stepped over the last, thin dividing line between Clausewitz's
settlement of political disputes by other means and the abattoir it can so
quickly become. The shame of surrender is often in the eye of the beholder
or the mind of the reader. Some causes are not worthy of the lives of many
soldiers denied the chance of successful resistance or escape. Accusations
of cowardice against those who surrender are often the response of those
in safety many miles from the battlefront. Faced with dismemberment or
evisceration for the cause in their comfortable living room, most would
give way very quickly and seek comfort in the fridge! 'Nuts' sounds so
splendid to read or to watch some actor mouth on celluloid, but if, in
consequence, all the audience does is to plunge their bayonets into your
intestines and tear them out, it is not such a smart response.

George Washington was the original 'surrender monkey' of Franco-
American relations when in 1755 he and his Virginian Militia
surrendered Fort Necessity to the French under Captain Louis Coulon
de Villiers.[9] There are many surrenders in the military history of every
nation. They do not necessarily imply anything that can be generalised
about national characteristics, except perhaps military incompetence.
The Americans surrendered to the Japanese at Bataan. By 8 April 1942,
they and their Filipino allies could fight no longer.

> As the Japanese approached Cabcaben, Bataan's commander,
> Major General Edward King, sadly concluded he had no
> alternative to surrender. Thus 79,500 men, the largest force in
> American military history to succumb to an enemy, put down
> their arms.[10]

# PICKING THE BONES

As if to prove that whatever the Americans could fail to do, the British could fail to do as well, the British surrendered Singapore to the Japanese in an even bigger capitulation than Bataan. Moreover, the British showed little of the fighting resistance the Americans had shown at Corregidor.

The collapse of 'Fortress Singapore' in February 1942 was the greatest defeat ever suffered by a British army and the most humiliating episode in the history of the British Empire. The Japanese conquest of Malaya that preceded it and the subsequent assault on the island of Singapore saw a dreadful collapse of military morale and a shameful loss of fighting spirit by the large garrison that, even as they surrendered, still outnumbered their opponents by nearly three to one.

Preconceptions about Japanese equipment and the fighting quality of their soldiers had not helped. Historian Louis Allen records an example of this in his book *Singapore, 1941–42,* quoting Brooke-Popham in a letter to General Ismay: 'I was amused by one battalion commander, who, while we were standing together looking at his men, said "Don't you think they are worthy of some better enemy than the Japanese?"' Allen comments pointedly that the colonel who feared himself too strong was, within a year, to lose his entire brigade to a single Japanese tank column. A further shock to British prestige came with the realisation that in their military technology the Japanese had advanced way beyond the Allies. It had been a popular belief that Japanese pilots and planes must inevitably be inferior to those of the Western powers. This was ethnocentrism perfectly expressed. When the Japanese A6M2 Zero-Sen naval fighter appeared over Malaya and promptly cleared the skies of the Allied planes it aroused a feeling of psychological shock. Surely only white men could build and fly such a plane? The pilots must be Germans and the plans based on those of a Western power. Such attitudes were an attempt to bolster belief in white supremacy and to discredit everything Japanese. However, even more than the United States, Britain refused to face the truth about the Japanese and by doing so ensured the destruction of her own position in the Far East.

As the Japanese advanced down the Malayan Peninsula, unit after unit of British, Australian and Indian troops cracked and began retreating in panic. As they did so, they drove before them huge numbers of refugees, fleeing from the fighting and crossing the causeway into Singapore to swell the civilian population. Australian morale cracked, as Brigadier Julian Thompson describes:

> The Australians have been going round saying that they can fit

three Japanese on to one bayonet because it's long enough . . . and all this sort of rather macho rubbish . . . and it comes as a huge shock when you suddenly find these people are better than you are.[11]

The truth was that the Australian component at Singapore displayed some of the worst aspects of an army in panicky rout. In the opinion of journalist Ian Ward, the upper echelons of the British garrison were little more than a 'cocktail-party army' and General Wavell summed it all up with, 'Britain's soldiers had lacked the "guts" to hold back a Japanese army a third of their own strength.'

Are you listening, Willie?

# CHAPTER 10

# *'Hell-roaring' Jake Smith*

*Time* magazine chose 'The American Soldier' as its Person of the Year for 2003. Its citation read:

> They swept across Iraq and conquered it in 21 days. They stand guard on streets pot-holed with scepticism and rancour. They caught Saddam Hussein. They are the face of America, its might and good will, in a region unused to democracy.[1]

We should be pleased to hear about the 'good will' of American soldiers as the USA clearly intends many parts of the world to be seeing a lot more of them in the near future. And in case the British soldier should feel neglected, the special relationship between Britain and America will assure him of many more opportunities for death in far-flung places. Even the Queen's Christmas speech fell into line with the Americans, coming as it did from a barracks in Windsor where Her Majesty stood alongside a light tank in order to thank her armed forces for helping the Americans, instead of staying at home as the majority of her subjects had wanted them to do.

American politicians have frequently assured us that the deployment of American troops over the past 100 years has been entirely different from the military activities of any other nation. Throughout the world, American servicemen have been exponents of the 'American Way', carrying democracy in their knapsacks, liberty on the tips of their bayonets and freedom writ large on their helmets. They are international 'good guys' who do not commit 'war crimes', unlike the soldiers of

America's enemies. They are more like the 'Salvation Army' than the soldiers of other nations.[2]

As Abraham Lincoln so wisely observed, 'You can fool all the people some of the time, and some of the people all the time, but you cannot fool all the people all the time.'[3]

The American people came face to face with the reality of war crimes when the story of Lieutenant William Calley's massacre of 500 South Vietnamese villagers at My Lai first broke in 1968. It seemed like a 'one-off' atrocity, a unique occurrence that showed that even American servicemen were susceptible to the horrors of war in the Far East. But generations of American soldiers were unable to maintain eye contact with their wives and mothers, knowing, as they did, that American soldiers had been as willing as those of any other nation to break the so-called 'rules of war'. War crimes were no longer simply a product of human cruelty committed by the minions of evil dictators and corrupt regimes. The assumption that Christian soldiers – fighting a 'just war' with families at

**A War Crimes Tribunal**

home waiting to read their letters – do not commit atrocities was wrong. Historians, and a few reporters, began to whisper the name Jacob Smith – 'Howling' Jake or 'Hell-roaring' Jake to his friends.

On 21 December 1898, President William McKinley of the United States made the following declaration about the future of the Philippines, newly conquered during the Spanish–American War:

> It should be the earnest and paramount aim of the military administration to win the confidence, respect and affection of all the inhabitants of the Philippines by assuring them in every possible way that full measure of individual rights and liberties which is the heritage of a free people, and by proving to them that the mission of the United States is one of 'benevolent assimilation', substituting the mild sway of justice and right for arbitrary rule.[4]

The Filipinos had assumed that once their 300-year occupation by Spanish colonial rulers was brought to an end, the Americans would be true to their word and grant freedom to the indigenous people. They did not expect the Americans to begin any 'assimilation', benevolent or otherwise. The Americans, however, had come to the Philippines to build schools and, by God, anyone who got in their way would learn a sharp lesson. US General Shafter had suggested that it might be necessary to kill half the population of the Philippines in order to bring justice to the other half.[5] This might have involved torture and genocide but these were not crimes, apparently, if the end goal was to create a democratic society. It was the argument of the Inquisition all over again – burn the heretic to save his soul. It was how the advocates of bombing civilians have justified themselves in wiping out whole cities to save their inhabitants from Nazism, Communism, terrorism, fundamentalism and so on.

Laws are silent in times of war and memories are conveniently short. In 1902, in an example of imperialist amnesia, President Theodore Roosevelt called the recent American war to suppress the Filipino Revolt the 'most glorious in US history' and a 'triumph of civilisation over the black chaos of savagery and barbarism'. This alone should have been enough to send the rock carvers back to Mount Rushmore to remove his likeness from the cliffs there. In fact, the war was one of the most disgraceful episodes in the whole history of Western imperialism.

Only atrocities like the German suppression of the Herero people between 1904 and 1908, and the brutalisation of the Congolese natives by the officials of King Leopold of Belgium during the 1890s bear comparison with the American treatment of the Filipinos.

The American press was driven by jingoism. As the *Baltimore American* wrote, 'It is the same old law of the survival of the fittest. The weak must bend to the strong and today the American race is the sturdiest, the noblest on earth.'[6]

Although by 1902 some of the allegations of atrocities were being leaked by the press, the *New York Times* predicted that the response of the American people would be that they would 'take another sip of their coffee and remark, "How very unpleasant!" before continuing with their breakfast'. They were right precisely because politicians like 'Teddy' Roosevelt had so convinced the voters that US troops could do no wrong. He conceded that there were 'a few acts of cruelty' in retaliation for 'the hundreds committed by the Filipinos' but these were a small price to pay for the advance of civilisation. One American journalist wrote:

> There is no question that our men do shoot niggers somewhat in the sporting spirit . . . They do not regard the shooting of Filipinos just as they would the shooting of white troops. This is partly because they are only niggers.[7]

In recent years, American textbooks have downgraded the Filipino rebellion from a war to an insurrection against US rule. This is a complete distortion of the truth. There never had been any American rule before the Spanish were driven from the Philippines and so how could the Filipinos be insurgents against something that the conquerors had never possessed? The Americans were trying to establish their rule against the wishes of the Filipinos and that is why they were facing resistance. It was all about freedom. But the Americans had a special view of freedom. Only they understood the meaning of a word that was infinitely flexible in their hands. Just as the Inuit are supposed to have many different words for snow, so the Americans had as many for freedom. German philosopher Theodor Adorno summed it up: 'People have so manipulated the concept of freedom that it finally boils down to the right of the stronger and richer to take from the weaker and poorer whatever they have left.' The concept did not exist in other languages. Ronald Reagan once claimed there was no word for 'freedom' in

Russian. There is. *Svoboda* is just not recognised by American readers.

This has been the eternal problem of US foreign policy. The Americans have insisted on being described as 'liberators' when they have often been invaders/conquerors. In the Philippines, nobody had asked them either to come in the first place or to stay when they had won their 'splendid little war' against Spain.

In 2003, the story of the Filipino Revolt earns little more than a footnote in books on American history. It is not difficult to see why. The racial attitudes of American soldiers, generals and enlisted men alike, provide a chilling introduction to a century that has seen genocide on a level undreamed of in earlier centuries. In a sense these American servicemen were only reflecting the prejudices of the age in America. The massacre of 3,000 Filipinos by US troops in Manila in 1899 provoked the following editorial from the *Chicago Tribune*:

> The slaughter at Manila was necessary but not glorious. The entire American population justifies the conduct of its army at Manila because only by a crushing repulse of the Filipinos could our position be made secure. We are the trustees of civilisation and peace throughout the islands.[8]

The *Salt Lake City Tribune* commented:

> The struggle must continue till the misguided creatures there shall have their eyes bathed in enough blood to cause their vision to be cleared, and to understand that not only is resistance useless, but that those whom they are now holding as enemies have no purpose toward them except to consecrate to liberty and to open for them a way to happiness.[9]

The trustees of civilisation and peace had acquired their own skills during the extermination of the Native Americans. Significantly, most of the senior American officers who served in the Philippines had experience of the Native American wars and some, including 'Howling' Jake Smith himself were at the massacre of 300 Sioux, most of them unarmed women and children, at Wounded Knee in 1890. For this atrocity, 18 Congressional Medals of Honour were awarded to members of the 7th Cavalry who carried out the killings.[10]

During the 1899–1902 war in the Philippines, American soldiers shared the nationalist and racist zeal of their officers and fought the

Filipino 'enemy' with a brutality that frequently tipped over into lawlessness. Racism, prevalent in the United States at this time, played a major role in the war crimes committed by American personnel. One of the most common forms of torture was the so-called 'water cure', which took this form:

> The water cure was the favoured method for extracting information from Filipino prisoners. The Filipino was held down and a funnel used to force water into their mouth. The prisoner was made to swallow water until their stomach was distended and near bursting. Then the Americans would pump the water back out. If the prisoner still wouldn't talk, the process was repeated, sometimes as many as a dozen times. In a crueller version of the water cure, Americans simply poured water continuously over the prisoner's head. The prisoner couldn't breath without inhaling water, and they would slowly drown as their lungs filled up. The water torture rarely failed; even the most patriotic Filipino couldn't hold out for long. While most American commanders denied that the so-called 'water cure' was ever used, reports of it from Filipino prisoners and mentions in soldiers' letters and journals make it seem certain.[11]

The American soldiers were men of their time who knew of and might even have participated in racist lynchings in their hometowns and cities. Their white-supremacist attitudes were shared by even the most senior politicians, including the head of Princeton University and future President, Woodrow Wilson. A repeated theme of the veterans who told of their personal experiences is the dehumanisation they had grown up with as children, usually in the poorer areas of the old Confederacy long before they enlisted. This is clear from the language they used in their letters home and their willingness to kill and torture Filipino civilians whom they always referred to as 'niggers'. Serving soldiers felt no reason to conceal their actions from their families. One US soldier wrote home: 'I am in my glory when I can sight my gun on some dark skin and pull the trigger . . . Tell all my enquiring friends that I am doing everything I can for Old Glory and for the America I love so well.' Another wrote, 'Our fighting blood was up and we all wanted to kill "niggers".' A third added, 'No cruelty is too severe for these brainless monkeys . . . the boys fill the blacks full of lead before finding out whether they are friends or enemies.'[12]

The officers set no better example. Six American officers were officially 'reprimanded' for torturing prisoners and then shooting them, whilst one officer – a persistent offender – was fined $300 for 'acute' torture of prisoners. When an officer was actually sentenced to 5 years' imprisonment for killing a prisoner, the verdict was quashed by President Theodore Roosevelt and substituted by the loss of 35 places in the seniority list for promotions. Major Edward Glenn admitted that he made 47 prisoners kneel and pray before having them bayoneted to death.[13] The list of such atrocities is seemingly endless. The ex-Confederate general 'Fighting Joe' Wheeler tried to explain away American atrocities by saying that the Filipinos had mutilated their own dead, murdered women and children, and burned their own villages to discredit the US army. He was disproved by his own officers, like Captain Elliott of the Kansas Regiment, who wrote, 'Talk about war being "hell", this war beats the hottest estimate ever made of that locality. Caloocan was supposed to contain 17,000 inhabitants. The 20th Kansas swept through it, and now Caloocan contains not one living native.' Leonard F. Adams of the Washington Regiment added:

> I don't know how many men, women and children the Tennessee boys did kill. They would not take any prisoners. One company of the Tennessee boys was sent into headquarters with 30 prisoners, and got there with about 100 chickens and no prisoners.

Colonel Funston of the 20th Kansas Volunteers wrote:

> The boys go for the enemy as if they were chasing jackrabbits . . . I, for one, hope that Uncle Sam will apply the chastening rod, good, hard, and plenty, and lay it on until they come into the reservation and promise to be good 'Injuns'.[14]

The US army later strongly denied killing prisoners and injuring Filipinos, but their explanation for the extraordinary battle statistics might have originated from Gestapo headquarters. Whereas casualty figures from nineteenth-century wars, including the American Civil War, recorded a usual proportion of five injured men to each man killed, the figures from the Philippines were unprecedented: fifteen Filipinos killed to each man wounded or captured. Successive US commanders, General Otis and General Arthur MacArthur, had deeply racist explanations, clearly at odds with the truth. Otis attributed the high kill-count to the excellent marksmanship of the rural Southern soldiers; MacArthur added a nasty twist by explaining that Filipinos simply died more easily than the Anglo-Saxons because they were of an inferior race.[15]

Such treatment of prisoners and civilians, if carried out by Germans or Japanese soldiers in the Second World War, would have seen the perpetrators tried by post-war courts. Instead, the Americans who committed these atrocities returned home to America with their crimes on their consciences but not on their records. These men were military heroes to the American people, even though their crimes were as cruel and terrible as those committed by men who today face international outrage. At the time, Dr Henry Rowland excused actions of American soldiers because of the heat and the fact that the vertical sun impairs judgement.

For an army bringing 'democracy' to a benighted people, there was a shameful amount of looting of the much-abused Filipinos by the superior representatives of 'civilisation'. The following could have been written by a latter-day Goth or Vandal pillaging ancient Rome:

> I have six horses and three carriages in my yard, and enough small plunder for a family of six. The house I had at Santa Ana had five pianos. I couldn't take them, so I put a big grand piano out of a second-storey window. You can guess its finish.

E.D. Furnam of the Washington Regiment wrote home:

> We burned hundreds of houses and looted hundreds more. Some of the boys made good hauls of jewellery and clothing. Nearly every man has at least two suits of clothing, and our quarters are furnished in style; fine beds with silken drapery, mirrors, chairs, rockers, cushions, pianos, hanging-lamps, rugs, pictures, etc. We have horses and carriages, and bull-carts galore, and enough furniture and other plunder to load a steamer.[16]

On 27 September 1901, following the killing of 59 US soldiers in Balangiga on the island of Samar, military command of Leyte and Samar was handed over to Brigadier-General Jacob Smith, a man with a reputation for giving no quarter and who was responsible for much of the slaughter of what he called the 'savages' in Batangas. Famed for his terrifyingly loud voice, he was originally called 'Hell-roaring' Jake. In the aftermath of the Balangiga incident Smith allowed his emotions to get the better of his judgement, issuing the famous order to Major Littleton Waller, 'I want no prisoners. Kill and burn and the more you kill and burn the better you will please me.' Smith said that anyone over the age of ten was old enough to be a rebel and should be shot. He ordered Waller to turn Samar Island – the centre of Filipino resistance – into a 'howling wilderness'.[17]

Waller marched 300 Marines through the central part of Samar during which he carried out atrocities as Smith had ordered, only to find on his return he was facing court martial. At his trial he defended himself by claiming that he was only following General Smith's orders and was exonerated. However, when the American press became aware of 'Howling' Jake's activities they demanded the general's court martial as well. During Smith's trial much evidence was found of his cruelty earlier in the war. He had routinely fired on Filipinos carrying white flags, imprisoned prisoners in crowded railroad trucks with no toilet facilities and posed for photographs in front of his 'cattle pens', boasting to the press about the death rates he had achieved. The *New York Evening Post* advocated his execution if found guilty of atrocities.

General Smith was found guilty of 'conduct to the prejudice of good order and military discipline' but he was sentenced only to be 'admonished'. The court insisted that Smith had not meant what his famous order to Waller had seemed to imply. Outside the court, however, Smith immediately declared that he had meant every word of it and that burning and shooting the Filipinos was the only way to win the war.

In Washington, the decision was taken to have Smith declared insane in an attempt to silence him but before this could be done a letter from a soldier in the Philippines revealed that 1,300 prisoners in Batangas had been forced to dig their own graves before being shot over a period of 6 days. Even the Catholic priest who had heard the confessions of the prisoners had been hanged to silence him.

When 'Howling' Jake Smith returned to the United States he was welcomed as a national hero. The docks at San Francisco were lined with people cheering the returning general and his medical officer defended him to the press:

> It makes me sick to see what has been said about him. If people
> knew what a thieving, treacherous, worthless bunch of

scoundrels those Filipinos are, they would think differently than they do now. You can't treat them the way you do civilised folks.[18]

Perhaps the American people of 1902 got the army they deserved. Was the same true in Vietnam in 1968?

On 16 March 1968, 'Charlie' company of 1st Battalion, 20th Infantry led by Second Lieutenant William Calley Jr was ordered to enter the village of My Lai in search of Viet Cong. Only in unusual circumstances – and the Vietnam War was one of them – would a man of Calley's low intelligence have been given command over men in battle. During the operation, Calley ordered his men to kill the villagers and up to 80 US soldiers participated in the massacre of 500 unarmed people. Vietnamese women, children and elderly men were stabbed with bayonets, women and young girls raped and then shot in the back of the head or blown to pieces by grenades. At his subsequent court martial, Calley, the only person convicted in the case, said, 'I felt then – and I still do – that I acted as directed, I carried out my orders, and I did not feel wrong in doing so.'

The rights and wrongs of soldiering have never been more brutally exposed than on this day. While the massacre was taking place in My Lai, from a helicopter flown by US army pilot Hugh Thompson, the crew could see groups of Americans killing helpless villagers. There was no enemy fire. Only the Americans were firing their guns. As Thompson flew over the eastern side of the village he saw dozens of bodies piled in an irrigation ditch, while US soldiers were standing nearby, taking a cigarette break. Thompson set his helicopter down near the irrigation ditch full of bodies. He asked a sergeant if the soldiers could help the civilians, some of whom were still moving. The sergeant suggested putting them out of their misery. Thompson turned to Lieutenant Calley in astonishment but was told to mind his own business. Next he saw several elderly adults and children running for a shelter chased by Americans. Thompson landed his chopper between the troops and the shelter, jumped out and confronted the lieutenant in charge. Asking for assistance in escorting the civilians from the bunker, Thompson was told the only help the 'gooks' would get was from a hand grenade. Thompson told his crewmen in the helicopter that if the American soldiers fired, they were to shoot them.

Thompson next coaxed the Vietnamese out of the shelter and radioed for other helicopters to land and fly the four adults and five children to safety, which they did within minutes. Before returning to base, Thompson saw something moving in the irrigation ditch – a child about four years old. He had a son of his own and was overcome by emotion. He immediately flew the child to a nearby hospital and then told his superiors what had happened.

The subsequent Pentagon investigation was cursory to say the least. It eventually concluded that nearly 80 soldiers had participated in the killing and cover-up, although only Calley was court-martialled. The eyewitness testimony of Thompson and his crewmen proved crucial. But instead of thanking them, America vilified them. Many saw Calley as a scapegoat for regrettable, but inevitable, civilian casualties. 'Rallies for Calley' were held all over the country. Jimmy Carter, then governor of Georgia, urged citizens to leave car headlights on to show support for Calley. Thompson, who got hostile letters and death threats, remembers thinking: 'Has everyone gone mad?' He feared that he might face a court martial for his command to fire, if necessary, on US soldiers. It was not until 6 March 1998, 30 years after the My Lai massacre, that Thompson and Colburn, his remaining crewman, finally received medals for their humanity in a ceremony at the Vietnamese Veterans Memorial in Washington.

It took 30 years for America to remember the humanity it shares with the rest of the world. Unfortunately, within 30 minutes of William Calley's court martial the racial prejudice that had underpinned the United States since its inception flared up everywhere. The idea that the only good 'gook' is a dead 'gook', just as the only good 'Indian' is a dead 'Indian' and the only good 'nigger' is a dead 'nigger' broke out like a rash on the face of America.

Calley had been court-martialled, like Smith 70 years before, and found guilty of murdering at least 22 South Vietnamese civilians. Sentenced to hard labour for life, Calley received more lenient treatment than he deserved when President Nixon intervened to reduce his sentence to three years house arrest at Fort Benning, with the privilege of having his girlfriend visit him regularly.

For many Americans, Calley was the hero. The governor of Indiana ordered all flags on state buildings to fly at half-mast because of Calley's conviction. The governor of Alabama showed similar support, saying, 'I can't believe an American serviceman would purposely shoot any civilian. Any atrocities in this war were caused by the Communists.'[19] Draft boards in Arkansas, Florida, Kansas, Michigan, Montana and Wyoming resigned in protest, while the American Legion and Veterans of Foreign Wars raised money to lodge an appeal against Calley's conviction. President Nixon received 100,000 letters and telegrams within 24 hours demanding Calley's release.

At Fort Benning, the Reverend Michael Lord told a church congregation, 'There was a crucifixion 2,000 years ago of a man named Jesus Christ, I don't think we need another crucifixion of a man named Rusty Calley.' A record entitled the 'Battle Hymn of Lt William Calley', in which Calley met the great commander in the sky and told him that he had followed orders and done his duty, enjoyed much success, selling 200,000 copies on its day of release. A biography of Calley took the title *The Making of a Hero*. Four out of five Americans felt the result of the trial was a disgrace, which must rank as one of America's most shameful displays of hysteria.[20]

In the aftermath of My Lai, the *Toledo Blade* published a report about the conduct of American troops in Vietnam. My Lai, it revealed, was just the tip of an iceberg. It reported that in 1967 a reconnaissance platoon in the 101st Airborne Division committed 'the longest series of atrocities in the Vietnam War'. For seven months, 'Tiger Force' soldiers moved across the Central Highlands, killing scores of unarmed civilians – in some cases torturing and mutilating them – in a spate of violence never revealed to the American public. Women and children were intentionally blown up in underground bunkers; elderly farmers were shot as they toiled in the fields; prisoners were tortured and executed – ears cut off to wear on necklaces and scalps taken for souvenirs. One soldier kicked out the teeth of executed civilians for their gold fillings like the Nazis in the death camps of the Holocaust.[21]

The army began a criminal investigation but no courts martial were brought. It was revealed that Tiger Force had not been a 'rogue unit'. Its members had done only what they were told, and their superiors knew what they were doing and were encouraging them to do it. The tactic, particularly in free-fire zones, was to kill indiscriminately to boost the body count as a measure of success and a reason officers were promoted. Officers as senior as colonels were boosting their body counts in this way.[22]

John Kerry, at the time of writing a senator and presidential candidate, delivered an impassioned speech to the Senate Foreign Relations Committee in April 1971. American troops in Vietnam, he said, had:

> . . . raped, cut off heads, taped wires from portable telephones to
> human genitals and turned up the power, cut off limbs, blown up

bodies, randomly shot at civilians, razed villages in fashion reminiscent of Genghis Khan, shot cattle and dogs for fun, poisoned food stocks and generally ravaged the countryside of South Vietnam in addition to the normal ravage of war, and the normal and very particular ravaging which is done by the applied bombing power of this country.

## The American Way of War

The final days of Operation Desert Storm in 1991 saw the American High Command walking a tightrope on war crimes. Through the use of high-technology weapons, American forces had moved away from their much-vaunted sanitised war towards a ruthless fundamentalism unknown in Western warfare since colonial days. The unnecessary slaughter of thousands of beaten Iraqi soldiers, unable to offer resistance to American firepower or even to surrender, was a shocking crime against humanity and a breach of the Geneva Convention.

The burial alive of Iraqi infantry in their trenches by US bulldozers in 24–5 February 1991 was the first of two incidents which clearly qualified as war crimes. Aware that the operation would be so emotionally charged that it was best hidden from the American people, the army command ensured that no journalists were allowed to witness it. Only through reports from the troops that participated did the details reach reporters and through them the American people.

Up to 8,000 Iraqi conscripts were occupying First World War-style trenches along a 70-mile front of what was called the 'Saddam Line'. Two brigades from the US army's 1st Infantry Division (Mechanized) – known as 'The Big Red One' – were equipped with ploughs mounted on tanks and combat earthmovers. As the vehicles approached the trenches, Iraqi resistance collapsed but the Americans had no intention of taking any prisoners. The Iraqis had no opportunity to escape or surrender before they were trapped under avalanches of sand.

As one witness reported, 'After so many thousands of prisoners, the order came down that it was endangering our men to capture any more. There were so many at once – it seemed like a trick. No one knows how many of those soldiers were trying to surrender.'[23]

Colonel Anthony Moreno, who commanded the lead brigade, reported on the attack, 'What you saw was a bunch of buried trenches with people's arms and legs sticking out of them. For all I know, we could have killed thousands.'[24]

Iraqi casualties will never be known as armoured combat earthmovers came behind the armoured burial brigade levelling the ground and smoothing away projecting Iraqi arms, legs and equipment. It was like a scene of biblical destruction. Not even the corpses were left behind to show that there ever had been an Iraqi army there.

Months later, the question posed by *Time* magazine was merely rhetorical: 'Were thousands of Iraqis buried alive during the allied operation against their front line last February?'[25] The army rationalised the operation, minimising casualties and blaming those who died for refusing to surrender. Under pressure from the media, an elaborate legal justification was sent to Congress by Secretary of Defense Dick Cheney. The Pentagon had decided that a gap in the laws governing warfare made it legally permissible for the US to have denied the Iraqi troops the chance to surrender. The issue was apparently one of 'reasonableness'. The Americans were reasonable and the Iraqis were unreasonable. And that was all that need be said to quieten any public unease about this merciless demonstration of war at its most brutal and unequal.

The other massacre of retreating Iraqis along the so-called 'Highway of Death' took place on 2 March after the ceasefire. Unlike the burial alive of the Iraqi conscripts, this was felt to be a prime-time television spectacular and was shown widely. The fact that it was an air operation against ground forces and Iraqi civilians would evoke a lesser emotional reaction. Or so it was thought. Yet the scene evoked images of hell for one soldier. 'It was like driving through Dante's inferno,' said Lieutenant Bill Feyk. Sergeant First Class Larry Porter admitted: 'I don't think my wife needs to know what took place out there. I do not want her to know that side of me.' A reporter from *The Independent* who later visited the scene of the carnage wrote, 'I lost count of the Iraqi corpses crammed into the smouldering wreckage or slumped face down in the sand.'

American aircraft bombed the front and back of the Iraqi convoys, trapping thousands of vehicles in a 'killing box', ten lanes wide by seven miles long. As if unwilling to miss the fun, American aircraft joined spirals of planes banked up and waiting their chance to join what they called a 'turkey shoot'. Not since the 'Marianas Turkey Shoot' in 1945 had war been such fun. The massacre went on for hours, during which time tens of thousands of vehicles were destroyed by US jets. There were few human survivors.

The degree to which the Pentagon and White House managed the news during the first Gulf War is exemplified by the systematic way that the human costs of the one-sided war were sanitised out. All photographs taken or owned by the major picture agencies and showing bodies were mysteriously ordered to be removed from circulation to the public through the mass media, and indeed from media files altogether. This disappearance and possible destruction of perhaps hundreds of news photos not only distorts both the conduct and the effects of the war; it also means that historians will never have the photographic record that has been available after other past conflicts involving the United States.

## Amherst and Amritsar

In case anyone assumes I am being unfair in concentrating on American war crimes, I cannot conclude without looking at two of the more infamous occasions where the British lowered their standards.

British Field Marshal Jeffrey Amherst had a fine military record during the late eighteenth century but his Native American policy in the 1760s cost him his command in North America and had him recalled to England. Amherst's total hatred for the Indians led him to plan their total extermination as atonement for their atrocities against the American colonists in general and two of his own personal friends, Sir Robert Davers and Lieutenant Robertson, in particular.

What he planned was one of the earliest examples of biological warfare, although the final proof of his success is elusive.[26] Amherst wrote to Colonel Bouquet, the commanding officer at Fort Pitt, to tell him of a plan to give blankets infected with smallpox to the Indians in the hope that the disease would spread throughout the entire Indian nation and kill as many as possible. Bouquet replied, 'I will try to inoculate the bastards with some blankets that may fall in their hands and take care not to get the disease myself.'[27]

Amherst was clearly planning genocide on the grounds that the Indians had 'forfeited all claims to the rights of humanity'. Documents and letters of 1763 testify that Amherst knew exactly what he was doing and that the blankets were given to the Indians. A soldier at the fort wrote in his journal, 'Out of our regard to them we gave them two blankets and a handkerchief out of the Small Pox Hospital. I hope it will have the desired effect.'[28] Apparently some blankets were given to the Indians and several tribes in the Ohio Valley did suffer an outbreak of smallpox a short time later.

174

The movement for Indian independence after 1918 was accompanied by many acts of violence against European civilians. The British establishment was frightened by the growing street violence in the Punjab and felt they needed a tough man of action. As a result, General Dyer, with just over 1,000 British, Indian and Gurkha troops, was moved to Amritsar, where he heard from the deputy commissioner about the savage beating of a missionary lady, Miss Sherwood. The commissioner had already issued a warning that assemblies of more than four Indians would be fired on, and Dyer received orders from the viceroy himself to the effect that if troops were used an example should be set.

When a meeting was called in the Jallianwala Bagh, an open space of about an acre surrounded by houses and walls, it was an intentional act of defiance. The people had been warned that the British would fire on such crowds, yet that afternoon nearly 20,000 of them assembled to hear speeches.

The British response was hysterical. One British surgeon suggested bombing the crowd from the air. The lieutenant-governor of the Punjab declared Amritsar under martial law and Dyer set off to deal with the crowds in the Jallianwala Bagh. With a small force of infantry, and 25 Sikhs and 65 Gurkhas, only half of whom were armed with rifles, he drove to the meeting accompanied by his 2 armoured cars. The entrance to the *bagh* was very narrow and so the cars were left behind and the troops marched up an alley and then straight into the arena.

Without hesitating, Dyer ordered his men to open fire into the crowd. At first there was a shocked silence and then someone shouted, 'They are only blanks.' But they were not blanks, and as the blood flowed people screamed and panicked, looking for a way out. Every exit was blocked and the only way out was the way Dyer's men had come in. The soldiers fired indiscriminately and once their magazines were empty they reloaded and kept firing. For some 10 minutes they kept up the killing, firing altogether some 1,650 rounds. Although Dyer claimed he had not seen any women or children, there were certainly many among his victims. Despite inflicting casualties of 379 killed and over 1,000 wounded, the British made no effort to help anyone, simply marching off the way they had come. Dyer had no doubts about what he had done and his decision was immediately endorsed by the lieutenant-governor. Among the British community Dyer was viewed as a hero and praised for his moderation.

It is doubtful if Dyer's mind was quite balanced during this period.

Because of the attack on the missionary, Miss Sherwood, Dyer ordered anyone wishing to use the lane where the attack took place to crawl down it on hands and knees. Anyone refusing to do so was promptly flogged. The spate of flogging spread to other parts of the Punjab, culminating in an extraordinary incident in which all the members of a wedding party at Kasur were flogged for breaking the curfew.[29]

When news of all this reached England, Winston Churchill denounced Dyer in the House of Commons for this 'monstrous event'. The Hunter Committee was immediately set up to investigate the Amritsar Massacre and condemned Dyer for firing on the crowd without warning and continuing to fire until he had exhausted his ammunition. Dyer was relieved of his command and ordered back to England where he was received as a hero and a public subscription raised over £25,000, making him a rich man – to the eternal shame of the British people.

To lower the tone a little, this chapter ends on a note of cynical humour from Will Rogers. It is something for the Americans to reflect upon: You can't say civilisation don't advance . . . for in every war they kill you a new way.

# CHAPTER 11

## *God Only Knows . . .*

Since the collapse of the Soviet Union, the United States of America has declared that it is a law unto itself, and the world has become suddenly lost in American dreams of how things are and how they should be. For many, the American victory in the Cold War was merely another sign of American exceptionalism, to use one description of the phenomenon, or sanctimonious self-deception, to use another, less kind, observation. Today, too many Americans believe that they are the 'chosen people', their actions ordained by God. The nation is dominated by a strident religiosity stemming from the language of the early settlers, which seems strange and frightening to foreigners, hinting as it does at fanaticism and fundamentalism.

In the aftermath of the 9/11 tragedy, President George W. Bush could have been excused for saying almost anything in the heat of the moment. Expletives can be deleted and if the destruction of the two giant buildings was not worth a 'F****** Hell!' then nothing ever has been. What cannot so easily be excused are the words that actually did pass his lips: Crusade, War and Civilisation. Osama bin Laden's victory on 11 September 2001 was not in the number of innocent victims who were killed in the World Trade Center and the Pentagon, nor in the fact that he virtually paralysed the will of the greatest military power on earth. The triumph of terrorism on 11 September was what it revealed about America. In a matter of minutes, the United States became frozen with fear and the terrorists were able to force the world's only superpower to dance to their tune. Not only did they force it to undermine its own democratic values by stifling free speech but they also caused it to stumble blindly into a mire of confused policy, which led to war in Afghanistan and Iraq.

When President Bush used the 'C' word – Crusade – he was sending a message to Muslims everywhere. Just as the Christian world had once before invaded the lands of Islam now it would do so again, and it would use its enormous military power to overthrow the 'one true faith'. And just as the faithful had fought then against the Christians they must now do so again, joining forces to resist the new threat. By talking of a 'clash of civilisations', Bush was adding an apocalyptic flavour to the struggle, which the terrorists would not be slow to exploit. While Bush and his advisers believed they were setting the agenda, they were, in fact, merely responding in the way it had been hoped they would.

The word 'crusade' carries historical and cultural baggage for whoever hears it. It triggers in the minds of any audience contentious issues of faith. For the Christian, it means something noble: a pilgrimage through hardship and adversity, both physical and spiritual, towards a destination where sins will be forgiven and service rewarded – to reach the spiritual Jerusalem will involve danger and suffering, but there is also the hope of redemption through violence.

Muslims naturally do not see it that way. In their view, at the time of the historical Crusades, it was their world that represented the height of civilisation. They were the heirs of the ancient world and had absorbed the legacy of Greece and Rome. Their cities in Egypt, Spain, Iraq and Persia were the world heritage sites of their time. In all the arts and sciences, the Muslims were far ahead of the Western Christians, while in medicine and mathematics the Arabs excelled.

Only, perhaps, in the art of warfare did the Westerners surpass their enemies. The Christian Crusaders were seen as uneducated barbarians of the sort Rome had faced in the fifth century. They were described universally as Franks and their love of fighting was only matched by their greed for land and loot. They were quite unlike the Byzantines – the Eastern Christians – alongside whom the Muslims had lived for centuries and whose civilisation was ancient and worthy. The Franks, on the other hand, were uncouth, unwashed and untrustworthy.

By the late eleventh century a concept of 'holy war' had evolved in Western Christendom. Built upon the Augustinian notions of the 'just war', the 'holy war' went well beyond Augustine's notion.[1] Not only was 'holy war' not offensive to God, it was actually thought to be positively pleasing to Him. Participants were not merely regarded as acting morally, they were fighting in a blessed cause that merited God's special favour. Those who travelled to the Holy Land did so as potential Christian martyrs. In 1095, those who took the cross were told:

> To kill Christians is a matter of horror; but it is not wicked to flourish your sword against Saracens. That is righteous warfare, and it is charity to risk your life for your brothers. Do not trouble about the concerns of tomorrow. Those who fear God want nothing, nor those who cherish Him in truth. Moreover, the possessions of the enemy will be yours, since their treasures will be the spoil for your victorious arms. Or if your blood gushes out, and you die, you will have gained everlasting glory.[2]

Towards the end of March 1096, crowds of poor Crusaders began to leave northern France on their way to the East led by Peter the Hermit, a fanatical French monk who expected God to show him the way, and a knight known as Walter Sans-Avoir, 'the Penniless'. First they moved through Germany, picking up large numbers of German Crusaders, including two monks named Gottschalk and Volkmar, and Count Eimich of Leiningen, who seemed to have his own agenda and claimed to have a cross miraculously branded on his back.

Unfortunately, some of the German Crusaders had no intention of following the cross to Jerusalem but were planning to exploit the opportunity to attack the Jews of the Rhineland cities. French Jews had written to those in Germany warning them of the danger of Peter's Crusaders but unwisely they assumed that the rowdier elements would be kept under control by their leaders, though with Count Eimich as one of the leaders this was never going to happen. In fact, Eimich used religious arguments to justify some of the pogroms that followed. As he claimed, why did one need to go all the way to Jerusalem to kill the Muslims who had seized the holy places of Christianity, when the people who had killed Christ were living as their neighbours?

At Worms, Eimich's Crusaders killed 500 Jews, even though they were under the shelter of the local bishop and the Crusaders had to violate the laws of sanctuary to do so. The Jews of Mainz sent Eimich a 7 lb weight of pure gold to pass by their city but it was not enough. They had begged the protection of the archbishop himself but Eimich's followers burned the archbishop's palace and killed up to 1,000 Jews. The Crusaders next moved on to Cologne, but warned by the news from Mainz the Jews scattered into the countryside or were sheltered by Christian families.

## PICKING THE BONES

The pogroms spread to Hungary, where the German Crusaders who had followed Volkmar began massacring Jews, but the Hungarians would not allow the atrocities and used force to resist what they saw as a barbarian invasion. After a series of small battles, the German Crusaders were heavily defeated. Count Eimich's Crusaders were not so easily defeated and it took a number of pitched battles by the Hungarians to turn them back at the border. Eventually, many of the German Crusaders were killed, but Count Eimich and some of the worst of his followers were able to return to Germany unharmed. The collapse of these disreputable expeditions cast a cloud over the whole crusading movement. For some observers it seemed to indicate God's disapproval of the whole enterprise.

Peter's own rag-tag army had also reached Hungary, where a dispute with local villagers – apparently over a pair of wooden clogs – escalated and finally resulted in the Crusaders overrunning the town of Semlin and killing as many as 4,000 of the local inhabitants, as well as capturing the citadel overlooking the Sava River. They then crossed the river and burned the city of Belgrade, after pillaging it as if it were the home of the infidels. When the Crusaders attempted to storm the city of Nish, the local Byzantine commander sent in his mounted troops and put them to the sword, killing hundreds, perhaps thousands, of the Christian rabble. The anti-Semitism of the followers of the First Crusade almost ended the crusading movement before it had started.

As soon as Peter's rabble crossed into Asia, they were annihilated by a Muslim army and it was not until Godfrey of Bouillon and the aristocratic commanders took over the crusade that the campaign made better progress. Even so, by the time they reached Jerusalem in the summer of 1099 the Crusaders had gone through many trials and much suffering. Their capture of the Holy City has set the pattern for Christian–Muslim relations ever since. The ferocity of the Christians in 1099 ensured a massacre on a truly appalling scale, accounts of which resonated down the ages.

On 15 July 1099, once they had forced their way into the city, a massacre ensued. The Christians hunted down every living thing in Jerusalem: man, woman, child, even animal. Much of the slaughter was carried out by the poor pilgrims who had accompanied the Crusade and who now fell to their work with any weapon that came to hand: axes, clubs and even sharpened staves. Almost intoxicated by the killing, they hacked at everything in their path. By torchlight, the Muslims of Jerusalem were hunted down, some dying by fire, some by the sword and others, abandoning hope, choosing to leap to their deaths from the highest buildings. As the Crusaders moved through the city it was as if the Angel of Death had passed by leaving nothing living. Even the pots and jars of oil and grain were smashed, and sacks of corn ripped open like the bellies of their human victims.

In the Muslim holy places of the al-Aqsa Mosque and the Dome of the Rock, the bodies lay so thickly piled up that they formed a veritable mound of flesh. Moreover, the Christians had hacked their victims horribly, slashing open their stomachs in search of the gold coins that it was rumoured the Muslims had swallowed to avoid losing them to the invaders. The result was that the blood was literally ankle-deep in some areas of the city, where drainage was impossible. For the Jews, a different fate was reserved. They were herded together into their chief synagogue and burned alive in the great conflagration that followed the assault on that building.

After the fighting was over, many of the Christian knights put aside their weapons and took off their armour, parading to the River Jordan carrying palm fronds like the penitential pilgrims they had been when they left France. Thousands more crowded into the Church of the Holy Sepulchre to celebrate their victory and to thank God for his great goodness, while around them in the streets were the unburied corpses of the Muslim population of Jerusalem. The heavenly city was now more like a medieval version of hell.

Ironically, when the Holy City was recaptured in 1187 by the Muslims under Sultan Saladin, there was no massacre. The Christian population was allowed to leave unharmed after having paid ransoms, and it was said that Saladin himself helped to ransom some of the widows and orphans of those who had fallen in battle against him at the Battle of Hattin.[3]

## And the Bible Begat Violence

How would our modern media report the campaigns of Joshua in Canaan? What would Fox and CNN say as the film of the destruction of Jericho's walls hit the screens? How would Old Deuteronomy – with excuses to T.S. Eliot and Andrew Lloyd Webber – justify the massacre, genocide, enslavement and ethnic cleansing of the Canaanites on the 24-hour news channels?

How do our priests and Sunday school teachers justify telling us, as children, 'And they utterly destroyed all that was in that city, both man and woman, young and old, and ox, and sheep, and ass, with the edge of the sword'?

We are all exposed to the Old Testament in our schools and churches. Yet the Bible relates the fall of Jericho to Joshua in words that would be chilling if we read them in a modern account. And the genocide described is apparently the work of God's 'chosen people'. As far as I am aware, Joshua never appeared before a war crimes tribunal, nor has anyone ever considered the actions of the ancient Israelites in acquiring the 'Promised Land' as genocidal.

## Redemptive Violence

When a nation uses military force to subdue an enemy considered by them to be violent, the 'righteous' nation need not view its use of violence as a product of the same negative force that inspired the enemy. Acting for the benefit of everyone concerned, the 'righteous' nation is justified in its use of violence.

The 'righteous' nation – for the sake of argument lets call them, say, America – by punishing 'unjust violence', 'redeems' its own violence as being 'for the good of the people'. Even the dead can lie happy in the knowledge that they are redeemed.

Gobbledegook, yet powerful gobbledegook.

Television violence, we are told, is often to blame in driving vulnerable, easily led youths to acts of violence. What if a whole society was raised believing that the violent actions of a chosen people might be justified because they were carrying out God's will on earth? This would be absurd if it could ever be proved. How could any ancient history lead a modern state to emulate the 'crimes' committed by a desert people 3,000 years before? Does violence in the name of the Lord redeem the perpetrator? How can he know that he does God's will? Is the argument that you are killing in God's name any better a defence than that used by Hitler's henchmen during the Holocaust: that they were merely following orders? It is the easiest thing in the world to do terrible things once you have surrendered the power to think rationally.

## Killing in the Name of God

On 14 August 1914, a correspondent for the *Catford Journal* wrote, 'What with the war and the rain, last Saturday was a most depressing day for the Catford cricket club.' On the same day more than 10,000

French troops were killed or wounded in the Ardennes and Lorraine. But who's counting?

The following week the *Catford Journal* was taking things in its stride, 'We may be at war in the technical sense with the German emperor but with the German people – never. We must fight; honour demands it. But we must not lose our tempers.'[4]

It would have been interesting, four years later, to have spoken to the same correspondent to see how his temper had stood up to the horrors of world war. Yet, once one has suppressed the modern tendency to sneer and dismiss such evidence of a simpler world, one is entitled to wonder how the people of the pre-war generation were able to adapt so readily to the truly terrible war that lay just ahead. In a word – God. They became Christian warriors in a battle between good and evil sold to them by politicians whose justifications for war could not have convinced anyone without the use of the 'God and my country' card.

In 1914, millions of Europeans with little or no military training answered the call of King and Country, *La Patrie*, Fatherland or Motherland. Patriotism brought them flocking to the recruiting offices but it was the old lie that made them sign up as it had done their ancestors for generations back: 'Dulce et decorum est pro patria mori'.[5] The men of religion – Catholic, Orthodox and Protestant – were the men who finally made the difference. They steadfastly answered the most FAQs of the civilian soldier:

> If it is right for a Christian to die for one's country, is it right for
> a Christian to kill for one's country?

It was the task of politicians to turn civilians into killers, reversing their entire civilian experience where they had been taught to avoid violence and to regard killing as the worst thing a Christian could do. While the instructors taught them the use of the bayonet, the propagandists demonised the enemy by telling lies about them to make it easier for new recruits to accept that it was right to kill them. The hardest job of all, however, was that of dealing with the conscience of Christians who needed to believe they were involved in a 'just war' where God was on their side and approved their violent actions.

Naturally many of the more intelligent recruits realised the irony that on both sides of No Man's Land, men of religion were at work convincing troops from Christian countries that God favoured their cause. The cynicism in this process, though unavoidable, must have undermined the faith of many. A British private summed up this problem:

> I saw some fellows with a German helmet, quite a massive affair with a spread-eagle and a scroll saying *Mitt Gott für König und der Vaterland*. Strikes me God must think we are a pack of fools: surely he can't be on both sides?

In fact, it was not God that was to blame. The politicians were competing for hearts and minds. And, in 1914, religion was the best way to both.

After 1 July 1916 on the Somme, however, it was apparent that God was on neither side.

### A Manhattan, Please

It is one of the oddities of the vast 'cocktail' that is modern America, that all races and creeds have been touched by the same self-righteousness, intolerance and exceptionalism of the original Puritan settlers. It is as if there is something in the spirit at the bottom of the glass. Why at times of crisis do Catholics, Evangelicals, Orthodox Greeks, Jews and even American Muslims use the language of seventeenth-century Puritans? It must be because to be American is to be one of God's Elect, chosen to carry out God's purpose on earth. In *Chosen People*, Clifford Longley explains this phenomenon as follows:

> American Exceptionalism is the doctrine that the United States of America is not just the fitting object of legitimate national pride by its citizens, but is unique among the nations. Thus generalisations which may apply to every other nation do not apply to it.

Essentially, America is a special case in whatever she does and, notably under Republican presidents, she 'can see things that others can't'.[6]

This worrying phenomenon would be laughable if it affected some world leaders with a sense of humour but American politicians, unfortunately, take themselves very seriously. They are, after all, in a line of succession from the ancient Israelites of Moses' time, who had a direct line to God. This idea is peculiar to Protestant biblical theology. As a basis for a nation's foreign policy it might be dismissed as absurd

**God's Chosen People**

if it were not backed up by the most terrifying military arsenal in human history. Even Bismarck and Palmerston would have resisted the urge to kick American diplomats in the butt for their sheer presumption if they had been facing a line of Abrams tanks armed with depleted uranium shells. Yet even the strongest of human weapons is not enough for God's Elect. The Americans, according to George W. Bush, can rely on apocalyptic weapons. Where Wagner's 'Ride of the Valkyries' was once good enough for Hollywood,[7] Bush can now invoke, 'An angel who rides the whirlwind and directs the storm'. Now *that* is impressive. It certainly trumps the Scuds that were the best Saddam Hussein could manage. One small thought does arise – is an angel classified as a weapon of mass destruction?

Faced with this worship of a 'vengeful God' one feels entitled to ask if the United States can still be recognised as a Christian country at all.

It seems to draw its inspiration from the God of Moses rather than the New Testament version favoured by most Christians. Biblical phrases attributed to Jesus like 'Blessed are the peacemakers' and 'The meek shall inherit the earth', no longer suit a people who worship violence so completely that a man who accepted death from his enemies without lifting a finger would today be condemned as a Frenchman. It seems that the Americans have got a crossed line to God.

And who opened this Pandora's box of apocalyptic weapons? The voters – or should I say, the vote-counters – of the great state of Florida. Since the election to the presidency of George W. Bush in 2000, America has been following an exceptionalist agenda in every respect, unilaterally invading Afghanistan and Iraq, rejecting the Kyoto Accord and refusing to be tied by any international agreement.

Longley develops his important thesis by offering two alternative explanations as to how the Americans ended up with the title 'chosen people'. The first is that the English were disqualified and the Americans were awarded the title instead. The same Puritans who won the title for America had originally been part of the group who lost it for England. And this group, of whom let us say Oliver Cromwell stands as a very good example, had originally won it for England when the Jews had been disqualified for participating in the death of Christ.

Until the War of Independence, the English and the Americans had shared the title because God had singled out Anglo-Saxondom for special favours. Britons, for example, were going to 'rule the waves', 'never be slaves' and 'tame haughty tyrants'. However, British policies towards her colonies, and the tyranny of King George III in particular, meant that Britain lost the title, which passed solely to the Americans upon them winning their independence in 1783.

## Republic of Fear

The passage of centuries and the dilution of the Elect by millions of immigrants from throughout the world has not succeeded in giving the Americans the broad multiculturalism that might truly have created a nation that had the best of all the world. Instead of widening experience, emigration to the United States seems to have narrowed perspectives, and freedom has produced fear and paranoia amongst those who previously had nothing to lose. The 'Land of the Free' has become the 'Republic of Fear'. One recalls the words sung by Porgy in Gershwin's opera *Porgy and Bess*: 'Folks with plenty of plenty they've got a lock on the door, afraid somebody's gonna rob 'em while they're out a'making more – what for?' Porgy's question is one for all Americans today. Porgy is closer to the original freedom that America offered than all the corporations with their angst-ridden executives. ''Cause the things that I prize – like the stars in the skies – are all free.'

Irving Berlin's Annie Oakley echoed these sentiments as she sang, 'I've got the sun in the morning and the moon at night.' Ironically, the anti-materialist views expressed here and in Whitman's 'Falling asleep on the gather'd leaves with my dog and my gun by my side' are exactly what Americans have feared to lose, and by doing so have lost already. The conflicting work ethic of the Puritan settlers that brought economic freedom has triumphed over the natural freedom of the frontiersmen like Davy Crockett and Daniel Boone.

I have sought in vain for my source but the impression remains of two grizzled cowpokes discussing the state of things. One says to the other, 'I tell you, things ain't what they wuz.'

To which his partner responds, 'And I'll tell you somethin' else, they never wuz what they wuz.'

Embodied in this half-remembered exchange is much that the historian, as well as the politician, experiences in using history. The passage of time covers past events in so much value-added material that it is a wise event that knows its father.

American history, as used by politicians like Ronald Reagan and George W. Bush, is so romantic and nostalgic that it is either designed to mislead or – to credit the presidents with some integrity – to sacrifice content in order to concentrate on its presentation. To listen to that old showman Ronald Reagan giving his farewell presidential address we might as well have been listening to an actor like Gielgud reading from *The Vision of Piers Plowman*. The world envisioned by Ronald Reagan was not that of 1980s America but that of the Puritan divine John Winthrop. For Reagan, America was that 'shining city upon a hill'.

But the rest of the world has got to live with this seventeenth-century America, armed as it is with the weaponry of the twenty-first century and run not by Puritans but by 'born-again' Christians and by multi-billion-dollar industries committed to their shareholders and keeping their markets. At the same time as Reagan thought of the vision of Winthrop, he was funding the biggest increase in arms in human history. The 'shining city upon a hill' sure knows how to protect itself against any threat, real or, more likely, imagined.

# CHAPTER 12

## *Uncle Sam and the Poodle*

Nations do not have friends, they have interests. What may seem like friendship is merely a coincidence of shared interests. For politicians to read more into it is sentimental and dangerous because shared interests are as likely to cause conflict as widely differing ones. This was the lesson of Suez, when America's stumbling policy under John Foster Dulles forced Britain out of her strategic position in the Middle East.

British politicians since the Second World War have tried to give the impression that Great Britain and her people have benefited from a special relationship with the world's only superpower, the United States. There is some truth in this, but for every Falklands War, where American help was indispensable to Britain's success, there have been other occasions – Suez leaps into the memory – where Britain has had reason to feel aggrieved at an especially unhelpful relationship with America.

The special relationship between Britain and the United States has always seemed more apparent than real, based on wishful thinking on the part of Britons and pure sentiment for most Americans. The relationship has provided a number of marriages of convenience, not as in the novels of Henry James or Edith Wharton for the Old World to re-dress the New World in the trappings of royalty or at least titled nobility, but between politicians – like Winston Churchill and Franklin Roosevelt, Margaret Thatcher and Ronald Reagan, and George W. Bush and Tony Blair – where the New World can re-dress the Mother Country in something to cover her rags, while Britain can add an air of faded respectability to the more extreme American adventures.

The truth was that Old Europe ended after the Suez fiasco of 1956. The Anglo-French Entente was no more, as the new friends but even older enemies went their separate ways and a new relationship developed between Britain and the United States. The French recognised that they could no longer operate independently of America and decided that the only way they could hope to retain any influence in the world was as a part of an enlarged Europe. After 1956, therefore, France concentrated her attention on playing a leading part in the emergence of a powerful new Europe. The British facing the same challenge chose to remain within a special relationship with the United States, even if it was only as an outpost of the New World on the edge of the enlarged Europe. The Americans remembered Britain as their 'special ally' only when it suited them, as in 1991 and 2003 over Iraq. At other times, their 'special relationships' with Mexico and Israel weighed far more heavily with them.

The 'special relationship' has been a figment of Britain's imagination for over 60 years. It is a sad reflection on two generations of politicians that the blindness of Winston Churchill in 1940 should have been allowed to cause impaired vision in British politicians ever since. Rather than seeking a future based on a realistic assessment of Britain's condition in 1945 politicians from Churchill to Blair have built and maintained a version of events that has misled the British people and misdirected their efforts ever since. They have claimed that Britain enjoys favourable treatment at the hands of the United States both politically and economically. In times of crisis, the Stars and Stripes can always be relied upon to come to the aid of the Union Jack, the 'Mother Country', and relations between politicians, soldiers and intelligence personnel on both sides of the Atlantic will always be cordial and cooperative. However, George Bernard Shaw once observed, 'England and America are nations divided by a common language.'[1] Shaw's quip is closer to the mark than most. The language that divides us is that of the King James Bible and the Old Testament at that. In fact, Britain and America are different branches of the same evolutionary tree that have been developing seperately for over four centuries. And it shows.

**The Odd Couple**

## The Odd Couple

Britain and the United States have always been uneasy allies. The Americans saw this from the start; the British, deceived by the nostalgic rhetoric of Winston Churchill in 1940, did not. The problem was that Churchill, half American by birth, had grown up during a period of Anglo-Saxon pseudo-culturalism, based essentially on white racism in the 1890s, with its theory that the 'English-speaking peoples' had a divinely inspired mission to take up the 'White Man's Burden' as Kipling put it.

The USA was, in fact, Britain's natural rival as an economic, imperial and naval power. In Paris in 1919, Woodrow Wilson made his anti-British feelings clear when he warned, 'If England insists on maintaining naval dominance after the war, the United States could and would show her how to build a navy.' Later he made matters even clearer, 'You must not speak of us who came over here as cousins, still less as brothers; we are neither.'[2]

Geography, which had given the English the Channel, had been even kinder to America by giving her the Atlantic and the Pacific oceans. Her expansion, when it came, would be far faster and more dynamic than the gradual development of the British Empire over three centuries. Without the German threat in the twentieth century there would have been inevitable Anglo-American naval wars like those between England and Holland in the seventeenth century. Germany presented the threat that brought the two naval powers temporarily together. However, the Americans always resented the Royal Navy, the manifestation of British arrogance that Americans had always felt they left behind when they found a world of their own during the seventeenth century. Significantly, while the Kaiser built bigger and better yachts to out-sail his uncle Edward VII at the Cowes and Kiel regattas, it was eventually the Americans who beat them both.[3] More important even than their opposition to the Royal Navy was America's fundamental hatred of the British Empire.

The relationship that developed between Roosevelt and Churchill, of course, was very special. Churchill was a good dinner companion and great raconteur but was this enough upon which to build a foreign policy? Sometimes it seemed that unlike the American President, Churchill was unable to keep public and private affairs separate in his mind. He was prepared to make concessions to a friend that he would never have made to the leader of another foreign country. Roosevelt, on the other hand, never lost track of the fact that there were many things about Britain and her empire with which he could never agree. Roosevelt's anti-imperialism was always specifically anti-British, while his economic policies sought to benefit from the decline of the British Empire, something on which Churchill tragically miscalculated, forgetting the Americans had their own agenda that was very different from Britain's.[4] Nations could never afford to conduct their affairs like friends, over a drink and a late-night chat.

Like his predecessor Woodrow Wilson, Roosevelt hoped to create a New World Order, no longer dominated by the Europeans but built around the American way of democracy and self-determination. There was no room in this vision for Britain's Victorian legacy of King-emperors in India. Once de-colonisation had taken place, the ex-British lands would provide opportunities for an expanded American economy.

As became clear even before the negotiations at Versailles, many Americans saw no intrinsic benefit for the world in a victorious Britain.

To the Americans, Britain – as much as Germany – stood as the natural obstacle to America's New World Order. The truth is that Britain could have remained a great power only by avoiding war in both 1914 and 1939. In terms of realpolitik, it was America that was Britain's quintessential economic, naval and colonial enemy in the twentieth century. Hitler, on the other hand, was an emotional, symbolic enemy from the past, like Napoleon or Philip of Spain.

## Appeasement

Between 1941 and 1945, Winston Churchill, who had avoided appeasing Germany in the 1930s, appeased America instead. Ironically, he sacrificed Britain to preserve the Empire, and in doing so saved Europe instead and was left with the Commonwealth. From Anglo-American bipartisanship, which grew out of the wartime alliance of Churchill and Roosevelt, what emerged were unilateralism, globalisation and the birth of a superpower. Britain was the nest in which the American superpower incubated.

A mythology has built up that it was in Britain's interests to follow an aggressive policy towards Germany in the inter-war years and that Appeasement was therefore the wrong policy for Britain. The very term 'appeasement' now provokes knee-jerk reactions, being equivalent to the accusation of cowardice in the face of the enemy. Few have stopped to consider what Britain had to gain from fighting a resurgent Germany, either in 1935 or even finally in 1939. The post-war demonisation of Hitler and the German nation has prevented a realistic interpretation of Britain's policy towards Germany in the inter-war years. Nobody in 1935 knew the Hitler of *Kristallnacht* or the 'Final Solution'; nobody in 2003 can ever really understand the Hitler of 1933. One is presented with two Hitlers – the Hitler before and after the Holocaust. Without a triumph of empathy or a chilling objectivity as yet never achieved, even historians can at best try to limit the colouring provided by their own experiences. When politicians speak with certainty about 'appeasement' the listener should take warning.

Britain began the war in 1939 as a net creditor of £3.5 billion, only to end it in 1945 as a net debtor to the extent of £2 billion. The reason was simple – Britain was trying to punch above her weight militarily. The world power of 1890 was trying to fight a world war in 1939–41 on the old battlefields of France and Flanders, North Africa, the Middle East, India, Singapore and Burma, on and under her coastal waters, in the

Mediterranean, in the Atlantic, even in the Indian Ocean and in the air over Britain and Malaya. With an unmechanised army in 1939, she was dependent on the French for any hope of victory over Germany and had no chance of honouring her pledges to Poland.

With defeat staring Britain in the face after the disaster at Dunkirk, it was not in the national interest for Britain to fight on alone, risking bankruptcy as well as invasion. In 1940, Hitler had not proved himself as terrible a dictator as Josef Stalin in Russia and yet Churchill was willing to swallow his profound anti-Communism in order to vanquish the Hun once again. Certainly Hitler was a blackguard by 1940 but he was still a human one. Demonisation was still 18 months away. As John Charmley has shown in *Churchill's Grand Alliance*, the only real beneficiary from a war in which Britain emerged nobly victorious but grievously wounded would have been the United States. Even though Churchill believed Britain would be compensated in some way for her sacrifice, this was never going to happen. That may have been what happened at Harrow when you took the rap for a chum and he repaid you with extra tuck, but in the real world a scornful snort from de Gaulle or an annual Christmas tree from Norway was all you could expect. And for that Britain lost her wealth, her industry and her future: the heaviest price any state has ever had to pay since Carthage fell.

Churchill's monochrome view of Germany and rose-tinted view of the United States required an optician. Yet between 1940 and 1945 Britain was to experience the whole gamut of emotions: from the nadir of Dunkirk and Singapore to the euphoria of the battles of Britain and El Alamein. Yet, all the time Britain believed she was saving the world, she was suffering a financial bankruptcy supervised by our own greatest financial rival.

Few politicians shared Churchill's heroic blindness to the fact that he was fighting America's war for them. If the truth of lend-lease had been revealed earlier, Churchill would have looked like a fool. Anthony Eden had been embarrassed by the 50 destroyers agreement as a 'grievous blow to our sovereignty',[5] but Churchill was less concerned with the destroyers than with winning American good will. America would win Britain the war and save the British Empire from destruction. But, of course, Churchill was wrong. America was a far greater threat to the British Empire than Hitler was. Churchill's misguided sentimental investment in 1940 helped the USA more than Britain. Britain's 'finest hour' was an indirect invitation to the USA to take the world away from

Europe. It was also an invitation for Roosevelt to take Britain's overseas assets and replace Britain as the world power.

Franklin D. Roosevelt was always – at best – Churchill's 'imaginary friend'. This was true because Roosevelt was the US President and America had its own agenda, which was not the same as Britain's. As a politician, Roosevelt was a juggler of interests – he had to be. While Britain stood alone against Hitler in 1940 and 1941, Roosevelt was content to keep Britain in the fight at all costs. If Britain succumbed, then Europe was lost to America and that meant that Germany 'inherited the earth' not the United States. While the price of keeping Britain fighting was merely financial, America could urge Churchill's lion to keep roaring.

Anthony Eden recognised that Britain in 1939 had no realistic war aims other than to maintain the Empire, which could have been achieved by keeping out of the war in the first place. Hitler may have offered a challenge to Britain's traditional 'balance of power' philosophy, for which she had fought Kaiser Wilhelm II, Napoleon and Louis XIV, but he offered no threat to the British Empire as such. Instead, by opting to allow the United States to win hegemony, Britain abandoned her traditions and accepted a junior partnership with an emerging giant. And by doing so, Britain chose to be diminished in victory rather than maintained in defeat – an odd decision for the pragmatic British. A bitter Lord Cherwell observed that the 'fruits of victory which Roosevelt offers seem to be safety for America and virtual starvation for us'.[6] By 1945, Britain had won a 'virtual victory' (it is amazing what you can do with special effects, and America provided the rose-tinted glasses through which generations of Britons could appreciate it).

### The Modus Vivendi

During the latter part of the Second World War, one of the most important if most secret parts of the Anglo-American special relationship was the cooperation in research on an atomic bomb. The collaboration (CPC – Combined Policy Committee) between Britain and America had been agreed at Quebec in 1943, where it was given the code name 'Tube Alloys', and it was later confirmed in the Hyde Park Aide-Memoire of 1944. It was something that was very much tied up in the personal friendship of Churchill and Roosevelt and was supposed to continue after the war ended. However, Roosevelt already had a future role for Britain in his mind. Armed with atomic weapons, Britain could become America's outpost in Europe, 'the sentinel for the New World in the Old'.[7] Unaware of this, of course, Churchill had his own plans for Britain's future and they revolved around a continuing British Empire with great power status based on the same military technology as the United States.

Cooperation on the atomic bomb was always uneasy, with each side prepared to shift from softball to hardball depending on the current status of their own research. Before 1942, Britain was definitely ahead in the work and it was America who was keenest for cooperation. However, once American research moved ahead, it was the British who favoured a pooling of resources and research.

Whereas Roosevelt was content with full cooperation with Britain, his advisers, notably Vannevar Bush and James Conant, were much less willing, realising the significance for the United States of holding the secret of the bomb unilaterally. World leadership was the prize they envisaged and they were not prepared to share this with anyone. The director of the Manhattan Project, General Leslie Groves, sided with Bush and Conant and he gave British scientists grudging access to the research.

The death of President Roosevelt shortly after he and Churchill had signed the secret Hyde Park Aide-Memoire was a blow to the special relationship, followed, as it was, by the defeat of Churchill in the 1945 election and his replacement by Clement Attlee. Britain no longer received anything very 'special' from the Anglo-American relationship and once the Americans had developed the atomic bomb and used it against Japan, the flow of information from America to Britain dried up. This was not a political decision on the part of Truman, but stemmed instead from General Groves and his specialists.

Time and again the Americans revealed that they were not as easygoing as the British might have liked, when negotiating on an issue of national security. They found the British living in a bygone age, where the word of a gentleman still meant something. Once they had seen the immense potential of the new wonder weapon, America's leaders were not keen to share it even with Britain. Having tasted the heady experience of superpower status, the Americans now passed the McMahon Act, which forbade sharing atomic information with any state. Attlee realised that without the atomic bomb Britain would be finished as a great power. His colleague Ernest Bevin wrote in October 1946, 'We have got to have this thing over here whatever the cost . . . we've got to have a bloody Union Jack flying on top of it.'[8]

Following five years of research, Britain had gained co-ownership with America of the Congo uranium ore vital to bomb-making, and in 1947 she had her 50 per cent of it brought to Britain. Then, even at the height of austerity, the Labour government reached the momentous decision that Britain would develop her own atomic bomb independently of the Americans. This turned the tables on the Americans who now found that they could not increase their stocks of uranium to continue their own bomb-making. In the end, to get their hands on some of Britain's uranium America agreed to a 'modus vivendi' by which they would exchange atomic information with Britain in return for access to the uranium. Even so, it was not until 1952 that the British successfully exploded their first atomic bomb, and by that stage America had moved on to thermo-nuclear weaponry.

## Friendly Fire Averted

Much of the bitterness associated with the Suez Crisis was a direct result of the personal relationship that existed between British Prime Minister Anthony Eden and the American Secretary of State, Foster Dulles. In simple terms, they loathed each other. Their relationship was once described like this: 'They were like two lute strings whose vibration never coincided.' Winston Churchill was no great fan of Dulles either, describing him, typically, as 'Dull, Duller, Dulles'.[9]

When Eisenhower became President in 1952, Churchill, once again Prime Minister in Britain, hoped that the close relations that he had had with Ike during wartime would be resumed. He was mistaken. The Americans had changed and Churchill was disappointed to learn that America had no intention of restoring the special relationship, or of treating Britain any differently from her other allies. In fact, Eisenhower found Churchill's hopes for a return to the wartime relationship 'childlike'. As he said, 'In the present international complexities, any hope of establishing such a relationship is completely fatuous.'[10] The period of severe anti-Communism in American life dominated the thinking of the Republican administration, notably that of Foster Dulles himself who was obsessed with the need to combat the Soviets. For this he did not see Britain as the sort of useful ally she had once been. She and France were old colonial powers who would be hostile to the new ex-colonial nationalists America wanted as her allies against Soviet Russia.

When Eden replaced Churchill as Prime Minister in 1955, a major change towards the United States was inevitable. Eden had never taken the same view on the special relationship as Winston Churchill, for whom it meant almost everything. Eden felt that his old boss had sacrificed too much in wartime to maintain the relationship and Eden intended to run a more independent path as Prime Minister.

The erosion of the British position in the Middle East began with the overthrow of King Farouk in Egypt in 1952 by General Neguib and the establishment of a republic. The power behind the movement, Colonel Gamal Abdel Nasser, eventually replaced Neguib in 1954 and negotiated the British evacuation of Egypt and the Suez Canal zone. On 26 July 1954 Nasser proclaimed, 'A new era of friendly relations based on trust, confidence and cooperation exists between Egypt, Britain and the Western countries.'[11] Nasser was seeking to build the Aswan Dam to help modernise Egypt and had secured loans from the World Bank with Anglo-American support.

However, fighting on Egypt's borders with Israel persuaded Nasser to seek arms from the West and when these were refused he turned instead to the Soviets, who fed him arms through the Czech Arms Deal of July 1955. When news of Nasser's shift towards the Communists reached Washington early in 1956, Dulles thought Egypt was blackmailing America and withdrew funding for the Aswan Dam scheme, humiliating Nasser who responded with a knee-jerk reaction. On 26 July 1956, the Egyptian leader nationalised the Suez Canal Company, which had been mainly owned by British and French shareholders, seizing its assets and announcing that in future the canal would be managed by Egyptians for Egypt's benefit. In fact, he hoped to benefit from the tolls charged to ships using the canal, as well as to demonstrate his independence of the Western powers.

From this moment onwards the Suez tragedy was inevitable. John Foster Dulles had blundered by insulting Nasser but it was the British who were going to suffer the consequences. Britain's attitude towards the Suez Canal was proprietorial to say the least. In both world wars the defence of the canal had been a major part of British strategy, which saw it as a hinge for the whole British Empire in India and the Pacific region beyond. Eden, as a foreign policy expert of the old school, could not imagine the canal in hands other than British and regarded its takeover by the nationalist Nasser, who also seemed to be inclining towards the Soviets, as an action that needed a military response from the West. Appeasement of the Fascist dictators in the 1930s, notably over the Rhineland and Czechoslovakia, weighed heavily with British diplomats of the 1950s and Eden feared that if Britain allowed Nasser, a kind of

Mussolini figure, to strike an anti-British stance unchallenged, it would create a domino effect throughout the Middle East, affecting General Glubb in Jordan and Nuri as-Said in Iraq. More than the Suez Canal was at stake in opposing Nasser. Nothing less than the future of Britain as a great power was the real issue and for this Eden was prepared to fight. He found in the French a willing ally and expected Eisenhower to take a similar line. His misreading of the Americans was to prove fatal to Eden's Suez policy as well as to his own premiership. He contacted President Eisenhower by telegram, saying, 'My colleagues and I believe we must be ready, in the last resort, to use force to bring Nasser to his senses. For my part we are prepared to do so. I have this morning instructed our chiefs of staff to prepare military plans accordingly.'[12]

Eisenhower's main concern in the autumn of 1956 was the forthcoming presidential election and his actions convey a fundamental reality of US foreign policy. When an election is in the offing, America has no foreign policy, only a domestic one. In spite of the fact that the crisis over the Suez Canal had grown out of America's failed policy towards Nasser, the settlement of the Egyptian question would have to wait until the incumbent President was comfortably returned to power. What did it matter if the Soviet Russians were on the point of invading Hungary to suppress an independence movement there or that two of the most powerful members of NATO were about to go to war with Egypt in order to restore their colonialist hold on the Suez Canal?

The American chiefs of staff were apparently willing to support a British military response. Eisenhower, however, was not. He was adamant that there were no votes to be won through military action in Egypt. He therefore told Eden, 'I must tell you frankly that American public opinion flatly rejects the thought of using force.'[13] A widening gulf was beginning to develop between the British and the Americans. Both Eden and Macmillan thought Eisenhower would at least stay neutral if Britain did use force to regain the canal and Macmillan thought the President would definitely 'lie doggo' until after the election. The last thing the British leaders expected was an outburst of moral outrage from their favourite American, the only living 'unknown soldier', Dwight D. Eisenhower.

The essential hollowness of the special relationship was revealed in the next few weeks. The threat posed by Hitler's Germany had been enough for Roosevelt to play down the problems he felt about having Britain as a close ally. Operating on a basis of 'sufficient to the day is the evil thereof', Roosevelt realised that one day he would need to face up to the problem of Britain's trade policies and her Empire. However, with a potential German threat to America's world domination unresolved, Roosevelt knew that he dare not endanger the war-winning alliance with Britain and the Soviet Union.

Ironically, it was Roosevelt's death in 1945 that meant that the essential differences between Britain and the United States did not immediately come out into the open. With the onset of the Cold War under Roosevelt's successor, Harry Truman, America's continued need for Britain as an ally kept their major differences hidden. Clearly when Churchill became Prime Minister again in 1951, he presumed the old relationship with America would continue. But the first Republican government in America for 20 years put an end to this hope.

Eisenhower's plans to end Britain's dominant position in the Middle East meant that America could not allow herself to be seen to support such an obvious act of colonial aggression as that which Eden planned in Egypt. Arab opinion would swing away from the United States towards the Soviet Union and in 1956 this could not be allowed to happen. American economic interests in the Middle East were too deeply entrenched to be put at risk. If it came to a choice between old friends and new friends, America would look to the future. Foster Dulles explained this in October 1956:

> For many years now the US has been walking a tightrope between the effort to maintain our old and valued relations with our British and French Allies on the one hand, and on the other try to assure ourselves of the friendship and understanding of the newly independent countries who have escaped from colonialism.[14]

Eisenhower was between a rock and a hard place. Already facing one international crisis with Russia's invasion of Hungary, it seemed inconceivable that Britain of all nations would bring on the sort of incident that she would have condemned out of hand if perpetrated by Italy or Japan in the 1930s. If the US President had known that Britain and France were secretly colluding with Israel to invade Egypt, he would have been convinced that Anthony Eden had lost his senses. As it was, Eden did not give Eisenhower advance notice of the Anglo-French invasion and this was the final straw as far as Ike was concerned. He telephoned Eden in a fury: 'Anthony, have you gone out of your mind? You've deceived me.'[15] For the moment, any idea of a special relationship went out of the window as America used all the diplomatic, economic and financial pressure at her disposal to force Britain to withdraw from Egypt. The Americans engineered a Sterling crisis and when Britain approached the International Monetary Fund for support, she was told by George Humphrey:

> You will not get a dime from the United States Government if I can stop it until you have gotten out of Suez. You are like burglars who have broken into someone else's house. So get out. When you do, and not until then, you'll get help.[16]

On 5 November 1956, Eden accepted a ceasefire. The naughty puppy had come home.

The truth was there had been blunders on both sides, but there was more excuse on the British side than the American. Eden had reacted to Nasser's nationalisation of the canal in the way that great powers had always reacted and, in an era of de-colonisation, the Americans could not be seen to support it. However, if he had resisted American pressure and succeeded in reoccupying the canal zone and toppling Nasser, Eden would have been a hero of the same type as Thatcher after the Falklands. What could not be accepted was his duplicity with France and Israel, and the lies he used to justify himself before Parliament. Here the parallel is surely with Tony Blair in the run up to the 2003 Gulf War when the arguments used to justify his military action fell apart one by one.

The American conduct during the Suez Crisis was deeply unhelpful in many ways. After the crisis, during which Foster Dulles was seriously ill, his judgement and that of the President were revealed as profoundly flawed. Just before his death in 1959, Dulles admitted, 'Perhaps I made a mistake at Suez. I would not have made some of the decisions which I made about Suez had I not been sick at the time.'[17] The Americans, including Dulles, had wanted Eden to overthrow Nasser but he must do it quickly and without seeming to implicate them. They, in the meantime, would get the best of both worlds by winning the friendship of the neutrals but gaining secretly from the 'burglary'. When world opinion exploded in the United Nations against Britain and France, America was forced to climb off the fence and take sides. Eisenhower decided that America had more to gain from kicking her old friends than endangering links with her new allies. As a cynic might observe, with friends like this who needs enemies?

The Americans deserved none of the kudos associated with the British evacuation of Suez. Eisenhower had stabbed an old friend in the back and had humiliated Britain for all the world to see. It was hardly surprising that the level of anti-Americanism in Britain was very high. Nobody could defend Eden for his collusion with France and Israel but neither could they accept that he alone was guilty. Had the Americans supported action against Nasser's seizure of the canal, which after all had been a reaction to American policy, not British, a compromise settlement with the Egyptian leader would have been far more likely. Cinemas and shops refused to serve Americans and at one stage it seemed likely that the United States would be asked to give up her air bases in Britain.[18]

Eventually sentiment saved the day. While France made the brave and decisive decision to ditch her links with America and develop her position in Europe, it was Churchill who was brought out of retirement to carry out repairs to the special relationship. He wrote to Eisenhower:

> Whatever the arguments adduced here and in the United States for or against Anthony's action in Egypt, it will now be an act of folly, on which our whole civilisation may founder, to let events in the Middle East come between us.[19]

This was well received in America and once Eden was sent back to the kennels in disgrace, Macmillan became Prime Minister and the special relationship was resurrected. Nobody spoke of it but it had changed. The ageing British bulldog had become America's poodle.

The most extraordinary, and certainly the most dangerous, event in the history of the Anglo-American special relationship arose from the Suez Crisis. It is not well known to the general public on either side of the Atlantic but its potential for disaster had been very great.

With the American record on 'friendly fire', it is positively amazing that the Anglo-French landings at Suez in 1956 passed off as peacefully as they did. As the Anglo-French fleet of 200 ships, including 5 British aircraft carriers and the French battleship *Jean Bart* approached the Egyptian port of Alexandria on 31 October 1956, the US Sixth Fleet, under orders to evacuate American civilians from Alexandria, decided to place itself directly in the path of the invasion fleet. Clearly the Americans had a secret agenda by which they were instructed to embarrass and obstruct the Allied fleet by any means short of war. When Admiral 'Cat' Brown was ordered to 'go to sea with [his] bombers up, ready to fight anything', there was no evidence of hostile forces in the vicinity of the Egyptian coast, or any forces at all other than the ships of his NATO allies, Britain and France. Unsurprisingly, the admiral asked for clarification of the order. 'Who's the enemy?' asked Brown, to which the reply came: 'Don't take any guff from anybody.' Brown admitted later, 'I didn't know who the enemy was.'[20]

With the politicians calling the shots if not firing them, Secretary of State John Foster Dulles asked Admiral Arleigh Burke if the Sixth Fleet could stop the Anglo-French operation. Burke replied, 'We can stop them but we will blast hell out of them.'[21] Dulles asked if there was any other way. 'If we're going to threaten,' said Burke, 'then you've got to be ready to shoot. We can defeat them – the British and the French and the Egyptians and the Israelis – the whole goddam works of them we can knock off, if you want. But that's the only way to do it.'

And so, on 31 October 1956, a *totentanz* in mime began. While the British and French ships prepared to put troops ashore, the Americans fouled their sonar and radar, illuminated their warships at night with searchlights and buzzed Allied ships. One commander reported, 'Have been continually menaced during past 8 hours by US aircraft approaching low down as close as 4,000 yards and on two occasions flying over ships.' The operation commander, Sir Charles Keightley was quite clear what was happening and reflected that the Sixth Fleet 'endangered the whole of our relations with that country [USA]'.[22]

Just 13 years before, during the Anglo-American landings at Sicily, American naval gunners had demonstrated how 'trigger-happy' they could be as British and American airborne troops flew over them in gliders and C-47 transports. They had massacred 1,200 elite troops from US 82nd Airborne and the British First Airborne in one of the worst ever friendly fire incidents. The proximity of hundreds of Allied and American ships off the Egyptian coast, with the Americans determined to be as provocative as possible, was a formula for just such another tragic incident. What may have saved the situation was the complete lack of fire from the Egyptians, which had it occurred would have complicated matters out at sea.

When the British commanders asked the Sixth Fleet if they would 'kindly' move out of the way so that Britain could get on with her invasion, they were informed – just as kindly – that the Sixth Fleet was in precisely the position ordered by Washington. The message was clear: America disapproved of what Britain was doing and was not prepared to move aside for anyone.

What the British commanders feared most was that the Americans would issue an ultimatum to them to stop the invasion. In this event a major incident was virtually certain, as American planes might have been mistaken for Egyptian ones and American submarines for enemy – possibly Russian – ones. As it was two American submarines were detected around the British ships and ordered to the surface. Meanwhile, American planes were making repeated 'dummy runs' on French warships. With droll statement of the obvious, Admiral Sir Manley Power posited the thought, 'I consider it quite possible that they are obstructing us on purpose as their aircraft flying in the area rendered our air warning virtually useless.'[23]

The political orders to the Sixth Fleet were symptomatic of American confusion over the whole Suez Crisis. Washington was so concerned with that bane of American foreign policy, a presidential election, that even the special relationship was on hold. The problem was that the only British leader to have ever challenged this Churchillian chimera, Anthony Eden, was at that very moment trying to undermine it – and failing.

### Things are Quieter Now

At the time of writing, the trappings of Empire and global power have a Ruritanian flavour as they are unpacked for the state visit of President George W. Bush. Britain is still very much the master of ceremonies even if Britain Inc. is no more than an outlying theme park for USA Inc. where presentation, not content, counts for everything.

### The Special Relationship – Let's Call the Whole Thing Off . . .

- The Americans are empire-building; the British are downsizing.
- The Americans are 'born again' Christians; Britons hardly Christians at all.
- America is the 'Land of the Free'; Britain is the 'Land of the Freebie'.
- The Americans are the 'chosen people'; the British were telephoned first but politely refused.
- The Americans have developed their sense of power; the British their sense of humour.
- The Americans 'liberate' people; the British laugh at them.
- The Americans meet triumph and disaster; the British treat those two impostors just the same.

# CHAPTER 13

## Thanks for the Selective Memory . . .

The most important battle in American history has still to be fought – the one to repair and reclaim the 'collective memory' of the American people. Control of history has been for so long the possession of politicians that only academic historians know the real issues that have made the United States the country it is today. Where a textbook entitles itself the 'triumph' of the American nation or where a politician casually tells people that America is the greatest nation on earth, it is time that the listeners demanded to know on what basis they are being 'sold' these ideas. No country is above criticism and America attracts only contempt and ridicule for its pretensions. With problems in race relations, poverty, crime, human rights and ecological issues, it is madness for anyone to believe that America is the greatest nation on earth. Either that or the world is in a lot more trouble than it seems.

The absence of America's true history is in my opinion the new form of slavery for its people – the slavery of the mind. What is needed is someone to give back the freedom that Americans boast is theirs to give others. They are wrong. Ignorance of their history means that they live in a collective coma, manipulated by politicians whose only aim is to keep them in a state of unease and fear by putting themselves forward as the only men who can save Americans from what lies 'out there' beyond Winthrop's 'shining city on the hill'.

### Lies, Damned Lies and Politics
Presumably 'Saving Private Lynch' was just too good an opportunity to

miss for the Pentagon caption writers. Within weeks everybody would have unconsciously linked the story of Jessica Lynch with the famous Spielberg film and would think 'Ryan' and 'Lynch' virtually interchangeable.[1] Look out collective memory, here comes another slight adjustment. Sit tight and you won't feel a thing. Surely it would be just another of the many lies that had gone into the making of the most duplicitous war in history. Forget the 'crucified Canadians', the 'bayoneted babies' and the 'corpse factory' of the First World War, things are more sophisticated in 2003.

Lynch's story was the stuff of wartime legend. More like Rambo in Vietnam than Nellie Forbush in *South Pacific*, it was reported that Jessica had not given in to her Iraqi assailants but had fought them in a stand-up fight. Jessica, however, later admitted that her weapon had jammed and she had not fired a single shot. According to government propaganda she had been seriously injured in the action behind enemy lines, was captured, tortured and, although severely injured, raped. This story was refuted by Lynch, who said, 'No one even slapped me.' Specialists in the United States later admitted that in view of her injuries had she been raped she would not have survived. The 'feel-good' finale – the dramatic rescue from hospital by US troops – had been staged like a Hollywood scene and filmed.

Jessica Lynch faced an avalanche of publicity after her return from Iraq, much delayed as it had been by her lengthy medical treatment. On 9 November 2003, NBC had broadcast the made-for-TV film *Saving Jessica Lynch*. The following Tuesday, the book *I Am A Soldier, Too: The Jessica Lynch Story*, by Rick Bragg, was published, and the same evening ABC aired its much-hyped interview with the former soldier, conducted by Diane Sawyer. Lynch appeared on the morning talk shows, ending with an appearance on *Late Night with David Letterman*. She was also chosen for the cover of *Time* magazine.

Jessica suspected she was being used as a piece of propaganda and in her own words, 'It hurt.' Suddenly she realised who her real enemies were and was prepared to face up to them. The events surrounding her capture and rescue had been 'massaged' into shape by the Government to boost morale at home and among the troops in Iraq. Jessica had been close to becoming just another piece of false history manipulated by the malignant guardians of America's past.

## A British Civil War

When it comes to military affairs, the Americans are convinced that they can recognise a 'just war' when they see one. Two in which they were involved were just about the 'justest' that anyone ever saw. Surely nobody could find fault with the Second World War, that American crusade against fascism, while their own struggle for independence from Britain was a 'noble' struggle against a tyrant king who threatened to enslave them all. Unfortunately, American accounts of this war have carried such a burden of propaganda that, as Hugh Bicheno and Richard Holmes have shown, history has been almost obliterated.[2] Deliberately falsified versions of the American past have been used to create a national 'collective memory'.

The events of the period from the end of the Seven Years' War in 1763 to 1783 have become ammunition for modern politicians to fire at any critics of their current policies. George III has become as demonised a tyrant as Saddam Hussein, his troops (who between 1756 and 1763 had fought to protect the American colonists against the French in the Seven Years' War) portrayed as little better than Nazis or war criminals;[3] the Loyalists or colonial Tories – numbering between 20 and 30 per cent of all the colonists – are shown as traitors standing in the way of America's divine purpose. This is an example of the winners writing the history. How can those who remain loyal to their king be regarded as unpatriotic? It was the so-called 'Patriots' who were untrue to their heritage. They were traitors not patriots and the Founding Fathers knew that if they failed they would suffer for their treason.[4]

The Founding Fathers were a self-perpetuating oligarchy in the same mould as that which governed the British political establishment – they were not elected, democratic nor respected by the common people they claimed to represent. George Washington and many of his senior commanders were ex-British army officers, and some had settled in America after the Seven Years' War, like Horatio Gates and Arthur St Clair. The foremost slave and plantation owners, men like Washington himself, Charles Carroll of Maryland and Henry Middleton of South Carolina have in the eyes of modern Americans been transformed from immensely wealthy oligarchs into freedom fighters and democrats. These rich landowners are not regarded as the aristocrats they would have been in England at the time but men of the people, a view of themselves they would never have accepted.[5] A survey of US presidents by Forbes.com in 2004 revealed that George Washington had in fact been the richest President in American history.

Any enemy of the Americans became, to the propagandists, evil incarnate – like the British officer Banastre Tarleton, who was demonised by American historians, accused of atrocities, suffered trial by Hollywood in the film *The Patriot* and was found guilty and executed by Mel Gibson. The incident that was shown in the film – the burning of villagers in a church – was taken directly from Nazi SS atrocities at Oradour-sur-Glâne in France during the Second World War. Gibson's decision to feature this unhistorical incident is mischievous to say the least and strongly anti-British. Using the film in this way as propaganda must suit an agenda he is employing without declaring himself, something I believe to be harmful to an impressionable and ill-informed audience. As Richard Holmes writes, 'popular history should not be allowed to get away with murdering the truth.'[6] Film-makers have always hidden behind the defence that their films are entertainment, not history. However, the same defence could have been used by D.W. Griffith and his inflammatory *The Birth of a Nation* which directly incited racial hatred in the United States and helped to boost membership of the Ku Klux Klan after 1916.

The truth about Banastre Tarleton is uncomplicated. 'Bloody Ban', as he came to be known, became a useful propaganda figure for his enemies. His command, the 'British' Legion, was composed mainly of American Loyalists from New York and Pennsylvania, who wore green jackets to distinguish them as a Tory regiment. The 'massacre' at Waxhaw, for which he has been cited as a war criminal, is the sort of incident that occurs many times in the history of war. Tarleton's unit caught up with a contingent of 350 Virginians, commanded by Colonel Abraham Buford. Tarleton called on Buford to surrender but the Patriot leader refused and so Tarleton attacked. Although outnumbered by more than two to one, Tarleton's legion smashed into Buford's regiment and forced the Americans to raise a flag of surrender. What happened next is unclear. According to Tarleton, his horse was shot and he was pinned underneath, unable to control events at all. His men, thinking their commander had been shot down under a flag of truce, were enraged and attacked Buford's men again, killing all they could, even those who were kneeling on the ground with their hands up. The slaughter went on for at least 15 minutes and the phrase 'Tarleton's Quarter' became a rallying cry for Patriots throughout the south. Militarily, nothing is ever gained by the slaughter of prisoners. Every soldier knows that the fortunes of war are capricious and that the next day it might be his turn to surrender to the mercy of his enemy. Probably Tarleton did not do enough to control his troops and is thereby culpable.[7] But to consider this an atrocity, or Tarleton a war criminal, is to misunderstand the nature of close-contact warfare, where surrendering is a far from precise activity. Richard Holmes compares Tarleton's so-called 'massacre' to one committed by the Patriot general 'Light Horse Harry' Lee in 1781.[8] As he says, though, such comparisons serve not to exonerate Tarleton but to demonstrate the harsh realities of warfare.

A fair and balanced picture of the period 1763–83 has become increasingly difficult in American terms because the *myths* of the period are so tightly bound around the *history* that to untie them would require an entire revaluation of America's past. Admittedly this would grant the American people the greatest freedom of all, freedom from the myths that have constricted them ever since the birth of their nation. Yet sometimes freedom can be won at too great a price and perhaps it is asking too much of a people accustomed to feeling good about themselves and ready to reject even constructive criticism such as that emanating from left wingers apparently envious of what Americans have achieved. The situation was neatly summed up by Leslie Fiedler in 1969 when he wrote:

> To be an American is precisely to imagine a destiny rather than
> to inherit one, since we have always been, in so far as we are
> Americans at all, inhabitants of myth rather than history.[9]

The danger facing the American Dream was always its very essence – its unreality.

So the American 'Humpty Dumpty' fell off the wall and 'all the king's horses and all the king's men could not put Humpty together again'. Once colonial America was broken there was no chance to restructure her. The future beckoned too forcefully for the 'glue' of the past to hold and Humpty Dumpty was put together wrongly. George III, poor mad Kraut that he was, just did not understand. His comment at the end of the war says it all: 'We meant well by the Americans – just to punish them with a few bloody noses – and then to make laws for the happiness of both countries.'[10] In 1776, the British – even if they called themselves Americans – would not allow Germans, either kings or Hessian mercenaries, to punch them in the nose without retaliating.

In 1783, as in 1645, the King lost again and Oliver Cromwell (for whom read George Washington) once again triumphed over the monarchy. Ironically, just as Cromwell was offered the Crown by his military commanders and rejected it, so George Washington was also offered the Crown by the army and also rejected it. Yet it was a close thing. Washington may have had absolutely no desire to replace a despised king with his own person, yet there were some who were suspicious of the idea of a republic with its danger of mob rule and its consequent threat to the sanctity of property. So, the American republic almost started life as the kingdom of America, ruled if not by King George I with a slave-owning aristocracy, at least by some other general supported by the army, perhaps General John Stark of New Hampshire.

Like the Holy Roman Empire which was neither 'Holy', 'Roman' nor an 'Empire', the American War of Independence was not really 'American', nor a self-contained 'war' and certainly not concerned with 'independence'. It was a British civil war, a colonial version of the struggle that had taken place in England a century earlier. There were few Americans involved – if by 'American' anybody visualises the independent, buckskin-clad frontiersman Daniel Boone who has become the modern view of the Americans fighting for freedom and independence.

The struggle was between different elements within British society. The Patriots were less the peace-loving farmers of the American myth and more the wealthy decentralisers who wanted to control their own finances and had already made preparations for a separate struggle by allying with the French. These men were not concerned with liberation or democracy but with financial independence from London. To achieve this they were prepared to win the support of their fellow colonists by creating a myth of British tyranny and cruelty. They accused the British of using German troops – the dreaded Hessians of *Sleepy Hollow* fame – against their own compatriots, entirely overlooking the fact that they were in turn going to use French troops from the most autocratic power in Europe. Moreover, as Hugh Bicheno shows, the 'peace-loving American farmers' had been receiving military aid from France, including heavy artillery, muskets and four million livres, under the eyes of the Redcoats even before hostilities had broken out.[11]

From the point of view of the British – meaning the inhabitants of the British Isles – the 'war' was just a theatre of a much larger 'world war'. Britain's real enemies were not George Washington and the colonists, but France and her allies – Spain, Holland and, in the Armed Neutrality of the North, Russia. Fighting took place from India to the West Indies and at one stage in 1777 Britain faced a possible French invasion. In the light of such a serious threat, Britain could not devote her main attention to events in the New World. In the words of Richard Holmes, 'The British lost because victory never mattered as much to them as it did to their opponents.'[12] Although in the eyes of posterity, Saratoga or Yorktown may seem 'decisive' battles, in the eyes of the British the decisive battle of the period was won in the West Indies when Rodney defeated de Grasse at the Battle of the Saints on 12 April 1782 and regained control of the seas, something upon which the British were never prepared to compromise.

## Comrade Robin Hood of Nottingham

As Marc Ferro wrote of America, 'There is no other country in the world where there is such a large gap between the sophisticated understanding of some professional historians and the basic education given by teachers.'[13]

Freedom of thought is not guaranteed by the American Bill of Rights. In fact, its very opposite is more likely to be found in American schools. School textbooks have been the battleground for every kind of outlandish interference and history texts have probably suffered the most.

- From the 1960s those responsible for bringing up healthy children in Oregon have decreed that no school text may ever be used that speaks slightingly of the Founding Fathers.
- In 1961, a group calling itself Texans for America pressed two publishers to delete extracts from their history texts. In one, the offending passage suggested that the Second World War might have been avoided if the United States had joined the League of Nations. The other stated that the United States needed to maintain friendly relations with other countries who might sometimes disagree with them. This passage was replaced with a passage stating the other countries were less free than America.
- In the 1920s, the Hearst Corporation criticised certain history texts as unpatriotic, un-American and pro-British. One account of the battle of Bunker Hill was removed because of a sentence saying, 'Three times the British returned courageously to the attack.' The author, when asked to alter this, rewrote it as 'Three times the cowardly British returned to the attack.'[14]
- In the 1920s, the Daughters of the American Revolution complained about several history texts as they were not stressing military history in enough detail.
- Also in the 1920s, the Ku Klux Klan complained that history texts contained too much pro-Jewish and pro-Catholic material.

- Religious fundamentalists have for many years protested against the teaching of evolution theory and some biology texts have been purged of all reference to evolution.
- In 1939, Dr Harold Rugg used the 'S' word on the first page of his text. 'Socialism' in a school textbook aroused the wrath of various pressure groups, including the Advertising Federation of America, the American Legion and the Hearst Corporation. Rugg was accused of advocating socialism or even communism and sales fell from 289,000 in 1938 to just 21,000 in 1939. After that the book was taken off the market.
- A prize should go to Ada White of the Indiana Textbook Commission. She believed that Robin Hood had been a Communist. She therefore insisted that the story of Robin Hood should be banned in all Indiana schools.
- The Texas State House of Representatives insisted on a loyalty oath from all textbook writers and passed a resolution that, 'American history courses in the public schools emphasise in the textbooks our glowing and throbbing history of hearts and souls inspired by wonderful American principles and traditions.'
- During the 1950s, in the words of Frances FitzGerald, school textbooks embodied militant self-righteousness:

According to these books, the United States had been a kind of Salvation Army to the rest of the world: throughout history, it had done little but dispense benefits to poor, ignorant and diseased countries. In the nineteenth century and the beginning of the twentieth, it had opened doors for the Chinese, saved Cuba from the Spanish, protected Puerto Rico, separated Panama from Colombia in order to wipe out yellow fever, and taken on the Philippines in order to 'educate' and 'civilise' the Filipinos – just as President McKinley said. American motives were always altruistic . . . In the twentieth century, the United States had spent most of its time – apart from a short period of isolation – saving Europe and Asia from militarism, Fascism and Communism . . . According to an unnamed group of Oxford scholars, 'We are too little astonished at the unprecedented virtuousness of US foreign policy and at its good sense.'[15]

I cannot go on!

# PICKING THE BONES

MARCHING TO BASRA
(to the tune of 'Marching Through Georgia')

Bring the good ol' F-16! We'll set some people free,
Bomb them like we bombed the Japs at good ol' Nag'saki,
Bomb them like we used to bomb them back in Germanee,
When we were marching to Basra.

Hurrah! Hurrah! We bring them liberty,
Hurrah! Hurrah! The bombs that make them free,
So we liberated folks from Baghdad to the sea,
When we were marching to Basra.

How Iraqis shouted when they heard the joyful news,
Yanks have come to free them from the goddamn'd Saddam blues,
How the buildings tumbled when we shot them with our Cruise,
When we were marching to Basra.

Hurrah! Hurrah! We bring them Coke and fries,
Hurrah! Hurrah! That's magic to their eyes,
Shame the bombs and guns and planes have silenced all their cries,
When we were marching to Basra.

Down came Saddam's statue to the joy of one and all,
Up went Dubya's ratings when the Black Hawks came to call,

Strafed the tourist hotels where the foreign press men fall,
When we were marching to Basra.

Hurrah! Hurrah! Fox Network leads the way,
Hurrah! Hurrah! It's like Thanksgiving Day,
We don't find hidden weapons? So? It's the 'merican Way,
When we were marching to Basra.

Can't say what we're doing here, don't really give a Shi'ite,
'raqis stink, there's rats and flies, mosquitoes buzz all night,
God has sent his chosen folk an' we have got the right,
When we were marching to Basra.

Hurrah! Hurrah! Caught Saddam down a hole,
Hurrah! Hurrah! Don Rumsfeld's scored a goal,
Dubya's re-elected and Bush Senior's saved his soul,
When we were marching to Basra.

## American Fascism

Is America a fascist state? Or does it merely act like one? Certainly, it has elements that when compared to similar features in Nazi Germany and fascist Italy seem convincing. Moreover, its combination of militarism and corporatism do conjure up unfortunate memories of Europe in the 1930s.

Here are just a few pointers drawn from recent events:

- Government use of empty slogans and Orwellian double-talk
- The dumbing-down of public issues noted by US observers like Paul Fussell
- The collective memory of the nation has become the property of right-wing intellectuals like Lynne Cheney, the vice-president's wife
- Government control of the media through the Patriot Act
- USA ruled by mythocracy through myth-information
- Political pressure groups control education and school textbooks
- Fear or paranoia being used as social control
- Undemocratic elections – as an example, the presidential election in 2000

- Contempt for international agreements such as the Kyoto Accord
- Contempt for the United Nations, notably the General Assembly
- Ignorance within the US population of its own history
- Lack of free speech as evidenced by period after 9/11
- Ignorance of and contempt for other cultures and nations
- Militarism on an unprecedented scale
- Aggressive nationalism and foreign policies
- Secret security forces – FBI, CIA etc.
- US exceptionalism and intolerance
- Continuing acceptance of racism and white supremacy within the mainstream public
- Possession of guns by a violent society and support for National Rifle Association
- Large prison population and extreme penalties including death penalty
- Lack of real political variety – no liberal or left-wing party
- More and more middle-class Americans living behind security gates and employing private guards to protect them from their less fortunate neighbours

Gore Vidal wrote in 1991:

> The corporate grip on opinion in the United States is one of the wonders of the Western World. No First World country has ever managed to eliminate so entirely from its media all objectivity – much less dissent.[16]

And in the 13 years since then things have got much worse. In a sense, the United States has become 'post-democratic' and its system of government one of 'virtual democracy'.

The prevailing idea that the world is envious of the United States seems to have become widespread amongst modern Americans. Anyone who tries to criticise the policies of the United States is shamelessly brushed off by the accusation that they are jealous of American democracy and love of freedom. It would be funny if it were not so sad. Such an attitude places the United States beyond help. What might have been true during the nineteenth century when the USA was a land of opportunity and offered chances unattainable in Europe is no longer so, except for the young and immature who associate the wealth and excess to be seen in American popular culture as a desirable aim in itself.

Today, America seems more like a giant lottery with inequality guaranteed. The few winners will gain prizes beyond the imagination or interest of the majority but most will lose their stake and many will endure lives of poverty far below the average European level. Without the safety net of the welfare system expected in Europe many Americans would do better to reverse the nineteenth-century process and emigrate back across the Atlantic. Moreover, the emptiness of modern American life, with its rampant materialism and its formula of dumbing-down has meant that there is as large an intellectual inequality as there is a material one. From the stars to the bars is a very long way.

The United States of America is a hegemony inside an empire within a superpower. It has been the most interventionist state of the last 100 years, an 'economic' imperialist on a scale that dwarfs the territorial empires of Britain, France and Spain. Complaining that these old colonial powers represented a past that was tainted by the control of indigenous peoples, the truth was that the colonial powers prevented American financial interests from getting control of their areas of interest. To the Americans, therefore, decolonisation was aimed at opening markets for their own corporations. The world must be made safe for democracy in the name of the US economic system.

In 1948 George Kennan wrote the memorandum of the next half century for the United States:

> We have about 50 per cent of the world's wealth but only 6.3 per cent of its population. In this situation, we cannot fail to be the object of envy and resentment. Our real test in the coming period is to devise a pattern of relationships which will permit us to maintain this position of disparity. We need not deceive ourselves that we can afford today the luxury of altruism and world benefaction – unreal objectives such as human rights, the raising of living standards and democratisation.[17]

This seems to say it all.

Or, perhaps, not quite.

# PICKING THE BONES

## VOTE RIGGERS IN THE SKY
(to the tune of 'Ghost Riders in the Sky')

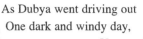

As Dubya went driving out
One dark and windy day,
Upon a ridge he rested as
He drove along his way,
When all at once a mighty crowd
Of rednecked voters passed,
A-hurryin' to the Florida count
That Dubya'd won at last.

Yippee-yi-ya, yippee-yi-yo,
Vote riggers in the sky.

The rednecks rushed on past him and
He heard one call 'Take care',
If you want to save your soul from hell
You'd better play it fair,
'Cos next time, Dubya, change your ways
Or like us you will fly
To chase these same bewildered
herds
Whose votes you cannot buy.

Yippee-yi-ya, yippee-yi-yo,
Vote riggers in the sky

**Advice for George W. Bush**

It's not the voting that's democracy, it's the counting.
Tom Stoppard, *Jumpers*

216

**Advice for Tony Blair**

The last temptation is the greatest treason;
To do the right deed
For the wrong reason.
T.S. Eliot, *Murder in the Cathedral*

# *Afterword*

Democratic politicians have always faced the problem of controlling ever-growing populations without the tools available to totalitarian states, like the army and secret police. Universal suffrage in modern nation states has created, to use Walter Lippmann's phrase, an immense 'bewildered herd' of voters, who cannot be allowed to exercise independence of thought. Yet these masses are the essence of democracy and unless their thoughts can be moulded and directed, they point the way to chaos and mob rule.

Over the last 100 years, politicians have cultivated the art of controlling the masses while at the same time convincing them that they are the masters and the politicians their obedient servants. They have manufactured consent from the 'trampling and roar' of the aforementioned herd, who are guided by mere emotion and impulse. To achieve this consent, 'potent simplification' is combined with 'necessary illusions'. In other words, politicians will put whatever spin is necessary on the facts of any situation to convince the voters that the actions of their representatives in Parliament or Congress have been those for which they were elected to perform. As Noam Chomsky put it so bluntly, 'Propaganda is to a democracy what the bludgeon is to a totalitarian state.'[1]

I hope that, in this book, I have been able to demonstrate some of the ways in which politicians have achieved this control of the public mind and how much of their success has been due to their misuse of history. The democratic media has been both a tool in this misuse and a battleground where opponents of the political control of history have fought for the conscience of the nation.

## AFTERWORD

In Britain in 2003, the objectivity of the British press and visual/sound media was compromised by its need to play the part of 'People's Tribune' against a government prepared to resort to presentational trickery to portray the facts in a way that supported its agenda. The reality was that this agenda had already failed to win support from the United Nations, and was, furthermore, probably unrepresentative of the majority of British opinion; this rendered the role of the BBC during the 2003 Iraq War and the subsequent Kelly case and Hutton Inquiry vital to British democracy. In the United States, however, the press and the visual/sound media enabled President George W. Bush and his advisers to ensure that the public was exposed to the 'right kind' of data. This assured Bush of massive support for his pre-emptive war against Iraq. Led by the Fox Network, US television set new lows of partisan bias, with no attempt at objectivity or balanced coverage. In the press, the coverage of the war was so one-sided that one was reminded of US novelist John Dos Passos's comment about his own people in 1917, 'Once lead this people into war and they will forget there ever was such a thing as tolerance.'[2] During the Iraq War, the erosion of free thought in America was everywhere apparent, as was the cheapening of Christian theology that has become second nature to American politicians. Even the most questionable foreign adventure is dressed up in biblical robes to represent God's divine mission or purpose so that support for American policy becomes unquestioningly a matter of faith.

Few Americans, other than academics, have studied their history with any rigorous intention to get at the truth. Most have been content to inhabit a comfortable land of myths, fed on a diet of 'freedom', 'democracy' and 'liberty', without any evidence that what they are told is true or ever has been. American school textbooks are full of meaningless slogans like 'Land of the Free' and 'All Men are Created Equal', which any knowledge of US history would be enough to refute time and time again. But any challenge to the 'democracy' they hold so dear produces an unthinking patriotism of the kind described by Dos Passos. It is a brave man who, at such times, tries to maintain objectivity and a respect for the standards of history as a subject.

From the late nineteenth century, demagogues like Theodore Roosevelt, allied to media tycoons and, since 1945, a military–industrial sector, have exerted a malign influence over American voters. Using rhetoric and metaphor, demonising political and foreign opponents in a dualistic struggle between 'good' and 'evil', and mythologising and falsifying events in the past, these politicians have created a kind of democracy which is individual to America and unrecognisable to other democratic states, notably those in western Europe. The American slogan 'Log Cabin to White House' has never been further from the truth, with the presidency a prize to be won only by the astronomically wealthy. No modern 'Honest Abe Lincoln' will ever emerge again.

The euphemising of the language of war has been the most obscene semantic crime in history. How American politicians can describe the heavy civilian casualties of the wars of the post-Vietnam period as representative of the sanitisation of war beggars belief. One of the repulsive consequences of this has been a popularisation of war, notably as the result of the fact that it is now so one-sided that Americans need fear few of the normal consequences.

During the 1991 Gulf War, the *Washington Post* spoke of the need to instil in people respect for 'martial value'. As Chomsky observed:

> If you want to have a violent society that uses force around the world to achieve the ends of its own domestic elite, it is necessary to have a proper appreciation of the martial virtues and none of these sickly inhibitions about using violence.[3]

Someone who knew more about war than most was ex-Supreme Allied Commander, Dwight D. Eisenhower. In a speech in Washington in April 1953, President Eisenhower warned of America's love affair with the military which in the half century since has led his country inexorably towards fascism and away from a democracy in which free speech and political debate are valued.

> Every gun that is made, every warship launched, every rocket fired signifies, in the final sense, a theft from those who hunger and are not fed, those who are cold and are not clothed. This world in arms is not spending money alone. It is spending the sweat of its labourers, the genius of its scientists, the hopes of its children.[4]

As part of America's Global War on Terror, President George W. Bush chose to settle scores with the *bête noire* of his father, George Herbert Bush. Lacking any evidence that the overthrow of Saddam Hussein would make the world a safer place and ignoring substantial evidence that it would do the contrary, Bush launched a war of aggression not against Saddam Hussein but against the people of Iraq. In case anyone thinks this is an unfair description of what took place in February 2003 let them answer this question: if you were in the position of an Iraqi civilian, would the news that Saddam Hussein had been overthrown have done any of the following:

1. Restored your life if you or your family had been killed by US bombing?
2. Restored your arms, legs, sight, hearing, nerves or other mutilation you suffered while the Americans inflicted Shock and Awe on you?
3. Rebuilt your house and replaced property destroyed in the bombing?
4. Restored your shop or place of business if it had been wrecked through bombing or fighting in your town or city?
5. Restored water, electricity, gas, oil, food, and law and order to the area in which you lived?
6. Educated your children in the schools destroyed by the bombing, provided medical treatment in the hospitals ruined or overcowded with war casualties?
7. Made the streets safer for your family to walk in or your children to play in?
8. Improved any single legal aspect in your life?
9. Caused you to thank the Americans for coming to liberate your country?

In conclusion, let Amnesty International speak for all those who have been liberated by American troops:

> The scenes at al-Hilla's hospital on 1 April showed that something terrible had happened. The bodies of the men, women and children – both dead and alive – brought to the hospital were punctured with shards of shrapnel from cluster bombs. Videotape of the victims was judged by Reuters and Associated Press editors as being too awful to show on television. Independent (UK) newspaper journalists reported that the pictures showed babies cut in half and children with their limbs blown off. Two lorry loads of bodies, including women in flowered dresses, were seen outside the hospital. Injured

survivors told reporters how the explosives fell 'like grapes' from the sky and how bomblets bounced through the windows and doors of their homes before exploding. A doctor at al-Hilla's hospital said that almost all the patients were victims of cluster bombs.[5]

George W. Bush seems content to blame the failure to find weapons of mass destruction on faulty intelligence, never for a moment linking this failure with the collapse of his entire justification for fighting an illegal, aggressive, pre-emptive war against the Iraqi people. Tony Blair, on the other hand, is not content to simply blame the intelligence community. For him, any hint of criticism is too personally felt. He believes that he must have been right to go to war because it felt right to him as an honest man and a Christian. Just as was said of Woodrow Wilson, the danger with Blair is that he cannot imagine that he is ever wrong. Others must apologise for their mistakes, but such human weaknesses are for lesser men. While George Bush shrugs and moves on to the next subject, Tony Blair is enmeshed in a self-righteous struggle to prove that he was justified whatever the damage to his public image or the image of his country. While Hans Blix has utterly disproved the argument that Britain and the United States were enforcing previous UN resolutions, something that can never be done unilaterally and without total UN support, Blair clings to the Attorney General's interpretation of international law which he, alone, has seen, but which remains hidden from everybody else. As a man of the law, Tony Blair should realise the appalling example he is presenting to the jury.

Ah, but I forget, the Court of History is not yet in session and by the time it does sit to consider the Iraq War of 2003, Tony Blair hopes that Iraq will present such a splendid example of Anglo-Saxon democracy and American investment that few will remember the thousands of Iraqi civilians who died to make it so.

And then the end will have justified the means.

Won't it, Tony?

# *Notes*

## Chapter 1: Shock and Awe

1. George Orwell in *Shooting an Elephant,* quoted in *Oxford Dictionary of Quotations*
2. George W. Bush quoted in Sheldon Rampton and James Stauber, *Weapons of Mass Deception* (Penguin, New York, 2003), p. 130
3. Rampton and Stauber, *Weapons of Mass Deception*, p. 123
4. Interview with Harlan K. Ullman on CBS News, 'Iraq Faces Massive US Missile Barrage', 24 January 2003
5. Robin Cook, 'Iraq's Phantom Weapons and Iran', *New Perspectives Quarterly*, Vol. 20, Issue 3 (July 2003), p. 29
6. Jessica Stern, 'How America Created a Terrorist Haven', *New York Times*, 20 August 2003
7. Vincent Cannistraro quoted in Walcott, 'Some in Administration Uneasy Over Bush Speech', *Philadelphia Inquirer*, 19 September 2003
8. Michael Ignatieff, 'Why Are We in Iraq?', *New York Times Magazine*, 7 September 2003, p. 71
9. Winston Churchill quoted in Ralph Raico, 'Politics of Hunger: A Review', *Review of Austrian Economics*, Vol. 3, No. 1 (1989), p. 253
10. H.G. Wells cited in Raico, op. cit., p. 253
11. Colonel House quoted in Raico, op. cit., p. 255
12. C. Paul Vincent, *The Politics of Hunger* (Ohio State University Press, 1985), p. 68
13. Ibid., p. 85
14. General Sir Herbert Plumer quoted in Vincent, op. cit., p. 110
15. Vincent, op. cit., p. 149
16. Ibid., p. 150
17. Ibid., p. 151

18. Geoffrey Regan, *Air Force Blunders* (Carlton Books, London, 2002), pp. 127–8
19. Churchill quoted by George Rosie in 'Stink of Hypocrisy', *Sunday Herald*, 9 February 2003, www.sundayherald.com/print31247
20. Ibid., see also Prime Minister's Personal Minutes, Serial No. D.217/4 for General Ismay and COS Committee
21. Michael Beschloss, *The Conquerors* (Simon and Schuster, New York, 2002), p. 27
22. Ibid.
23. John Dietrich, *The Morgenthau Plan* (Algora Publishing, New York, 2002), p. 98
24. W. Friedman quoted in Dietrich, op. cit., p. 118
25. Roosevelt quoted in James Bacque, *Other Losses* (Little Brown (Canada), 1999), p. 7
26. Churchill quoted in Beschloss, op. cit., p. 125
27. Ibid., p. 131
28. Roosevelt quoted in Beschloss, op. cit., p. 149
29. Dietrich, op. cit., p. 135

## Chapter 2: Homo Hostilis

1. Kevin Hearne, 'The Demonization of Pan' www.mc.maricopa.edu/~tomshoemaker/StudentPapers/pan.html
2. Sam Keen, *Faces of the Enemy* (Harper San Francisco, 1988), p. 76
3. Chalmers Johnson, 'Blowback: The Costs and Consequences of American Empire', www.thirdworldtraveler.com Blowback_CJohnson/Blowback_CJohnson.html
4. Robert Ivie, 'Evil Enemy Versus Agonistic Other: Rhetorical Constructions of Terrorism', *The Review of Education, Pedagogy and Cultural Studies* (2003)

## Chapter 3: The Noble Art of Dying

1. John Pilger, 'The Unthinkable Is Becoming Normal', *The Independent*, 20 April 2003. In his article, Pilger refers to the injured child, Ali Ismaeel Abbas, who lost his parents and both of his arms during the war in Iraq. When he heard of the case, Tony Blair said he would do everything he could to help him. This must be the ultimate insult to the memory of all the children of Iraq who have died violently in Blair's war and as a result of the embargo that he enthusiastically endorsed. The saving of Ali substitutes a media spectacle of charity for our right to know the true extent of the crime committed against the young in our name. Let us now see the pictures of the 'truckload of dozens of dismembered women and children' that the Red Cross doctors saw.
2. Winston Churchill cited in *Oxford Book of Quotations*
3. Paul Fussell, *The Great War* (Oxford University Press, 1975), pp. 21–9

4. George Lakoff, 'Metaphor and War, Again', 18 March 2003, www.alternet.org/print.html?StoryID=15414

5. Paul Fussell, *Wartime* (Oxford University Press, 1989), p. 151

6. *Hansard*, 4 June, 1940, col. 796

7. John Charmley, *Churchill's Grand Alliance* (Harcourt, London 1995)

8. Geoffrey Regan, *Military Anecdotes* (Carlton Books, London, 2002), p. 130

9. Ibid., p. 5

10. Barbara Tuchman quoted in Fussell, *The Great War*, p. 175

11. W. Beach Thomas, *Daily Mirror*, 22 November 1916 quoted in Fussell, *The Great War*, p. 175

12. John Ellis, *The Sharp End of War* (Simon and Schuster, London, 1983), p. 103

13. Ibid., p. 113

14. Frank Richardson quoted in Richard Holmes, *Firing Line* (Penguin, London, 1987), p. 70

15. Regan, op. cit., p. 76

16. Ibid., p. 128

17. Chris Hedges, *War Is a Force That Gives Us Meaning* (PublicAffairs, New York, 2002), pp. 30–1

18. Ibid., p. 177

19. Ibid., p. 25

20. Ibid., pp. 158–9

21. Ibid., p. 143

## Chapter 4: History in Black and White

1. Lynne Cheney's *A Patriotic Primer* begins: 'We live in a land of shining cities [note the use of Winthrop's image] and natural splendours, a beautiful land made more beautiful still by our commitment to freedom. I wrote this book because I want my grandchildren to understand how blessed we are [note Longley's 'chosen people' theme]. I want them to know they are part of a nation whose citizens enjoy liberty and opportunity such as have never been known before. Generations have passed from the earth never dreaming that people could be as fortunate as we Americans are.'

2. I would like to acknowledge the use of the 'Court of History' to Alan Bennett's play, *Forty Years On*, where I find his treatment of Neville Chamberlain both brilliant and hilarious.

3. James Parton, *Life of Thomas Jefferson* (James R. Osgood and Company, Boston 1874)

4. Sir John Harington, quoted in *Oxford Book of Quotations*

5. Niall Ferguson, *Empire* (Allen Lane, London, 2003), p. 89

6. Eric Foner, *The Story of American Freedom* (W.W. Norton & Company, New York, 1998), p. 33

7. Gabriel Prosser quoted in Foner, op. cit., p. 44

8. James W. Loewen, *Lies My Teacher Told Me* (Touchstone Books, New York, 1996), p. 143
9. Abraham Lincoln quoted in Loewen, op. cit., p. 180
10. The Internet is full of articles concerning the death of the 100-year-old US Senator and his family's revelations of his black daughter, now 78 years old.

## Chapter 5: Selling the USA

1. James W. Loewen, *Lies My Teacher Told Me* (Touchstone Books, New York, 1996), p. 32
2. Ibid.
3. Ibid., p. 31
4. Frances FitzGerald quoted in Loewen, op. cit., p. 217
5. Loewen, op. cit., p. 217
6. Madeleine Albright quoted in William Blum, *Rogue State* (Zed Books, London, 2002), p. 7
7. Marilyn B. Young, 'The Age of Global Power', in Thomas Bender (ed.) *Rethinking American History in a Global Age* (University of California Press, 2002), p. 282
8. Smedley Butler cited in Loewen, op. cit., p. 220
9. Congress Joint Resolution 19, Public Law 103–150, 23 November 1993
10. Gary Leupp, 'The Rosy Dawn of US Imperialism', www.counterpunch.org/leupp01162003.html
11. Colonel Charles E. Stanton in a speech at the tomb of American revolutionary war hero General Marquis de Lafayette, reported in *New York Tribune*, 6 September 1917
12. Loewen, op. cit., p. 140
13. Ibid., p. 27
14. Ibid., p. 28
15. Tim Madigan, *The Burning* (Thomas Dunne Books, New York, 2001), pp. xvi–xvii
16. Ibid., p. 46
17. Ibid., p. 144
18. Ibid., p. 216
19. Loewen, op. cit., p. 23
20. Ibid., p. 24
21. Ibid., p. 26
22. Wilson cited by Margaret Macmillan in *Peacemakers* (John Murray, London, 2001) p. 11
23. Macmillan, op. cit., p. 11
24. Ibid., p. 13
25. Warren Harding quoted in Ralph Raico, 'World War One: The Turning Point' in John V. Denson (ed.), *The Costs of War* (Transaction Publishers, New Brunswick, 1998), p. 238

26. Excerpt from *New York Times* quoting Elihu Root in Howard Zinn's *A People's History of the United States* (HarperCollins, New York, 2001), p. 369
27. Macmillan, op. cit., p. 16
28. John Terraine on Haig in *The War Lords* (Little Brown, London, 1976), p. 41
29. J.P. Harris, *Amiens to the Armistice* (Brasscy's, London, 1998) p. xi
30. Woodrow Wilson quoted in Macmillan, op. cit., p. 18
31. Ibid., p. 19
32. Ibid., p. 21

## Chapter 6: The Evil Empire

1. Robert Ivie, 'Fire, Flood and Red Fever', *Presidential Studies Quarterly*, 29, No. 3 (September 1999), p. 574
2. Ibid., p. 570
3. William Blum, *Killing Hope* (Zed Books, London, 2003), p. 8
4. Ibid., p. 12
5. Ibid., p. 10
6. Ivie, op. cit., p. 574
7. Senator Myers cited in Ivie, op. cit., p. 585
8. Ibid., p. 587
9. Ibid.,
10. Blum, op. cit., p. 12

## Chapter 7: Barefaced Doctorin'

1. Sam Keen, *Faces of the Enemy* (HarperSanFrancisco, 1988), p. 46
2. Eric Foner, *The Story of American Freedom* (Rutgers University Press, New Brunswick, 1993), p. 321
3. William Blum, 'Anthrax for Export: U.S. companies sold Iraq the ingredients for a witch's brew' in *The Progressive*, April 1998, www.progressive.org/plaintexts/anth0498.html
4. Jeane J. Kirkpatrick cited in Clarence Lusane, 'U.S. should not have aided mass murderer', The Progressive Media Project, 12 March 2002, www.progressive.org/Media%20Project%202/mplm1202.html

## Chapter 8: Stillbirth of a Nation

1. Clifford Longley, *Chosen People* (Hodder and Stoughton, London, 2002), pp. 111–12
2. Extract from the *Washington Post* cited in Geoffrey Regan, *Snafu* (Avon Books, New York, 1993), p. 247
3. Howard Zinn, *A People's History of the United States* (HarperCollins, New York, 2001) p. 493
4. Michael K. Smith, *Greatest Story Never Told* (Xlibris Corporation, USA, 2001), p. 326
5. Ibid., p. 325

6. *Maariv*, Israel, 12 June 1983
7. Noam Chomsky, *Media Control* (Seven Stories Press, London, 2002), p. 33
8. H.W. Brands, *The Devil We Knew* (Oxford University Press, 1993), p. 177
9. *Wall Street Journal* quoted in Brands, op. cit., p. 177
10. Paul Warnke quoted in Brands, op. cit., p. 178
11. Ibid.
12. Bruce Franklin, *M.I.A. or Mythmaking in America* (Rutgers University Press, New Brunswick, 1993), pp. 133–4
13. Rod Edelman of *Cineaste* quoted in Franklin, op. cit., pp. 141–2
14. Franklin, op.cit, p. 151
15. Ibid., p. 155
16. Richard C. Thornton, *The Falklands Sting* (Brassey's, Washington, 1998), p. 226
17. Sam Keen, *Faces of the Enemy* (HarperSanFrancisco, 1988), pp. 31–2
18. Regan, *Snafu*, p. 124
19. Ibid., p. 132
20. Ibid., p. 128
21. Ibid., p. 124
22. Ibid., pp. 125–6
23. Lord Christopher Soames quoted in Jonathan Steele's 'Regime Change – The Prequel', *The Guardian*, 13 October 2003
24. Eric Alterman cited in Smith, op. cit., p. 325
25. Ibid., p. 347
26. George Bush Snr. quoted in Smith, op. cit., p. 347
27. Smith, op. cit., p. 375
28. Moshe Arens cited in Regan, op. cit., p. 153
29. Regan, op. cit., p. 156
30. Ibid., p. 160
31. Sheldon Rampton and John Stauber, *Weapons of Mass Deception* (Penguin, New York, 2003), pp. 86–7
32. Ibid., p. 87
33. Gustave Gilbert, *The Nuremberg Diary* (Da Capo Press, New York, 1995), pp. 278–9

### Chapter 9: A History of Cartoon Violence

1. Dominic Hilton, 'Weapons of War', opendemocracy.net/other_content/article-1075-worlddiary.jsp, 20 March 2003
2. Linda Feldman, 'The Impact of Bush Linking 9/11 and Iraq', *Christian Science Monitor*, 14 March 2003, www.aaiusa.org/news/must_read03_14a_03.html
3. Robert Byrd, 'We Stand Silently Mute', *The Modern Tribune*, 12 February 2003, www.themoderntribune.com/robert_byrd_-_we_

stand_silently_mute_-_robert_byrd_  february_12_2003_war_on_
iraq.htm
4. Statistics from T.N. Dupuy and R.E. Dupuy, *Encyclopedia of
Military History* (Macdonald and Jane's, London, 1970)
5. Hugh Bicheno, *Rebels and Redcoats* (HarperCollins, London, 2003),
pp. 246–7
6. Geoffrey Regan, *Military Anecdotes* (Carlton Books, London,
2002), p. 18
7. Geoffrey Regan, *Snafu* (Avon Books, New York, 1993), p. 186
8. Norman Gladden cited in William Moore, *See How They Ran* (Leo
Cooper, London, 1970), p. 32
9. Fred Anderson, *Crucible of War* (Faber, London, 2000), pp. 52–66
10. Belote and Belote, *Corregidor* (HarperCollins, New York, 1967),
p. 104
11. Julian Thompson quoted in Regan, *Great Military Blunders*
(Channel 4 Books, London, 2000), p. 83

## Chapter 10: 'Hell-roaring' Jake Smith

*1. Time,* 21 December 2003
2. Frances FitzGerald quoted in Loewen, *Lies My Teacher Told Me*
(Touchstone Books, New York, 1996), p. 217
3. Abraham Lincoln quoted in *Oxford Book of Quotations*
4. J.C. Miller, *Benevolent Assimilation* (Yale University Press, 1982),
p. 52
5. Ibid., p. 94
6. Ibid., p. 15
7. Geoffrey Regan, *Great Military Blunders* (Channel 4 Books,
London, 2000), p. 73
8. Ibid., p. 72
9. Miller, op. cit., p. 74
10. Ibid., p. 195
11. Rebecca Dowell and Kendra Kuhl, 'The Philippine–American War',
www.geocities.com/Athens/Crete/9782/main.htm
12. Miller, op. cit., p. 189
13. Ibid., p. 189
14. 'Soldiers' Letters: Being Materials for the History of a War of
Criminal Aggression', from Jim Zwick (ed.) *Anti Imperialism in the
United States* 1898–1935, http://www.boondocksnet .com/ai/ailtexts/
soldiers.html
15. Miller, op. cit., p. 189
16. Zwick, op. cit.
17. Miller, op. cit., p. 220
18. Ibid., p. 256
19. Joanna Bourke, *An Intimate History of Killing* (Granta Books,
London, 1999), p. 193

20. Ibid., p. 194
21. 'Elite unit savaged civilians in Vietnam', *Toledo Blade*, 23 October 2002
22. Cincinnatus, *Self Destruction: The Disintegration and Decay of the United States Army during the Vietnam Era* (Norton, New York, 1982). See Chapter 3.
23. J.P. Zmirak, 'The Bulldozer Assault' *National Catholic Register*, Dec. 8–14, 2002, www.ncregister.com/Register_News/120802war.htm
24. Ibid.
25. Ibid. See also www.digitaljournalist.org/issue0211/sloyan.html
26. Fred Anderson, *Crucible of War* (Faber, London, 2000), pp. 542–3
27. J.C. Long, *Lord Jeffrey Amherst: A Soldier of the King* (Macmillan, New York, 1933), p. 187
28. John W. Harpster, *Pen Pictures of Early Western Pennsylvania* (University of Pittsburg Press, 1993), p. 103
29. Geoffrey Regan, *Military Blunders* (Andre Deutsch, London, 2001), p. 80

### Chapter 11: God Only Knows . . .

1. Jonathan Riley-Smith, *What Were the Crusades?* (Palgrave Macmillan, London 1991)
2. Geoffrey Regan, *First Crusader* (Sutton, London, 2001), p. 236
3. Geoffrey Regan, *Saladin and the Fall of Jerusalem* (Croom Helm, London, 1988) and Geoffrey Regan, *First Crusader*
4. Extracts from *Catford Journal* quoted in Denis Winter, *Death's Men: Soldiers of the Great War* (Penguin, London, 1998), p. 23–4
5. See Wilfred Owen's poem, 'Dulce et Decorum Est', which ends with these lines: 'My friend, you would not tell with such high zest / To children ardent for some desperate glory / The old Lie: Dulce et decorum est / Pro patria mori.'
6. Clifford Longley, 'Unique among the nations', *The Tablet*, 31 August 2002. For the argument in full, see Longley, *Chosen People* (Hodder and Stoughton, London, 2002)
7. In reference to the surfing scene in *Apocalypse Now* (1979) which is followed by the 'Ride of the Valkyries' in the shape of helicopter gunships.

### Chapter 12: Uncle Sam and the Poodle

1. Quote attributed to George Bernard Shaw, though there is no evidence of it in any of Shaw's published writings.
2. Margaret Macmillan, *Peacemakers* (John Murray, London, 2001), pp. 28–9
3. Robert Massie, *Dreadnought* (Random House, London, 1991), pp. 152–7
4. Essentially, this is the theme of John Charmley's book, *Churchill's*

*Grand Alliance* (Harcourt, London, 1995)

5. Charmley, op. cit., p. 21
6. Lord Cherwell quoted in Charmley, op. cit., p. 23
7. Martin J. Sherwin, *A World Destroyed: Hiroshima and Its Legacies* (Random House, London, 1975), pp. 113–14
8. Septimus Paul, *Nuclear Rivals* (Ohio State University Press, 2000), p. 111
9. John Dickie, *'Special' No More* (Weidenfeld & Nicholson, London, 1994), p. 87
10. W. Scott Lucas, *Divided We Stand: Britain, the U.S. and the Suez Crisis* (Hodder & Stoughton, London, 1991), p. 19
11. Dickie, op. cit., p. 90
12. Eisenhower cited in Dickie, op. cit., p. 92
13. Dickie, op. cit., p. 93
14. Foster Dulles quoted in Lucas, op. cit., p. 277
15. Dickie, op. cit., p. 94
16. Ibid., p. 95
17. Foster Dulles cited in Lucas, op. cit., p. 307
18. Ibid., p. 314
19. Churchill quoted in Dickie, op. cit., p. 97
20. Neff, *Warriors at Suez* (Random House, New York, 1983), p. 21
21. Ibid., p. 409
22. Kyle, *Suez* (Weidenfeld & Nicholson, London, 1988) pp. 411–12
23. Admiral Power cited in Kyle, op. cit., pp. 411–12

## Chapter 13: Thanks for the Collective Memory . . .

1. A US soldier, Private Jessica Lynch, was severely injured in an engagement with Iraqi forces. She was the only survivor of her unit and was taken prisoner in a military hospital. A dramatic rescue by American troops took place, and she was brought out alive. The incident was exploited by the US government to popularise the war. It turned out to be a propaganda stunt.
2. Hugh Bicheno, *Rebels and Redcoats* (HarperCollins, London, 2003), p. xxv
3. Ibid., p. xxviii
4. Benjamin Franklin at the signing of the Declaration of Independence, *Oxford Book of Quotations*
5. Bicheno, op. cit., p. 5
6. Richard Holmes, *Firing Line* (Penguin, London, 1987), p. 16
7. Ibid., p. 17
8. Ibid.
9. Leslie Fielder, 'Cross the Border – Close the Gap', *Collected Essays Vol. 2* (1971)
10. Bicheno, op.cit., p. 19
11. Ibid., p. 23

12. Holmes, op. cit., p. 18
13. Marc Ferro, *Use and Abuse of History* (Routledge, London, 2003), p. 25
14. Frances FitzGerald, *America Revised* (Little Brown, Boston, 1979), p. 35
15. Ibid., p. 129
16. Gore Vidal, 'Cue the Green God, Ted', *A View from the Diner's Club*, www.eserver.org/cyber/media-quotes.html
17. George Kennan, quoted in James W. Loewen, *Lies My Teacher Told Me* (Touchstone Books, New York, 1996), p. 216

### Afterword

1. Noam Chomsky, *Media Control* (Seven Stories Press, London, 2002), pp. 20–1
2. John Dos Passos, *Mr Wilson's War* (1917), quoted in *Oxford Dictionary of Twentieth Century Quotations*
3. Chomsky, op. cit., p. 34
4. Dwight D. Eisenhower, speech in Washington, 16 April 1953, quoted in the *Oxford Dictionary of Twentieth Century Quotations*
5. 'Iraq: Civilians Under Fire', Amnesty International, 8 March 2003, http://web.amnesty.org/library/index/ENGMDE140752003

# Select Bibliography

This is not intended to be the sort of bibliography found in an academic study. It consists of the works that I have found most useful in writing my book and, to the authors of these books, I express my sincere thanks. I would like to acknowledge the particular assistance of James Loewen's book in chapters 4 and 5; John Charmley's work on Churchill in the chapter on the special relationship; Frances FitzGerald in Chapter 13; Bruce Franklin on Hollywood mythmaking; Robert Ivie on the Truman Doctrine; Tim Madigan on the Tulsa Massacre; Stuart Miller on war crimes in the Philippines; and C. Paul Vincent on the British naval blockade during the First World War.

Bender, Thomas (ed.), *Rethinking American History in a Global Age*, University of California Press, Berkeley, 2002

Beschloss, Michael, *The Conquerors: Roosevelt, Truman and the Destruction of Hitler's Germany, 1941–45*, Simon and Schuster, New York, 2002

Bicheno, Hugh, *Rebels and Redcoats*, HarperCollins, London, 2003

Blum, William, *Killing Hope: US Military and CIA Interventions Since World War II*, Zed Books, London, 2003

Brands, H.W., *The Devil We Knew: Americans and the Cold War*, Oxford University Press, New York, 1993

Charmley, John, *Churchill's Grand Alliance: The Anglo-American Special Relationship 1940–1957*, Harcourt, London, 1995

Denson, John V. (ed.), *The Costs of War: America's Pyrrhic Victories*, Transaction Publishers, New Brunswick, 1998

FitzGerald, Frances, *America Revised: History Schoolbooks in the Twentieth Century*, Little Brown, Boston, 1979

Foner, Eric, *The Story of American Freedom*, W.W. Norton & Company, New York, 1998

Franklin, H. Bruce, *M.I.A. or Mythmaking in America*, Rutgers University Press, New Brunswick, 1993

Fussell, Paul, *The Great War and Modern Memory*, Oxford University Press, 1975

Fussell, Paul, *Wartime: Understanding and Behaviour in the Second World War*, Oxford University Press, 1989

Hedges, Chris, *War Is a Force That Gives Us Meaning*, PublicAffairs, New York, 2002

Holmes, Richard, *Firing Line*, Penguin, London, 1987

Ivie, Robert L., 'Evil Enemy Versus Agonistic Other: Rhetorical Constructions of Terrorism', *Review of Education, Pedagogy and Cultural Studies*, 25, 2003

Ivie, Robert L., 'Fire, Flood, and Red Fever: Motivating Metaphors of Global Emergency in the Truman Doctrine Speech', *Presidential Studies Quarterly*, 29, No. 3, September 1999

Keen, Sam, *Faces of the Enemy: Reflections of the Hostile Enemy*, HarperSanFrancisco, 1988

Loewen, James W., *Lies My Teacher Told Me: Everything Your American History Textbook Got Wrong*, Touchstone Books, New York, 1996

Longley, Clifford, *Chosen People*, Hodder & Stoughton, London, 2002

Macmillan, Margaret, *Peacemakers*, John Murray, London, 2001

Madigan, Tim, *The Burning: Massacre, Destruction and the Tulsa Race Riot of 1921*, Thomas Dunne Books, New York, 2001

Miller, Stuart Creighton, *Benevolent Assimilation: The American Conquest of the Philippines, 1899–1903*, Yale University Press, 1982

Paul, Septimus H., *Nuclear Rivals: Anglo-American Atomic Relations, 1941–1952*, Ohio State University Press, 2000

Pilger, John, *The New Rulers of the World*, Verso Books, London, 2002

Rampton, Sheldon and Stauber, John, *Weapons of Mass Deception: The Uses of Propaganda in Bush's War on Iraq*, Penguin, New York, 2003

Smith, Michael K., *The Greatest Story Never Told*, Xlibris Corporation, USA, 2001

Vincent, C. Paul, *The Politics of Hunger: The Allied Blockade of Germany, 1915–19*, Ohio State University Press, 1985

# SELECT BIBLIOGRAPHY

Vistica, Gregory L., *Fall from Glory: The Men Who Sank the U.S. Navy*, Touchstone Books, New York, 1997

Zinn, Howard, *A People's History of the United States: 1492–Present*, HarperCollins, New York, 2001

# Index

# INDEX

# INDEX